# 3D Game Textures

D0206879

# 3D Game Textures

## Create Professional Game Art Using Photoshop

## Luke Ahearn

### Third Edition

AMSTERDAM • BOSTON • HEIDELBERG • LONDON
NEW YORK • OXFORD • PARIS • SAN DIEGO
SAN FRANCISCO • SINGAPORE • SYDNEY • TOKYO

Focal Press is an imprint of Elsevier

Focal Press is an imprint of Elsevier
225 Wyman Street, Waltham, MA 02451
The Boulevard, Langford Lane, Kidlington, Oxford, OX5 1GB, UK

© 2012 Elsevier Inc. All rights reserved

No part of this publication may be reproduced or transmitted in any form or by any means, electronic or mechanical, including photocopying, recording, or any information storage and retrieval system, without permission in writing from the publisher. Details on how to seek permission, further information about the Publisher's permissions policies and our arrangements with organizations such as the Copyright Clearance Center and the Copyright Licensing Agency, can be found at our website: www.elsevier.com/permissions.

This book and the individual contributions contained in it are protected under copyright by the Publisher (other than as may be noted herein).

**Notices**
Knowledge and best practice in this field are constantly changing. As new research and experience broaden our understanding, changes in research methods, professional practices, or medical treatment may become necessary.

Practitioners and researchers must always rely on their own experience and knowledge in evaluating and using any information, methods, compounds, or experiments described herein. In using such information or methods they should be mindful of their own safety and the safety of others, including parties for whom they have a professional responsibility.

To the fullest extent of the law, neither the Publisher nor the authors, contributors, or editors, assume any liability for any injury and/or damage to persons or property as a matter of products liability, negligence or otherwise, or from any use or operation of any methods, products, instructions, or ideas contained in the material herein.

**Library of Congress Cataloging-in-Publication Data**
Ahearn, Luke.
  3D game textures : create professioal game art using Photoshop/
Luke Ahearn. — 3rd ed.
      p. cm.
  Includes bibliographical references and index.
  ISBN 978-0-240-82077-4 (pbk.)
    1. Computer games—Programming.   2. Computer graphics.
    3. Adobe Photoshop.   I. Title.
  QA76.76.C672A42154 2012
  794.8'1526—dc23                                    2011033195

**British Library Cataloguing-in-Publication Data**
A catalogue record for this book is available from the British Library

For information on all Focal Press publications
visit our website at www.elsevierdirect.com

11 12 13 14   5 4 3 2 1

Printed in the United States of America

Working together to grow
libraries in developing countries

www.elsevier.com | www.bookaid.org | www.sabre.org

ELSEVIER   BOOK AID International   Sabre Foundation

For Julie, Ellen, and Cooper

# Contents

# Acknowledgments

Brian Grabinski, Mark Birge-Anderson, and Jose Vazquez, the concept artists.

Ann Sidenblad, a great friend and one of the best digital artists I know, for providing her invaluable feedback.

Jeffrey C. Huff, Assistant Professor of Computer Graphics at Missouri State University, for technical editing on this version of the book.

Unigine Corp., developers of the Unigine technology.

Nick Marks, for his initial input on this book many, many years ago.

NVIDIA: Doug Rogers, Kevin Bjorke, Gary King, Sébastien Dominé, Carrie Cowan, and Derek Perez, for information and help developing the shader section.

Maggie Quale at Smith Micro Inc.

Alkis "Atlas" Roufas, for the Genetica3 demo on the disk.

Michael S. Elliott, for the use of the Tengwar-Gandalf font.

The Focal Press people, who are too numerous to name; specifically, I worked with Laura Lewin, Lauren Mattos, Amanda Guest, Sarah Binns, and Katy Spencer. In addition, Becky Golden-Harrell, who was at Focal Press for the first edition of this book.

# Introduction

Welcome to the third edition of this book. Game development is still booming! Many more books have been written, even more information is available on the Internet, and many more colleges are offering courses, or even degrees, in game development—and many use this book. Thanks to all the students and instructors who e-mailed me with suggestions and feedback over the years. I loved the praise, but I really appreciate the suggestions and feedback the most; you have made this a better book. Yet I find that of all the numerous topics that fall under the large umbrella of game development, texture creation is still not getting thorough treatment. People still trumpet the virtues of the Offset filter in Photoshop—hence the need for this third edition.

I wrote this book after having held many positions on various game projects, from president and art director to in-the-trenches artist working through crunch times. I worked with many artists on numerous projects, and no matter what their education or background, their knowledge of game development came largely from actually doing it. No one school or book can adequately train you for an industry that changes so fast and requires that professionals have a rather large set of skills in order to function. Even an experienced game developer must frequently face a learning curve. The reality is that most game projects are one-time, unique ventures that are never to be done the same way twice. Things change too fast: the technology, the processes, the marketplace. And the industry is still a bit transitory, so you could find yourself in a new town, at a new company, at work on a new genre of game, with tools that you have never used before.

You would think that writing a book about something that is so constantly changing and affected by so many variables would be an impossible task. But given all the change and evolution in our industry, there are some core skills and practices that don't change from year to year. My goal with this book is not only to show you how to create textures but also to give you a basis for understanding the larger picture of game development as it pertains to texture creation. The difference between a good artist and a good artist who can function as a member of a high-performance game development team is the ability to do good work fast and efficiently—and to contribute to the forward momentum of the project. I approached each of the projects in the book with all of this mind and tried to give you a feel for the various situations in which you may find yourself as a game artist.

**Note:** Remember that although specific game tools are not the focus of this book, in the job hunt you will want to master at least one set of commercially useful game development tools—at the expert level, if possible.

## The Photoshop Focus of This Book

I also developed the exercises in this book to rely heavily on Photoshop. I did this for several reasons:

- The only way to really get to know Photoshop well is to use it a lot and to use it with real-world examples, not just a limited three-step tutorial on the Offset filter.
- When you get to know your way around Photoshop, you will be more impressed by it. Every day I learn some new trick or feature that saves precious time.
- When you are truly proficient in Photoshop, you will develop a feeling for the best way to accomplish a task. When you develop this feeling, you know that you have left the learning curve far behind you. You can then focus on getting better and faster at using Photoshop until it becomes an extension of you. You will be less hindered in creating what you are envisioning.
- When you get to know the capabilities of Photoshop, you will be able to create anything you want and will be less dependent on resources that might not be available everywhere you go, such as premade texture sets, digital cameras, and other software.

When you are able to use other resources to create your textures, they will be much better—and not only visually. Your source files will be more flexible, better organized, and much easier to work with. This is very important because creating game art is a balancing act. You are always making decisions that involve not only aesthetics but also efficiency and technological limits. Having files that are easy to find and that can be quickly altered is as important as how good they look. The best-looking texture in the world is useless if you can't find it or it won't run in a game engine. And on a development team, you will most likely not be the only person using a file. If your layers are not named, grouped, and organized, the next person's job will be much, much harder.

One of the biggest challenges in game development is to avoid breaking any of the fragile connections between the thousands of parts of a typical game. A poorly organized file is one of the things that will threaten to break those connections; many poorly organized files will almost assuredly cause a break. These connections are called *dependencies*. The development team must function smoothly and efficiently as a whole because usually certain tasks and goals must be reached by one group, or one individual, in order for the other team members to move forward with their work.
A good number of poorly organized or missing files will cause the

guilty party to take longer to complete his or her work and cause the dependent parties to wait before starting their work. There is a snowballing effect, delays cause more delays, and the schedule starts to slip dramatically. The project may even grind to a dead standstill. What's worse is having no schedule and not knowing (until it's way too late) that the game you had hoped (or are contractually obligated) to develop is an impossibility given the lack of time and resources so late in development. The worst case is that this will cause the project to get cancelled. At best, this is where most of the infamous crunch time is created. Crunch time includes those last few months where the development team lives in the office day and night to finish a game. One day developers are going to realize that the reason they are crunching is that the project wasn't planned properly. Someone at a higher level didn't do his or her job a year or two earlier, and the developers end up paying for it. Sorry, free pizza isn't adequate compensation for working 24 hours a day for three months. So, beyond creating a wood or metal texture, the greater goal here is to learn to create assets in an efficient, organized, and flexible way. Working on a game development team, speed, accuracy, and flexibility are critical. The process in which you handle assets is called the *pipeline*. From concept to creation to in-game asset, tens of thousands of files pass through the pipeline. So, where you save your files; what you name them; and how you name, group, and organize the layers in a Photoshop file are all important details. You don't want to be the person responsible for losing or overwriting a file that took someone else hours or days to create. Not only will you be the cause of the loss of precious man-hours of work, but potentially you could be responsible for delaying the entire project.

## What This Book Is Not

There is much confusion when it comes to the vocabulary of game development. This book does not cover careers, characters, animation, lighting, modeling, NURBS, shader programming, or character skinning and is not a vague overview of all game art. This book is focused on creating 2D textures for various 3D game environments.

## Whom This Book Is For

This book is for game developers, architects, simulation developers, Web designers, and anyone who needs to create 2D imagery for a 3D computer application. I have come across two general types of individual in the art departments of game development teams: the artistically challenged technical person and the technically challenged artistic person. Most people are trained and/or simply more proficient at thinking in one of those ways. There's no shame in being a great programmer who can't draw a bloody talon or in being a great artist who can't do all that complex code stuff. This book will help the beginner get started in game texturing, but it will also help the technically oriented professionals who are artistically challenged create textures (in a way they can relate to), and it will teach the technically challenged artists to create their art in a fashion that will allow them to set up their work with an eye toward the important aspects of game development. There is no shame in being an artist who has focused solely on creating beautiful art, and not on the technical issues of game development, but it is limiting. The good news is that the creation of beautiful art is the hard part. All you have to do now is set up your art in a way that allows you to quickly find, alter, and output your textures for use in a game.

## Overview

### Chapter 1: A Basic (Game) Art Education

The basis of computer art is art itself, so in chapter 1, I discuss the most basic and important aspects of visual art. Although teaching you traditional fine-art skills is beyond the scope of this book, it is critical to have an understanding of some basic aspects of visual art in order to create game textures. The basic aspects of visual art we will focus on are shape and form, light and shadow, texture, color, and perspective.

### Chapter 2: A Brief Orientation to Computer Graphic Technology

We will talk technology very briefly. You will eventually need to learn a good deal about the technical side of computer art to decide upon the various issues that technology will present to you, but a brief orientation of technology is all you will need to start painting textures. Although creating art on a computer can be limiting, frustrating, and confusing for many people, once you understand the limits placed on you and learn to work within them, you are much more likely to create impressive work. The aspects of technology that we will look at are common features of graphic file formats, the power of two and the grid, UV mapping, and shader technology for artists.

### Chapter 3: Shaders and Materials

Shaders allow for a level of realism in games that is stunning and getting better all the time. Simply put, a shader is a mini-program that processes graphic effects in real time. For example, the reflections on a surface can move in real time instead of being "baked" or permanently painted into a surface. Shader effects are very powerful visually, even if viewers are unaware of what they are seeing. That is, the average player would have a hard time specifying why the game looks so good. It may be the real-time reflections, normal mapping, or the specular mapping being processed in real time.

### Chapter 4: Prepping for Texture Creation

In this chapter we will look at the various sources of digital resources for texture creation and each of the steps in the process of gathering, preparing, and storing your assets. The focus of this book is the creation of textures using Photoshop, so that you develop strong Photoshop skills, but in reality it is more common, easier, and more effective to use photo reference in texture creation. We will be using photo reference later in the book, and the CD contains a good collection of photo reference for you to use in your work. We also look at the use of overlays or overlay textures in this chapter.

## Chapter 5: The Sci-Fi Setting

This is the first tutorial chapter. A sci-fi scene looks complex due to the geometry and effects presenting use, but in actuality the texture set is very simple. We will start by taking from the concept sketch ideas for the base materials that we will create for the scene and from that base build a simple and versatile set of textures. This method produces textures that can be used in various ways and that are designed to be used with the newer technology coming out (shaders like bump and normal mapping, and so on).

## Chapter 6: The Urban Setting

In this chapter you will learn to work more faithfully to the detail in a concept sketch or any reference material that may be given to you. When you create textures for a game environment, you are usually creating them for a world that has been thought out, detailed, and developed to the point that showcasing your creativity is not the primary goal of your work. You are showcasing your talent and ability to recreate what you see in the materials in front of you. We will build a set of textures as they were traditionally created, in sets: base, wall, floor, and ceiling. This chapter focuses on breaking out not only the base materials that need to be created for a scene, but also the detail textures as well. Even though this approach is falling by the wayside due to technological advances, it is still an applicable skill to many games and applications and a good skill to have when you are required to work with more advanced technology. We always start with the basics to build a material (shape, color, texture) and then build detail on top of that. What you end up with is a full texture set that is easily altered and built upon. By the end of the chapter, you will have created all the textures needed for the urban environment as seen in the concept sketch.

## Chapter 7: The Fantasy Setting

This is a long chapter, so pace yourself. This chapter combines the creation of many high-detail textures that are used in a high-polygon-count scene. We will use the Path tool in Photoshop to create the fancy curves that you see in the scene, and we will do some basic hand-painting that will produce great results. Finally, we will look at the process of creating the textures used in a shader.

## Chapter 8: The Outdoor Setting

In this chapter we will create a set of textures for a forest that can be altered to look spooky, friendly, or fanciful. Using the basic approach presented here to break out the elements of an outdoor scene, you can also create a similar set of textures for any outdoor environment; jungle, desert, and so on. I will also introduce the use of photo source in texture creation. I mentioned in the very beginning of the book that the use of photo source to create textures is not only common but preferred. It makes your job faster and easier and gives your textures an extra layer of richness that can take a lot of time to achieve otherwise. Although working with overlays may take the most time and tweaking, they are generally added later in the creation process, after a good foundation is laid. Using digital imagery will greatly enhance and speed up your work, but you don't want it to be a crutch that you will always have to lean on. We will also look at the ways that the sky is typically handled in a game. We will also look at terrain painting, clouds, and water.

### Chapter 9: Game Effects

Games are full of visual effects—probably even more so than you realize. These effects are important, not just as eye candy, but for giving the player clues and information on what is happening in the game world. These effects also add a great deal to the level of immersion that a player will experience in a game. Typically, if you shoot at any surface in a game—wood, metal, concrete, and their variations—you will see and hear a different effect for each surface. Effects also include the glow around a candle, light shafts from a window, even raindrops. The assets for these effects are fairly easy to create. Actually, asset creation is the easy part of creating effects in a relative sense. It does take work to create the art and it must look good, but the systems that run the effects can be complex and challenging to work with. Generally, you will often create three types of effects: static, animated, and particle.

### Chapter 10: Normal Maps and Multipass Shaders

This chapter focuses on normal mapping; specifically, creating them in Photoshop with a look at creating them using a 3D program. We will also create the supporting maps for a typical environment: bump, normal, specular, illumination, and opacity. I will explain how 3D applications are used to do this, but of course we won't be doing that in this book.

Have fun!

## The Concept Artists

### The Urban Setting: Jose Vazquez

Jose was born in Mexico and raised in Chicago, Illinois, from the age of three. He still keeps a close connection with his Mexican heritage. Jose has a BA in Illustration from Columbia College and a BA in Media Arts and Animation from the Illinois Institute of Art. Jose has more than 15 years of professional experience that began with graffiti, then grew into contracted large-scale murals. Dabbling in airbrush art, portraits, and paintings of all media, Jose has a strong traditional art background, but due to his animation education, all his current works are digital. Jose currently develops characters in the video gaming industry.

## The Sci-Fi Setting: Brian Grabinski

Brian Grabinski was born and raised in Illinois. He graduated
from the Chicago-based American Academy of Art in 1997. Upon
graduation, he started working freelance and has worked as a full-
time illustrator/graphic designer for eight years. Brian has also
worked as a full-time concept artist for the video game company
Rainbow Studios/THQ, based in Phoenix, Arizona, and for the
Chicago-area animation studio Dreamation/Cineme. Brian continues
to work freelance for various clients and is employed full-time at
the Hoffman Estates and Illinois–based videogame company High
Voltage Studios as a full-time concept artist. You can contact Brian
Grabinski via e-mail at briangrabinski@aol.com or brian.grabinski@
high-voltage.com.

## The Fantasy Setting: Mark Birge-Anderson

Mark Birge-Anderson attended the Layton School of Art and Design in
Milwaukee, Wisconsin, and the Art Academy of Cincinnati. He works in
advertising in Chicago, coming up with original concepts and designs.
He has also done concept art for an animation studio in Chicago
and plans to pursue work in that exciting field. Mark does freelance
illustration as well and can be reached at mark@matrix1.com.

# Chapter 1

# A Basic (Game) Art Education

*Art is born of the observation and investigation of nature.*

—Cicero (Roman author, orator, and politician, 106 B.C.–43 B.C.)

## Introduction

The basis of computer art is art itself, so before we dive into any technical issues, we must first discuss the most basic, but important, aspects of visual art. Teaching you traditional fine art skills is beyond the scope of this book, but it is critical that you have an understanding of some basic aspects of visual art so that you can create game textures. Fortunately, these basic aspects of art are fairly easy to present in book form. By studying these basics of art, you will learn to see the world as an artist does and to understand what you see and then be better able to create a texture set for a game world.

The basic aspects of visual art that we will focus on are:

- Shape and form
- Light and shadow
- Texture
- Color
- Perspective

Learning to observe the basic visual aspects of the world around you is a strong foundation for the process of seeing the world as an artist does, communicating with other artists, and creating great game textures. Technology is, of course, critical to the larger picture of game textures, but the actual basics of art are where great textures begin. Too often, would-be game artists are thrown into a discussion on tiling or even game engine technology, when the skills that are most important for the creation of game textures are the ability to understand what you are seeing in the real world and the ability to recreate it in the computer. Often a texture artist is required to break a scene down to its core materials and build a texture set based on those materials, so learning this skill is essential. Although you don't need to have an advanced degree in art to create great textures, let's face it: Almost anyone can learn what buttons to click in Photoshop, but the person who understands and skillfully applies the basics of art can make a texture that stands out above the rest.

There are many types of art and aspects of visual art that you should further explore to develop as a game artist. Some of the things you can study and/or practice are:

- Figure drawing
- Still-life drawing
- Photography
- Painting (oil, water color, etc.)
- Lighting (for film, still photography, the stage, or computer graphics)
- Color theory and application

- Sculpture
- Drafting and architectural rendering
- Anatomy
- Set design
- Technical illustration

It is even worth the time to study other areas of interest beyond art, such as the sciences, particularly the behavior of the physical world. Game artists are processing light, for example, more and more in real time and not painting it into the texture to the extent it was just a few years ago. The more you understand and are able to reproduce effects such as reflection, refraction, blowing smoke, and so on, the more success you will find as a game artist. We now have technologies that reproduce the real world to a much greater extent than ever before, but it still takes an artist to create the input and adjust the output for these effects to look their best.

The areas of study that will help you deal with real-world behaviors are endless. You can start by simply observing the world. Watch how water drips or flows, the variations of light and shadow on different surfaces at different times of the day, how a tree grows from the ground—straight like a young pine or flared at the base like an old oak—and you will soon be staring at the cracks in the pavement and photographing the side of a dumpster while passersby stare at you. An excellent book to inspire this type of activity is *Digital Texturing and Painting,* by Owen Demers (New Riders, 2001). You can also take tours of museums, architectural tours, nature walks, join a photography club or a figure-drawing class—there is no end to the classes, clubs, disciplines, and other situations that will open up your mind to new inspirations and teach you new tools and techniques for texture creation. And, of course, playing games, watching movies, and reading graphic novels are basic food to the game artist.

## Chapter Overview

- Shape (2D) and form (3D) light and shadow
- Texture: Tactile vs. visual
- Color
- Perspective

There are many elements of traditional art, but we will narrow our focus to those elements that are most pertinent to texture creation. Let's start with shape and form.

## Shape (2D) and Form (3D)

A *shape* (height and width) is simply a two-dimensional (flat) outline of a form. Circles, squares, rectangles, and triangles are all examples of shape. Shape is what we first use to draw a picture before we understand such concepts as light, shadow, and depth. As children we draw what we see in a crude 2D way. Look at the drawings of very young children and you will see that they are almost always composed of pure basic shapes: triangular roof, square door, circular sun. Even as adults, when we understand shadows and perspective,

**Figure 1.1**
Here are some examples of shapes that compose everyday objects. These shapes range from simple to complex.

we have trouble drawing what we see before us and instead rely on a whole series of mental notes and assumptions as to what we think we are seeing. There are exercises to help develop the ability to draw what we actually see. Most notably, the book *The New Drawing on the Right Side of the Brain*, by Betty Edwards (Tarcher, 1999), offers many such exercises. One of the most famous of these involves the drawing of a human face from a photo. After you have performed this exercise, you then turn the photo upside down and draw it again. The upside-down results are often far better than the right-side-up ones, even on first try. This is because once you turn the image upside down, your brain is no longer able to make any mental assumptions about what you think you are seeing; you can see only what's really there. Your brain hasn't yet developed a set of rules and assumptions about the uncommon sight of an upside-down human face.

One of the first skills that you can practice as an artist is trying to see the shapes that make up the objects that surround you. Figure 1.1 has some examples of this shape training, ranging from the simple to the complex. This is a very important skill to acquire. As a texture artist, you will often need to see an object's fundamental shape amid all the clutter and confusion in a scene so that you can create the 2D art that goes over the 3D objects of the world.

*Form* is three-dimensional (height, width, and depth) and includes simple objects like spheres, cubes, and pyramids. See Figure 1.2 for examples and visual comparisons. You will see later that as a texture

**Figure 1.2**
Here are examples of shapes and forms. Notice how it is shadow that turns a circle into a sphere.

artist, you are creating art on flat shapes (essentially squares and rectangles) that are later placed on the surfaces of forms. An example is shown in Figure 1.3, where a cube is turned into a crate (a common prop in many computer games). When a shape is cut into a base material in Photoshop and some highlights and shadows are added, the illusion of form is created. A texture can be created rather quickly using this method. See Figure 1.4 for a very simple example of a space door created using an image of rust, some basic shapes, and some standard Photoshop Layer Effects.

Of course, mapping those textures to more complex shapes like weapons, vehicles, and characters gets more complex, and the textures themselves reflect this complexity. Paradoxically, as the speed, quality, and complexity of game technology increase, artists are actually producing more simplified textures in some cases. The complexity comes in the understanding and implementation of the technology. Don't worry—you will gradually be introduced to this complexity, culminating with some sections on shader technology.

As with shapes, you can practice looking for the forms that make up the objects around you. In Figure 1.5 you can see some examples of this concept.

## Light and Shadow

Of all the topics in traditional art, light and shadow are arguably the most important due to their difficulty to master and importance to the final work. Light and shadow give depth to and—as a result—define what we see. At their simplest, light and shadow are easy to see and understand. Most of us are familiar with shadow—our own shadow

**Figure 1.3**
A game texture is basically a 2D image applied, or *mapped*, to a 3D shape to add visual detail. In this example, a cube is turned into a crate using texture. A more complex 3D shape makes a more interesting crate using the same 2D image.

**Figure 1.4**
Here is an example of how shapes can be cut into an image and with some simple layer effects can be turned into a texture in Photoshop.

cast by the sun, making animal silhouettes with our hands on a wall, or a single light source shining on a sphere and the round shadow that it casts. That's where this book begins. Light and shadow quickly get more complicated, so the examples in this book will get more complex as well. The book starts by discussing the ability to see and analyze light and shadow in this chapter; moves up to creating and tweaking light and shadow in Photoshop using Layer Styles, for the most part; and finally looks at some basic hand tweaking of light and shadow. If you want to master the ability to hand-paint light and shadow on complex and organic surfaces, you are advised to take traditional art classes in illustration, sketching, and painting.

We all know that the absence of light is darkness, and in total darkness we can see nothing at all, but the presence of too much light will also make it difficult to see. Too much light blows away shadow, removes depth, and desaturates color. In the previous section, we looked at how shape and form differ. We see that

**Figure 1.5**
Here are some examples of the forms that make up the objects around you.

**Figure 1.6**
Here is the same door texture from the previous section. Notice the complete lack of depth as we look at it from angles other than straight on. The illusion of depth is shattered.

difference primarily as light and shadow, as in the example of the circle and a sphere. But even if the sphere were lit evenly with no shadows and looked just like the circle, the difference would become apparent when the object was rotated. The sphere would always look round if rotated, whereas once you began to rotate the circle it would begin to look like an oval until it eventually disappeared when completely sideways. In Figure 1.4, in which a shape was cut into an image of rusted metal and made to look like a metal space door using Photoshop Layer Effects, the highlights and shadows were faked using the various tools and their settings.

In Figure 1.6 you can see the same door texture rotated from front to side. Notice the complete lack of depth in the image on the far right. The illusion is shattered.

Understanding light and shadow is very important in the process of creating quality textures. We will go into more depth on this topic as we work through this book. One of the main reasons for dwelling on the topic is the importance of light and shadow visually, but in addition, you will see that many necessary decisions are based on whether light and shadow should be represented using texture, geometry, or technology. To make this decision intelligently in serious game production involves the input and expertise of many people. Although what looks best is ideally the first priority, what runs best on the target computer is usually what the decision boils down to. So keep in mind that in game development you don't want to make any assumptions about light and shadow—instead, ask questions.

This book covers different scenarios of how light and shadow may be handled in a game. It can be challenging to make shadows look good in any one of the situations. Too little shadow and you lack depth; too much and the texture starts to look flat. Making shadows too long or intense is an easy mistake. Unless the game level specifically calls for that on some rare occasion, don't do it. Technology sometimes handles the highlights and shadows. This feature is challenging because it is a new way of thinking that baffles many people who are unfamiliar with computer graphics. It can also be a bit overwhelming because you go from creating one texture for a surface to creating three or more textures that all work together on one surface. Naming and storing those textures can get confusing if you let the process get away from you.

Overall, you want your textures to be as versatile as possible, and to a great extent, that includes the ability to use those textures under various lighting conditions. See Figure 1.7 for an example of a texture in which the shadows and highlights have been improperly implemented and another one that has been correctly created. For this reason we will purposely use highlights and shadows to a minimal amount. You will find that if your texture needs more depth than a modest amount of highlight and/or shadow give you, you most likely need to create geometry or use a shader—or consider removing the source of the shadow! If there is no need for a large electrical box on a wall, for example, don't paint it in if it draws attention to itself and looks flat. If there is a need for an object and you are creating deep and harsh shadows because of it, you might need to create the geometry for the protruding element.

You will find that as game development technology accelerates, things like pipes, doorknobs, and ledges will be easily created with the larger polygon budgets or by using the advanced shaders at our disposal. Many texture surface properties are no longer painted on. Reflections, specular highlights, bump mapping, and other aspects of highlight and shadow are now processed in real time.

**Figure 1.7**
The crate on the left has conflicting light sources. The shadow from the edge of the crate is coming up from the bottom, is too dark, is too long, and even has a gap in it. The highlights on the edges are in conflict with the shadow cast on the inner panel of the crate, and they are too *hot*, or bright. The crate on the right has a more subtle, low-contrast, and diffuse highlight-and-shadow scheme and will work better in more diverse situations.

The rest of this book takes various approaches to light and shadow using Photoshop's Layer Effects to automate this process and other tools to hand-paint highlights and shadows. One of the main benefits of creating your own highlights and shadows in your textures is that you can control them and make them more interesting, as well as consistent. Nothing is worse than a texture with shadows from conflicting light sources: harsh, short shadows on some elements of the texture and longer, more diffuse shadows on others. See Figure 1.8 for an example. The human eye can detect these types of errors even if the human seeing the image can't quite understand why it looks wrong. One of the artist's greatest abilities is not only being able to create art but also being able to consciously know and verbalize what he is seeing. In Figure 1.9, you can see the various types of shadows created as the light source changes. This is a simple demonstration. If you ever have the opportunity to light a 3D scene or movie set, you will discover that the range of variables for light and shadow can be quite large.

Highlights also tell us a good bit about the light source as well as the object itself. In Figure 1.10, you can see another simple illustration

**Figure 1.8**
Here is a really bad texture created from two sources. Notice the difference in the shadows and highlights. The human eye can detect these errors, even if the human seeing it can't understand why the image looks wrong.

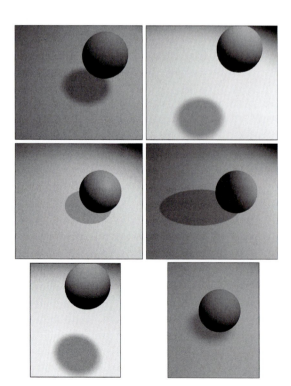

**Figure 1.9**
With one light source and a simple object, you can see the range of shadows we can create. Each shadow tells us information about the object and the light source, such as location, intensity, and so on.

**Figure 1.10**
With one light source and a simple object with various highlights on it, you can see that the object appears
to be created of various materials. Keep in mind that what you are seeing is only highlight and shadow. How
much does only this aspect of an image tell you about the material?

of how different materials will have different highlight patterns and
intensities. These materials lack any texture or color and simply show
the highlights and shadows created on the surface by one consistent
light source.

For a more advanced and in-depth discussion on the subject of
light and shadow for 3D scenes, I recommend *Essential CG Lighting
Techniques with 3ds Max,* by Darren Brooker (Focal, 2006).

## Texture

In the bulk of this book, as in the game industry, we use the term
*texture* to refer to a 2D static image. What we refer to as textures
in this book are also sometimes called *materials* or even *tile sets*

(from older games), but we will stick to the term *texture*. The one exception is that in this section we talk about the word *texture* as it is used in traditional art: painting, sculpture, and so on. A side note on vocabulary: Keep in mind that vocabulary is very important and can be a confusing aspect of working in the game industry. There is much room for miscommunication. Different words can often mean the same thing, and the same words can often mean many different things. Acronyms can be especially confusing: RAM, POV, MMO, and RPG all mean different things in different industries. POV means *point of view* in the game industry but *personally owned vehicle* in the government sector, and it also stands for *persistence of vision*. So to clarify, the term *texture*—usually meaning a 2D image applied to a polygon (the face of a 3D object)—in this section of this chapter refers to an aspect of an image and not the image itself. We draw this distinction for the following conversation on traditional art.

In traditional art, there are two types of texture: tactile and visual. *Tactile texture* is a term used when you are able to actually touch the physical texture of the art or object. Smooth and cold (marble, polished metal, glass) is as much a texture as coarse and rough. In art this term applies to sculptures and the like, but many paintings have thick and very pronounced brush or palette knife strokes. Vincent van Gogh was famous for this technique. Some painters even add materials such as sand to their paint to bring more physical or tactile texture to their work.

*Visual texture* is the illusion of what a surface's texture might feel like if we could touch it. Visual texture is composed of fine highlights and shadows. As computer game texture artists, we deal solely with this aspect of texture. So, for example, an image on your monitor might look like rough stone, smooth metal, or even a beautiful woman … and if you try to kiss that beautiful woman, she is still just a monitor. Not that I ever tried that, mind you.

There are many ways to convey texture in a two-dimensional piece of art. In computer games we are combining 2D and 3D elements and must often decide which to use. With 2D we are almost always forced to use strictly 2D imagery for fine visual texture. And though the faster processors, larger quantities of RAM, and the latest crop of 3D graphic cards allow us to use larger and more detailed textures and more geometry, a great deal of visual texture is still static; noticeably so, to a trained artist. This limitation is starting to melt away as complex shader systems are coming into the mainstream of real-time games. The real-time processing of bump maps, specular highlights, and a long list of other, more complex effects add to our game worlds a depth of realism not even dreamed of in the recent past. This book will teach you both the current method of building texture sets and the increasingly common method of building material sets that use textures and shader effects together. I will discuss this more at length later in the book, but for now you can see some visual examples of these effects. In Figure 1.11 you can see how in the 2D strip the object rotates but the effects stay static on the surface, whereas on the 3D strip the object rotates and the effect moves realistically across the surface.

**Figure 1.11**
Visual texture is composed of fine highlights and shadows. A shader allows for the real-time processing of visual texture, among other effects, and adds much more realism to a scene as the surface reacts with the world around it. In this example I used a specular map. These effects are best seen in 3D, but you can see here that the windows in the building on the top row have a reflection of the sky in them and that reflection moves as the players do. The windows in the building on the lower row are painted textures and stay the same no matter where the player walks. The bottom two rows are close-ups to help you see the effect. If you pick one window in the close-up images and look closely, you will see that the cloud reflections are in different places in each frame.

The game artist's job is often to consider what tools and techniques we have at our disposal and determine which one will best accomplish the job. We must often make a trade-off between what looks good and what runs well. As you begin to paint textures, you will find that some of the techniques of traditional art don't work in the context of game texturing. As traditional artists, we usually do a painting that represents one static viewpoint, and we can paint into it strong light sources and a great deal of depth, but that amount of depth representation goes beyond tactile texture and becomes faked geometry and looks flat in a dynamic, real-time 3D world. As mentioned earlier in this chapter, this approach will not work in a 3D game in which a player can move about and examine the texture. Once again, we must choose what to represent using a static 2D image, what can be processed in real time using a shader, and what must be represented using actual geometry. There are many solutions for this problem; among them are restricting the players' ability to move around the texture, removing the element of overt depth representation, or adding actual geometry for the parts of the texture represented by the overt depth representation (see Figure 1.12).

## Color

We all know what color is in an everyday fashion: "Get me those pliers. No, the ones with black handles." "I said to paint the house green. I didn't mean neon green!" That's all fine for civilian discussions of color, but when you begin to speak with artists about color, you need to learn to speak of color intelligently, and that takes a little more education and some practice. You will also learn to choose and combine colors, too. In games, as in movies, interior design, and other visual disciplines, color is very important. Color tells us much about the world and situation we are in.

At one game company we developed a massive multiplayer game that started in a small town—saturated green grass, blue water, butterflies—you get the picture; this was a nice, safe place. As you moved away from town, the colors darkened and lost saturation. The grass went from a bright green to a less-saturated brownish-green. There were other visual clues to the change as well. Most people can look at grass and tell whether it is healthy, dying, kept up, or growing wild. Away from town, the grass was long and clumpy, dying, and growing over the path. But even before we changed any other aspect of the game—still using the same grass texture from town that was well trimmed—we simply lowered the saturation of the colors on the fly and you could feel the life drain from the world as you walked away from town. As you create textures, you will probably have some form of direction on color choice—or maybe not. You might need to know what colors to choose to convey what is presented in the design document and what colors will work well together.

This section lays out a simple introduction to the vocabulary of color, color mixing (on the computer), and color choices and their commonly accepted meanings. I decided to skip the complex science of color and stick to the practical and immediately useful aspects of

**Figure 1.12**
There are several possibilities in dealing with overt depth representation. Upper left: The pipes are painted into the texture and totally lack any depth; notice how they dead-end into the floor. Upper right: Restricting the players' ability to move around the texture can alleviate some of the problem. Lower left: Adding actual geometry, if possible, for the parts of the texture that cause the overt depth is the best solution (this method uses less texture memory but more polygons). Finally, lower right: Adding the actual geometry into the recess is an option that looks pretty interesting and actually allows for a reduction of geometry. The removal of polygons from the backsides of the pipes more than offsets the added faces of the recess.

color. Color can get very complex and esoteric, but you would benefit from taking your education further and learning how color works on a scientific basis. Although this chapter will be a strong starting point, you will eventually move on from working with only the colors contained in the texture that you are creating to determining how those colors interact with other elements in the world, such as lighting. To start with, however, a game texture artist needs the ability to communicate, create, and choose colors.

First, let's discuss the way in which we discuss color. There are many color *models*, or ways of looking at and communicating color verbally. There are models that concern printing, physics, pigment, and light. They each have their own vocabulary, concepts, and tools for breaking out color. As digital artists, we use the models that describe light, because we are working with colored pixels that emit light. A little later we will take a closer look at those color systems from the standpoint of color mixing, but for now we will look at the vocabulary of color. In game development you will almost always use the red-green-blue (RGB) color model to mix color and the hue, saturation, and brightness (HSB) color model (both explained next) to discuss color. You will see that Photoshop allows for the numeric input and visual selection of color in various ways. When you discuss color choices and changes and then go to enact them, you are often translating between two or more models. Don't worry; this is not difficult, and most people don't even realize that they are doing it.

First, we will look at the HSB model, since this is the most common way for digital artists to communicate concerning color. In Figure 1.13 you can see examples of these aspects of color. These three properties of color are the main aspects of color that we need to be concerned with when discussing color:

- *Hue* is the name of the color (red, yellow, green).
- *Saturation* (or *chroma*) is the strength or purity of the color.
- *Brightness* is the light or darkness of the color.

## Hue

Most people use the word *color* when they really mean *hue*. Although there are many, many colors, there are far fewer hues. Variations of saturation and brightness create the nearly unlimited colors we see in the world. For example, scarlet, maroon, pink, and crimson are all *colors*, but the base *hue* is red.

Learning about color and its various properties is best done through visual examples. The most often used method is the *color wheel*,

**Figure 1.13**
In this image you can see a representation of HSB.

developed by Johannes Itten. We will look at the color wheel a little later. In Photoshop you will recognize the Color Picker, which offers various methods for choosing and controlling color, both numerically and visually. The Color Picker has various ways to choose color, but the most commonly used is RGB (Figure 1.14).

## Saturation

*Saturation* quite simply is the amount of white in a color. In Figure 1.15 you can see the saturation of a color being decreased as white is added. If you have access to a software package like Photoshop and open the Color Picker, you can slide the picker from the pure hue to a less saturated hue and watch the saturation numbers in the HSB slots go down as the color gets less saturated. Notice how the brightness doesn't change unless you start dragging down and adding black to the color. Also, you might want to look down at the RGB numbers and notice how the red in RGB doesn't change, but the green and blue do.

## Brightness

*Brightness* is the amount of black in a color. In Figure 1.16 you can see the brightness of a color being decreased. As in the previous discussion of saturation, you can open the Color Picker in Photoshop and this time, instead of decreasing the saturation, you can decrease the brightness by dragging down. You can look at the HSB and the RGB slots and see the brightness numbers decreasing. Also notice that this time in the RGB slots the red numbers decrease, but the blue and green are already at zero and stay there.

**Figure 1.14**
Here are Color Pickers from various applications.

**100% saturation**                    **0% saturation**

**Figure 1.15**
The saturation of the color red at 100%, decreasing to 0% by adding white.

**100% brightness**                    **0% brightness**

**Figure 1.16**
The brightness of the color red at 100%, decreasing to 0% by adding black.

Like most other aspects of color, brightness is affected by other factors. What colors are next to each other? What are the properties of the lights in the world? Another job of the texture artist is making sure that the textures in the world are consistent. That involves balancing the hue, saturation, and brightness of the color, in most cases. Figure 1.17 depicts an example of a texture that might have looked okay in Photoshop but that needed to be corrected to fit the scene. You can see that a great deal of contrast and intensity of color makes tiling the image a greater challenge.

### Color Systems: Additive and Subtractive

There are two types of color systems: additive and subtractive. *Subtractive color* is the physical mixing of paints, or *pigments*, to create a color. It is called *subtractive* because light waves are absorbed (or subtracted from the spectrum) by the paint and only the reflected waves are seen. A red pigment, therefore, is reflecting only red light and absorbing all the others. In the subtractive system, you get black by mixing all the colors together—theoretically. It is a challenge to mix pigments that result in a true black or a vibrant color. That is one of the reasons art supply stores have so many choices when it comes to paint. One of our advantages of working in the additive system is that we can get consistent and vibrant results with light. We won't dwell on the subtractive system since we won't be using it.

In the *additive system,* light is added together (as it is on a computer screen) to create a color, so naturally we deal with the additive system as computer artists because we are working with light. In Figure 1.18 you can see how the additive system works. I simply went into 3ds Max and created three spotlights that were pure red, green, and blue and created my own *additive color wheel,* or a visual representation of how the colors interact. Black is the absence of light (the area outside the spotlights), and white is all

PATCH OF EXPOSED STONE IN THE CONCRETE

**Figure 1.17**
Here is an example of a texture that might have looked okay in Photoshop but that needed to be corrected to fit in the scene correctly. This is a subtle example. Notice the patch of exposed stone in the concrete on the building that repeats?

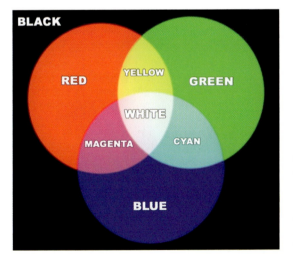

**Figure 1.18**
The additive system works by adding lights. Black is the absence of light (the area outside the spotlights), and white is all light (the center area where all three lights overlap each other): The combination of red, green, and blue is the additive system.

light (the center area where all three lights overlap each other): The combination of red, green, and blue is the additive system. If you look at the Color Picker in Photoshop (Figure 1.19), you will see a vertical rectangle of color graduating from red through the colors and back to red. This allows you to select a hue and use the Color Picker Palette to change the value and intensity.

**Figure 1.19**
The Color Picker in Photoshop has a vertical rectangle of color graduating from red through the colors and back to red. This allows you to select a hue and use the Color Picker Palette to change the value and intensity.

### Primary Colors

The three *primary colors* in the additive color system are red, green, and blue (RGB). They are referred to as primary colors because you can mix them and make all the other colors, but you can't create the primary colors by mixing any other color. Many projection televisions use an additive system where you can see the red, green, and blue lens that project these three colors to create the image you see.

### Secondary Colors

The *secondary colors* are yellow, magenta, and cyan. When you mix equal amounts of two primary colors together, you get a secondary color. You can see that these colors are located between the primary colors on the color wheel and on the Photoshop Color Picker vertical strip.

### Color Emphasis

Color is often used for emphasis. Look at Figure 1.20. All things being equal, the larger shapes dominate, but the small shapes demand your attention once color is added. Of course, there are many other forms of emphasis that you can use in creating art, but color can be the most powerful—and overused. Ever come across a Web page that has a busy background and every font, color, and mode of emphasis devised by man splashed across it? There is almost no actual emphasis, since all the elements cancel each other out. Let this be a cautionary tale to you: Often, less is more.

**Figure 1.20**
All things being equal, the larger shapes dominate, but the small shapes demand your attention once color is added.

In another example using a photograph, Figure 1.21, you can see that in the first black-and-white photo, your eye would most likely be drawn to the dark opening of the doghouse and you would most likely assume that the subject of this picture is the doghouse. In the second version, the colorful flower draws the primary interest; it still competes with the doghouse door for attention, but you would probably make the assumption that the focus of this picture was the flower.

In a game scene, you can see the use of color drawing the attention of a player to an important item. Look at Figure 1.22. In the first version of the scene, you are drawn to the fire and then to all the items in the shadows. In the second version, the red crate draws your attention and clearly means something. Depending on the world logic of the game you are playing, that could simply mean that you can interact with the object, or it could mean that the item is dangerous. That decision brings to our next topic: color expression.

## Color Expression or Warm and Cool Colors

When you start painting textures and choosing colors, you will want to know how they interact in terms of contrast, harmony, and even message. There is a lot of information on this topic, and once again, Johannes Itten (the guy who did the color wheel) enters the picture. Itten provided artists with a great deal of information on how color works and how colors work together. Itten was among the first people to look at color not just from a scientific point of view but from an artistic and emotional point of view. He was very interested in how colors made people feel. From his research we get the vocabulary of warm and cool colors.

We all are familiar with this convention, since it is mostly based on the natural world. When asked to draw a flame, we reach for the red or orange crayon. Ice is blue; the sun, yellow. Each warm and cool color has commonly associated feelings, both positive and negative.

**Figure 1.21**
Your eye is most likely
drawn to the opening of the
doghouse in the black-and-
white photo, but add color
and the flower draws the
primary interest.

The brighter or more pure the color, the more positive the association.
Darker and duller colors tend to have negative connotations associated
with them.

The warm colors are red and yellow, and the cool colors are blue
and green. Children will color the sun yellow and color ice blue and
use the black crayon to scratch out things they don't like. Traffic
lights are hot when you should stop or be cautious (red and yellow)
and cool when it is okay to go (green). Red and orange are hot and
usually associated with fire, lava, and coals. How many red and
black shirts do you see at the mall? Red and black together generally
symbolize demonic obsession. Red by itself can mean royalty and
strength as well as demonism. Deep red can be erotic. Yellow is a
hot color like the sun—a light giver. Yellow is rich like gold as a pure
color. A deep yellow (amber) window in the dark of a cold night can
mean fire and warmth. But washed out or pale yellow can mean
envy or betrayal. Calling a person yellow is an insult, meaning that

**Figure 1.22**
In a room full of normal objects, the players' eyes will be drawn to the fire and then equally to the objects. In a room full of normal objects, a red crate draws attention, especially given the fact that there are other normal crates around it.

he is a coward. Judas is portrayed as wearing yellow garments in many paintings. During the Inquisition, people who were considered guilty of heresy were made to wear yellow. For green, we think of lush jungles teeming with life. As green washes out, we get a sense of dread and decay (zombie and orc skin). Vibrant green in a certain context can be toxic waste and radioactive slime. Blue in its saturated state is cold like ice, but fresh like water and the sky. Darker blues indicate misery. Purple is mysterious and royal.

Keep in mind that color is context-sensitive. Water is generally blue (would you drink dark-green water?). But not just any blue will do. In the real world, if we come across water that is a saturated blue that we can't see through, we get suspicious. Was this water dyed? Are there weird chemicals in there? If anything lives in that, what could it be?! Blood is generally red, but what if an enemy bled green? What if the game you are playing is about an alien race taking over earth and one of your companions bleeds green from an injury during combat? In a fantasy game, you might come across coins. Which coin do you take: the one made of bright yellowish metal or the one made of gray-green metal? With no previous information on the color of coins in this world, most people would pick the brighter yellow. Look at Figure 1.23. What are some of the assumptions you might make about these three scenes?

**Figure 1.23**
These three scenes are the same except for the ax. What questions and/or assumptions run through your mind looking at each version?

Looking at color in this way might make it seem a bit mechanical, but it still takes a talented artist to make the right color choices. You can memorize all the information in the world, but it usually comes down to having a good eye and being able to convey that vision in your work and to your coworkers.

## Perspective

We discussed earlier in this chapter that dramatic perspective (Figure 1.24) is usually not used in the creation of a game texture, although sometimes perspective is present and needs to be understood. In addition, understanding perspective is not only a valuable artistic tool to have available but will also help you when you are taking digital reference images and when you are cleaning and straightening those images. We will look at the artistic aspects of perspective now; later, in the chapter on cleaning and storing your assets, we will talk about fixing those images.

Quite simply, *perspective* is the illusion that something far away from us is smaller than closer objects. This effect can be naturally occurring, as in a photo, or a mechanically created illusion in a painting. You can see samples of this illusion in Figure 1.25. In 2D artwork, perspective is a technique used to recreate that illusion and

**Figure 1.24**
Although dramatic perspective is used in traditional art, it is not used in a game texture. But there is some notion of perspective, so it is best to understand the concept.

**Figure 1.25**
Perspective is the illusion that something far away from us is smaller. Are the street lights actually getting smaller in this image? Are the train tracks really getting closer together?

give the artwork a 3D depth. Perspective uses overlapping objects, horizon lines, and vanishing points to create a feeling of depth. You can see in Figure 1.26 an image and the same image with the major lines of perspective as they converge on one point, called the *vanishing point*. Several types of perspective are used to achieve different effects.

## One-Point Perspective

*One-point perspective* is when all the major lines of an image converge on one point. This effect is best illustrated when you're looking down a set of straight railroad tracks or a long road. The lines

**Figure 1.26**
In 2D artwork, perspective is
a technique used to recreate
that illusion and give the
artwork a 3D depth.

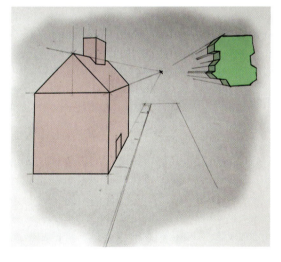

**Figure 1.27**
In one-point perspective,
all the lines that move away
from the viewer seem to meet
at a far point on the horizon.
This point is called the
*vanishing point.*

of the road and track, although we know they are the same distance
apart, seem to meet and join together at some point in the far
distance—the vanishing point. In one-point perspective, all the lines
move away from you (the z-axis) and converge at the vanishing point.

Vertical and horizontal or up and down and right and left lines (the
x- and y-axes) remain straight, as seen in Figure 1.27.

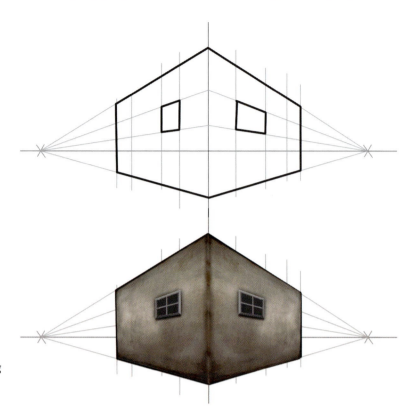

**Figure 1.28**
Two-point perspective has two vanishing points on the horizon line. All lines, except the vertical, will converge onto one of the two vanishing points.

## Two-Point Perspective

One-point perspective works fine if you happen to be looking directly at the front of something or standing in the middle of some railroad tracks, but what if the scene is viewed from the side? Then you shift into *two-point perspective*. Two-point perspective has two vanishing points on the horizon line. All lines, except the vertical, will converge onto one of the two vanishing points. See Figure 1.28.

## Three-Point Perspective

*Three-point perspective* is probably the most challenging of all. In three-point perspective every line will eventually converge on one of three points. Three-point perspective is the most dramatic and can often be seen in comic books when the hero is flying over buildings or kicking butt in the alley below as the buildings tower above. Figure 1.29 shows three-point perspective.

Perspective, from the texture artist's point of view while photographing surfaces for game art, can be the enemy. We will look at that issue in a coming chapter when we talk about collecting and cleaning your images. From the art education point of view, knowing what perspective is and what it looks like is enough for now.

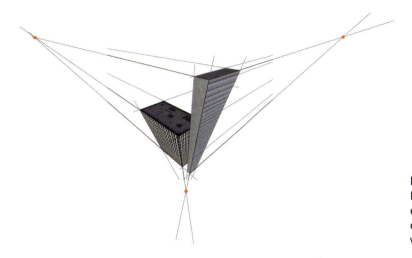

**Figure 1.29**
In three-point perspective, every line will eventually converge on one of three vanishing points.

## Quick Studies of the World Around You

The following pages display some quick studies that I did of random objects. I tried to work through each of them as a game artist might to give you some quick and general examples of how a game artist might break them down. We will do this type of exercise in more depth throughout the book, but in the tutorial portions of the book, those breakouts will be more specific and focused on the goal at hand. This is a general look and introduction on the thought process of recreating surfaces and materials in a digital environment. I covered all that was introduced in this chapter: shape and form, light and shadow, texture, and color, as well as considering other aspects of the object or material. I didn't touch on perspective in these exercises because I wanted to limit the exercise to recreating 2D surfaces (textures), and perspective is not as critical as the other concepts in this chapter. In the following pages, Figures 1.30 to 1.35 each have a caption that discusses the particulars of each study.

## Conclusion

This chapter was an overview of the most basic yet critical aspects of traditional art. Understanding the concepts in this chapter and further exploring them on your own will make you a much better texture artist. We are now ready to get more technical and look at the mechanical issues of creating game textures.

## Chapter Exercises

1. Examine and sketch your own series of basic shapes from world objects. Start with a ball, a cereal box, and other simple objects and work up to more complex items (what basic shapes is a car made from?). Pick three different objects and sketch each using only basic shapes. Compare the accuracy of your drawing by holding it at arm's length next to the object in the background. If you are having trouble with this exercise, it may help to use a

**Figure 1.30**
The upper-left image is a digital photo of some simple concrete stairs. You might have an art lead e-mail you an image like this and tell you that she wants a texture based on these stairs. Fortunately, this is a rather simple form; it doesn't have a lot of color or detail to distract us. Look at the simple recreation of the stairs to the right showing the basic light and shadow patterns on the stairs. The lower-left image shows the 2D texture created in Photoshop to be applied to a 3D model of the stairs. If you look at the yellow stripe on the stairs and compare it to the stripe on the texture, you can see the highlights painted in the texture where the edge of the step is and the shadow under the lip of the edge. If you were able to closely examine the original digital image of the stairs, you would see an almost infinite amount of detail. Part of the texture artist's job is to know when to draw the line. Here I didn't include every scuff and mark from the original stair image because that approach wouldn't work. You will learn in coming chapters that such details usually stand out and draw attention to the repeating pattern of a texture, or, in the case of fabrics and fine meshes, can create noise or static in the texture. I created this texture pretty quickly; given more time, I would experiment with the chips and wear on the edge of the steps to add more character.

picture so that you can work side by side and compare the two images—yours and the original.

2. Train your eye to see light and shadow. Start with a flashlight or one light source in a dark room and shine it at an object on a bare tabletop. The shadow should be pretty easy to identify. Move the

**Figure 1.31**
This is a straight-on photo of an interior plaster wall. I included this obviously unexciting image to demonstrate that even in such a simple surface, there can be complex highlight and shadow going on. Look at the color swatches of the highlight, shadow, and midtone. Notice that the colors are not simple black, white, and gray. The highlight is not pure white or light gray, but a very pale green. Look at the close-up of the image. You can clearly see the consistent behavior of light as it highlights the upper ridges of the plaster and shadow falls from the lower edges. Once you start studying such seemingly commonplace things, like a wall that you walk by a hundred times a day, you will start to notice, understand, and remember how various lights, materials, and other factors affect a surface. Do you convey that simple raised pattern in the texture using geometry or a shader? Of course, that depends on many factors, and hopefully by the end of this book you will know what questions to ask to determine the answers to such questions.

light back and at different angles and watch the shadow move. Now turn on another light source. Is it brighter than the light you are holding? Is it a different color? See how the dual shadows interact with each other. What happens to the shadow when the object is moved instead of the light? Also study how light and shadow affect color. Notice the various shades of color across a surface that may at first seem to be one solid color. Better yet, take an image into Photoshop and sample the various parts of the surface from darkest to lightest and take note of the range of shades the surface holds.

3. Focus on visual texture. Pick any object and look at it closely. A common mistake new artists make is to create a base texture and stop. A perfectly colored, shiny, and cleaner-than-clean plastic-looking object is going to look fake. In real life, even a new object has some texture—if not an actual texture, like a

**Figure 1.32**
This image simply shows the world that I need to wash my car. Seriously, look at the various parts of complex objects and you will see a variety of surface behaviors. Notice how the paint is highly reflective and mirrors the world around the car. The metal is not flat like a mirror, so notice the distortion of the reflected image. The windows, while reflecting the surrounding world as well, are translucent, so you can see what's behind the window and on the other side of the car. The window also has a patina of dirt and spots on it. If you needed to recreate this object as realistically as possible, you would have to take all those aspects into consideration and determine the best way to achieve the effect. Look at the close-up of the rim. You can see that the highlights are not mirror-like in their accuracy but rather are a diffuse notion of highlight. This looks simple to paint, but wheels rotate and will instantly look bad if not painted properly. Using a real-time process for highlights eliminates this problem. Though the tires are flat black and reveal only a faint notion of highlight, depending on the detail level, you may be dealing with complex mapping and shader effects here, too. All of this seems obvious, but taking the time to examine the object you are recreating and to understand what you are seeing and how to verbalize it helps when turning the object into game art. If you were to make materials or textures for this vehicle, you would need to know many things about the technology and how the car will be used in the game. Can we have real-time environmental reflections? Can we fake them using a shader? Do we have to carefully paint in a vague notion of metallic highlights that work in all situations the car may be in? And the windows: Can we do a translucent/reflective surface with an alpha channel for dirt? If the car is used in a driving game in which the vehicle is the focus of the game and the player gets to interact up close and personal with the car, I am sure a lot of attention will be given to these questions. But if this car is a static prop sitting on a street that the player blazes past, then over-the-top effects may only be a waste of development time and computer resources.

**Figure 1.33**

This sewer intrigued me: a simple shape of a common item that many might overlook as not worthy of serious attention. Some may have the attitude that it is only a sewer grate, so make it and move on. But a shiny new sewer grate with clean edges would stand out in a grungy urban setting. Look at this sewer grate. It is made of iron and looks solid and heavy. It was probably laid down decades ago and has had thousands of cars drive over it, people walk over it, millions of gallons of rainwater pour through it. On the image at the upper left you can look at the iron and see how it is rusted, but it's so well worn that the rust is polished off in most places. Dirt has built up in the cracks between the grate, the rim, and the concrete. Even little plants have managed to grow. Look at the close-up at the upper right and you can see just how beat up this iron is and how discolored it has become. At the lower left, I desaturated and cleaned up a portion of the image to see just how the light and shadow are hitting it and to get a feel for the quality of the surface. In this image, you can more clearly see the roughness of the cement and the metal, and although the circular grate looks round from a distance, up close there are no straight edges and smooth curves. All this detail can't be depicted 100% in a game texture, but knowing it's there and understanding what you are seeing will allow you to convey a richer version of the grate as you learn to focus on those details that add realism and character. On the lower right is a texture I did, and you can see that I was able to quickly achieve a mottled and grungy look for the metal and the edges. There are a few places at the top where I started the process of eating away at the concrete and the metal a bit.

leather grain, then a notion of the imperfection of the real world. Sometimes a subtle noise or cloud overlay is enough to create the almost indistinguishable texture that creates a more believable surface. Any object in the real world will have scratches from wear and tear, and other signs of use will develop pretty quickly. Study the texture of common objects and see what has created this object's texture. Is a wooden porch step smooth from use or rough due to weather and decay?

**Figure 1.34**
This image is similar to the sewer in approach. Here I wanted to point out how a simple shape can be turned into an ornate hinge with little effort. The top image is the original digital photo of the hinge. I drew the shape of the hinge in Photoshop. You may notice that I drew the screws separately. This is because you need the shapes separately to work with them in Photoshop—you will see why later in the book. In Photoshop I applied and adjusted the Layer Effects and then colored the hinge close to the overall color of the original. After that it was a matter of applying the right filters and doing some hand work to get the edges looking right. We will be doing this type of work throughout the book. I will remind you from time to time that although the best approach may be to use a photo source or any one of the other methods available, the focus of this book is to help you develop a set of Photoshop skills that will allow you to not depend on any one method. These skills will improve your abilities when you're working in any of the other methods.

4. Look closely at what color you are "really" seeing. As noted in this chapter, we mentally fill in a lot of blanks when it comes to trying to determine what we are seeing. Color is no exception. Look at images from the Internet, or better yet, take digital images with your own camera and load them into Photoshop or a similar image program. Sample the colors of various spots and see that almost no color is going to be pure, perfectly even, or at all where you

Source Image

Shape

Light and Shadow

**Figure 1.35**
This light switch is a common object that you might need to create. Instead of taking the time to clean up and manipulate a photo, you can just make one more quickly from scratch. The switch is composed of simple shapes with the Layer Effects applied. The wall behind the switch was a quick series of filters to add a base for this exercise.

might think it would be on the color selector. A red mug is not going to be a pure red mug; it will most likely be a shade darker or lighter or contain other colors.

5. Color expression: Can you make a puppy look evil? Try painting its eyes red. Take an image of a garden and desaturate it. What other images can you take and simply change the colors (all of them across the image or only one color) and create various moods and messages? A house with rich amber windows at night might seem inviting. How does a window with a red tint or a green cast make you feel? Try combining colors, too. An amber window with a predominantly black surrounding may feel like a lonely sight in the void, as opposed to the fanciful and richer blue surrounding.

6. Do your own quick studies of the world. Take pictures or just examine a surface or object and determine every bit of information you can based on what you learned in this chapter. Define the basic shape, note how light and shadow play on the object and how the object affects the light and shadow of the world around it, and sample and determine the colors of the object and the amount of variation of the color along the surface of the object. How would you begin to create the surface of this object in Photoshop? Don't try yet, but think about it. Later you will learn the tools necessary to create surfaces, but for now you need to be able to dissect a surface and determine what colors, shapes, and other qualities the surface contains.

# Chapter 2

# A Brief Orientation to Computer Graphic Technology

*Everything should be made as simple as possible, but not simpler.*

—Albert Einstein (1879–1955)

## Introduction

Now it's time to talk technology, but very briefly. You will eventually need to learn a good deal about the technical side of computer art to make the various decisions that technology will present to you, but a brief orientation of technology is all you need to start painting textures. I could have gotten away without including this chapter at all and instead launched directly into painting textures, but I believe that this small bit of information is critical to your long-term success as a texture artist. Learning to "button-click" from a tutorial might get you good results, but it won't give you the tools to eventually attack your own unique problems when you're asked to create a texture that will be used in a certain genre, platform, and so on. Understanding why textures are constructed the way they are, and why there are certain limits and restrictions placed on the game artist, will help you avoid a lot of wasted time. Later, as you are exposed to more information, complexity, and unique development situations, you will more easily assimilate that information and be able to use it more creatively.

Although creating art on a computer can be limiting, frustrating, and confusing for many people, once you understand the limits the technology places on you and learn to work within these limits, you will be much more likely to create impressive work. One of the first issues that you will run into is file formats. There are many graphic file formats, and each has many options and features. They are designed for different purposes, and their complexity and range of options reflect that fact. We will look not at the formats themselves as much as the options and features most often used by the texture artist. I find that starting with the gross oversimplification that I am just dealing with colored dots somehow helps me keep my mind wrapped around concepts and techniques that can otherwise get very complex in their implementation. Keep in mind that at the core, as a game artist you are always working with pixels—colored dots— and a file format is simply the way in which those pixels are stored, even in the case of the PSD file format, which we will look at later. PSD, the Photoshop file format, saves a great deal of information, but mainly it stores information about pixels and how they interact with each other. I am not trying to oversimplify a very complex subject and application such as Photoshop, but I am trying to tell you that you should not be intimidated by all the complexity. You can start very simple and assimilate a little at a time, rather than be overwhelmed all at once. Just remember that there is always more to learn, there is always a better and faster way to do something, and you should be having fun. Photoshop, with all its powerful tools and options, is simply giving you an almost unlimited number of ways to adjust the hue, saturation, brightness, and transparency of the pixels in an image to achieve many different results. One concept, which we will look at in more detail in Chapter 4, is layer blending modes.

In addition to being able to layer images on top of each other in Photoshop, you can control the way the pixels in each layer blend with each other. Blending modes are very useful and are used often in building textures. Quite simply, when you choose a blending mode, you are changing the way in which a pixel reacts with the pixels below it, thus affecting its hue, saturation, brightness, and/or transparency. The end result on screen is one pixel of a specific hue, saturation, and brightness.

We will look at image size, too. This topic is pretty straightforward, and we will talk about height and width, but knowing how big to make your images involves a bit of knowledge about the technology used, the method in which the game world is built, and how the texture will be used in that world. A texture that is huge but on a small sign that the player will never go near is a waste of texture memory. Likewise, a texture that covers 80% of the walls of your level, which the player will spend most of his time running past, probably warrants a much larger image.

In addition, we will talk about the *grid*. The grid is a bit of a throwback to games that required rigid geometry placement for various technical reasons. Nowadays, in most cases, we can literally build levels any way we like with no regard for right angles and grids, but if we do things that way, we run into problems. The grid is still very important for many reasons and makes building easier. Laying out textures on a grid makes them fit perfectly together—not just one texture tiling with itself, but a set of textures that will fit together when combined in the game world. When you are using a set of many textures you've built on the grid, in a game world built on the same grid, things will match up perfectly and look solid. When the textures and world elements are both built on the same grid, we can also more easily keep track of relative proportions of objects in the world as we work.

We will also look at UV mapping. Even though we won't be doing any UV mapping in the book, it makes texture creation a little easier, and the process will make more sense if you understand how your textures will be applied to the surfaces of the 3D game world. You will see how the textures you create in this book are applied to the 3D scenes they are decorating.

Finally, we will look at shaders at the end of this chapter. Shaders allow a level of realism in games that is stunning and getting better all the time. Very simply, a *shader* is a mini-program that processes graphic effects in real time. Shaders are used for image effects such as hair, fire, shadows, water, reflections, and so on. Although shaders play a huge role in game development, you still need to know basic texture creation to get the best results. Later in the book we actually build the assets for a shader.

Even though this book is focused on creating game textures, it is important to introduce some technical concepts. Since looking at every conceivable graphic file format or aspect of technology would be counterproductive, I will keep the discussion brief.

## Chapter Overview

- Common features of graphic file formats
- The power of two and the grid
- UV mapping
- Shader technology for artists

## Common Features of Graphic File Formats

Let's discuss graphic formats from a functional point of view rather than list every graphic file format available. The most common options that are typically available and used by the game artist are really what you need to know.

### Vector and Bitmapped Files

There are basically two types of graphic files: vector and bitmapped. A *bitmapped file* is the native format for the Windows environment and contains *pixels* (or colored dots). When you zoom into a bitmapped image, you can see the pixels. Though a bitmap is a type of image, a bitmapped image can be one of many different formats. Game developers deal almost exclusively with bitmapped images and the options associated with them, so they will naturally be our focus. There has been some gradual adoption of vector-based images in user interfaces (UIs) and menu construction in the form of fancy menu and UI systems, but these are very much like Flash-based sites on the Internet and are built in the same manner. Game content in a 3D game is still almost exclusively bitmapped.

### Source and Output Files: Distinctions

There is a distinction between the format of the output file (game-ready art) and the format of the original (source) file. The source file is what the game artist creates in Photoshop using large image sizes and many image options. The artist will then output a copy of that image and resize, convert, and optimize it. In actual production you will almost certainly work in Photoshop's proprietary file format (PSD) as the source file; these files get very large. Your source image will always be larger and of higher detail than the output file. The PSD file format is very flexible and saves a large amount of information. The output file—the game-ready art— is much smaller.

This book is focused on the creation of the flexible source file in the PSD format. When the time comes to output any of these images for use as a texture in a game, you will determine the size, format, and other details about the final image. The image you see in a game may only be 256 by 256 pixels (you can often see the pixels if you look closely) but is most certainly a smaller and more optimized copy of the original PSD file. Although the smaller compressed game image may be 43k in file size, the original PSD file may easily be 40 megabytes or larger. Photoshop saves lots of other data specific to the PSD format and useful in image creation, such as layers, levels, alpha channels, adjustment layers, layer effects, text layers, layer sets—and a great deal more, even audio files and attached notes. Don't let all this confuse you; you will be introduced to the PSD file later.

**Warning** One mistake that many new artists make is to work in Photoshop on a source image, forget they are editing the source, and then resize and convert the original and save it. Once you do that and close the file, you can't go back. When you are later asked to alter that image, you have only the small, low-detail version to work with. You will see exactly what I am talking about later in this chapter with the introduction of layers.

## Choosing a File Format

I use (and recommend) the following four criteria to choose a file format for output:

- *What looks best.* This is the most important consideration from the artist's point of view but often changes as a result of the other equally important criteria.
- *What the development technology requires.* Quite simply, if you don't generate assets to the specifications the game engine requires, the game might not run at all. Some game engines require a list of specifications be met in terms of size, ratio, color depth, format, and so on. Some technologies require the use of an exporter or converter to generate textures in a proprietary format. Still other technologies will take whatever you throw at them without complaining and then simply squish, resize, compress, and otherwise alter the texture to suit their needs.
- *What the target user system requires/will support.* Making a game that will run only on the most powerful computer that money can buy will severely limit your audience. If you are id Software (the creators of DOOM, Quake, and so on ... I don't have to tell you that, do I?) you can pull this off since people will actually upgrade their systems to play your game (I often spend hundreds of dollars to build or upgrade my computer so that I can play a $50 game). But that case is, of course, the exception and not the rule. Most developers must determine what computers their audience will most likely be using when their game is released. Console developers know almost exactly what they are developing for in terms of hardware configuration, but PC developers have to make complex decisions that always leave someone unhappy. Due to the vast variations in power, configuration, and compatibility of all the PCs in the world, game designers often need to develop significant amounts of technology and additional assets to deal with these differences by offering the user many configuration options. Or you develop to the least common denominator, knowing that you are not creating the best game you can because you are not developing for cutting-edge hardware. But game play is king, so often a low-tech game will break out on the sales charts.
- *What your boss tells you to use.* I am not trying to be flippant here. You could face circumstances in which a superior tells you what format an asset needs to be, and usually the reason is logical. You can ask why or simply obey, but I don't advise ignoring the instructions.

**Format Options**

Here are some of the most commonly used and critical features of graphic formats that game artists use most. As you work on different teams using different development technologies, you will learn about the numerous file formats and the options specific to each format. But the core functionality of these files will be fundamentally the same. So, understanding the basic information presented here will make the adoption of those varying formats and their options much easier.

**Note** *To Second Lifers and other virtual world creators:* Keep in mind that in most computer games, the final form of the texture you create is what is used by the engine, but in many online worlds, no matter what the texture is when it leaves your computer, it is common that it will be resized, converted, and compressed on the server to make things work smoothly in the virtual world. So, if the texture that you created looks terrible in the world, it may be that it has been heavily processed on the server side.

## Compression

*Compression* is simply the process of making a file smaller in size. It's easier said than done for a programmer. Creating compression routines that don't ruin visual quality is of course a complex programming task, but as artists we deal with compression primarily on a visual basis, judging whether we like the quality of the compressed image. We will make sure that our file meets the technical requirements and then press "Save As" and we are done. Most game artists want to learn more about the various compression schemes and their options so that they can create the smallest file size with maximum image quality.

Some image formats use absolutely no compression, preserving the image in its original state and losing no data. These are called *lossless* formats, whereas a *lossy* format will allow compression that strips out and reorganizes data in various ways and results in data loss for a smaller file size at the cost of visual quality to varying degrees. Compression is almost exclusively used on the output file and not on the source asset because it degrades quality. In Figure 2.1 you can see some examples of what compression can do to an image.

## Alpha Channels

*Alpha channels* are simply black-and-white or grayscale images. These images can be used in different ways, but typically they are used for transparency or masking. In other words, an alpha channel can make a portion of an image completely transparent or (depending on the quality of the alpha channel) semitransparent. In Figure 2.2 you can see a very common use for the alpha channel: foliage. The use of the alpha channel extends to other objects as well—objects that have details that would be better created using the alpha channel method rather than modeling the detail. Wire fences, tree branches, and other real-world objects are often created

**Figure 2.1**
Here are some examples of what compression can do to an image. On the upper left is the original uncompressed image, in the middle is a moderately compressed image, and on the right is a highly compressed image. Below are close-ups of the three images. Notice how the middle image appears to have a pattern of squares over it. This is due to the compression scheme. The image on the right has had many colors stripped out, so the image is very small but, lacking many colors, it looks blotchy. You need to know how close the player will get to this image to determine how small and compressed you can make it.

using alpha channels, and so are effects like muzzle blasts and scorch marks. Because alpha channels can give a semitransparent property to a model, they have been used on ghosts, water, fire, and other ethereal effects. Look at the ferns in the previous example. The use of alpha channels allows for much more complex and realistic shapes than can be efficiently created in 3D in some cases. If you modeled each fern in 3D, there would need to be so many polygons it would be impractical, the other option being terribly "geometric"-looking ferns if modeled using a low number of polygons.

Source

Alpha

Alpha in use

Alpha in use in scene

**Figure 2.2**
An alpha channel is typically used to make parts of an image transparent. Here you can see how a few polygons and one image can make these ferns look complex and organic because we can make parts of this image transparent.

When doing a "Save As" or "Export" of an image from Photoshop, you need to make sure that the format you are saving to supports alpha channels; otherwise that information may be lost. Typically, alpha channels are preserved in many formats, but not all formats. Keep in mind the distinction between *exporting to a format*, which typically means that you are creating another version of that file, and *saving a file*. As mentioned previously, if you resize and degrade your source asset and save the file, you will lose the ability to easily alter and re-export the asset. Usually the "Save As" or "Export" function will warn you about the potential for loss or tell you the options available to you in that format. In Figure 2.3 showing a "Save As" window, you can see that the software is warning the user that on this file being saved as a JPG, layers and alpha channels will not be preserved.

Sometimes the alpha channel or mask is part of the file format, and sometimes it is a separate image. In low-quality transparency schemes, it is sometimes only a certain color in the image itself that determines what part of the image is see-through, and there is no separate mask or alpha channel. You can see examples of these types of alpha in the next section on DDS format and DXTC.

## DDS Format and DXTC (Output Format)

DDS is a common file format that game developers output. DDS stands for Microsoft DirectDraw® Surface file format. This format stores textures as well as a lot of other information that is used

**Figure 2.3**
Typically, "Save As" or
"Export" in Photoshop will
warn you about information
that may be lost, such as this
file being saved as a JPG. The
warning is that layers and
alpha channels will not be
preserved.

in-game for various reasons that are both technical and visual in
nature. DDS is the file extension, and the compression scheme is
referred to as Direct X Texture Compression (DXTC). Several tools
allow you to save in the DDS format using DXTC. Douglas H. Rogers,
in the Developer Relations group at NVIDIA, develops Texture
Tools that support DXTC and stores textures in the DDS format. The
developer pages on the NVIDIA Web site contain many useful texture
manipulation tools and a mountain of information for programmers
and content creators:

http://developer.nvidia.com/ (NVIDIA's developer Web site)
http://developer.nvidia.com/object/nv_texture_tools.html (Texture
    Tools)

Figure 2.4 shows the NVIDIA DDS tools interface. This is an easy-to-
install plug-in that allows the exporting of the DDS file format from
Photoshop. After you select "Save As" in Photoshop and select the
DDS format, the NVIDIA tool activates. On the Texture Tools interface,
you will see a lot of options available for the output format of the
image and tools to view the choices you make. There are options
for compression, MIP map filtering, sharpening, fading, normal map
creation, and more. We will discuss only the compression options
here because the other options are outside the scope of this book.
Suffice it to say that you have a lot of control with this tool. Among
the various options, the two you will be most concerned with are
compression and the alpha channel. You can decide to compress an
image a great deal (8:1) if you can get away with it visually, or use no
compression if you want the highest possible quality. There is also a
3D preview window so that you can see various versions of the texture
before you save the image to disk. You can zoom, rotate, and move

**Figure 2.4**
This is the NVIDIA DDS tools interface, an easy-to-install (and very useful) plug-in that allows you to export the DDS file format from Photoshop. After you select "Save As" in Photoshop, there are many options and tools to view various versions of the file before committing to the version of the file you want to export.

the image in the window, and you can even assign a background color or background image to the preview window. By choosing the background, you can see your textures in context. It only makes sense that if you are developing a texture with an alpha channel—the bars of a cage, for example, that sit in front of another texture, maybe a dark stucco wall or bright canvas tent; it helps to see the two textures together. This method makes work flow much faster because you can see what you are getting before you commit to exporting the file, checking the results, exporting again, and guessing each time as to whether you made the proper adjustments to the image.

The DXT compression scheme can reduce texture size eightfold (fourfold if there is an alpha channel). In my experience, the images still look really good, especially considering the reduction in file size. You must examine both the visual and technical results of any file you output, and that's where the NVIDIA tools really come in handy. In general, the DDS format allows for the highest quality and most efficient output of assets and gives you the tools to make that balancing act much easier. There are many options, but most likely you will use four main compression options: DXT1 (with no alpha), DXT1 (with alpha), DXT3, and DXT5 (both have alpha).

- DXT1 with no transparency is the most compressed of the choices and results in the smallest file size.
- DXT1 with alpha transparency offers a simple version of alpha with an on/off alpha transparency scheme (which is not supported by some game engines). In this scheme the pixel is either completely transparent or completely opaque and results in jagged edges in the image. Consequently, this compression scheme has limited uses.
- DXT3 and DXT5 have more refined alpha channels, and both result in a larger file size. You can see in the previous figure of the DDS Viewer that the file size and compression scheme used are displayed below the image. These image sizes are larger because this format saves the alpha channel as a separate image inside itself. In case there is any confusion, you are effectively doubling your image file size because of the alpha but not the pixel dimensions of the image. Both these schemes result in the same file size. Then why the two choices? Though each has the same color compression scheme, they have different compression schemes for the alpha channel. They will each generate good or bad results depending on the texture. You should visually compare how the alpha looks in each format to choose the right one, but it is safe to say that you will be using DXT5 the most. The tool makes this visual comparison very easy. The example in Figure 2.5 shows a window with fine granularity in the alpha channel, so it requires DXT3 or DXT5. You can see that the less refined alpha scheme of DXT1 simply will not work on the window. But if you were doing a texture, such as a grate or vent, where a very exact edge between opaque and clear exists, DXT1 will do the trick. These formats are still lossy compression schemes, meaning that some data are lost from the original image.

In general, when using the NVIDIA texture tools, you should always try to compress your textures as much as possible. Use the tool and compare the various images side by side. You will find that DXT1 compression is very good for a lot of images and can save a ton of your texture memory budget, thus allowing you to possibly use more textures in the game. Of course, if you need an alpha channel, use DXT3 or DXT5.

Explore the options in the texture tools if you like; you will find a lot of them. Don't let yourself get overwhelmed, though. You know what you need for now and 80% of what you will most likely need to know in the near future.

**Figure 2.5**
DXT1 uses a more compressed and simplified scheme for transparency that does not always work well in every situation. If you were doing an object where a very exact edge between opaque and clear is needed, DXT1 would work. The grate in the upper-left corner works using DXT1, but the window, which requires a much finer alpha channel, needs DXT5. The file sizes of the two window images are displayed below them. It may be hard to read in the printed version, but they are left 87 k and right 174 k.

### PSD Format (Photoshop/Production Format)

PSD, as mentioned earlier, is the native file format for Photoshop and usually the production format of choice for game developers. This format's file size can get quite large, since it retains a lot of information in a very flexible way so that the artist can easily go back and tweak, or even drastically change, the art and re-output a new file quickly. One of the features of the PSD format that makes it so large and flexible a format is *layers*. We will look at layers in more detail in an upcoming chapter (as well as many of the other numerous tools and features available in Photoshop) and will also use Photoshop layers quite extensively throughout the book. This section provides a quick introduction to the concept.

**Figure 2.6**
At the upper left is the Layers Window as it appears in Photoshop. This tool allows you to move and manipulate layers. The stack of layers on the right is an illustration of the concept of layers and doesn't actually appear in Photoshop that way.

The functionality of layers is one of the first options you will come across in Photoshop. This is an option increasingly available in other formats used by high-end 2D paint programs. Storing an image in layers means that you can effectively store many images on top of each other and control how each layer affects the one under it. Imagine each image being a megabyte in size and storing a stack of those images on top of each other. That is one reason that the resulting file's size can get so large.

In Figure 2.6 you can see the Layers Window as it appears in Photoshop. This is the window that lets you move and manipulate layers and is not the actual image. The stack of layers on the right is an illustration of the concept of layers and doesn't actually appear in Photoshop that way. What you see in the Photoshop image window, the actual image you are editing, is what the final image will look like, whether it is in layers or flattened.

*Flattened* means what it sounds like: When all the layers are reduced to one layer, the image becomes one layer—one image. When this happens (if you save your file and thus can't undo the flatten operation), you lose all flexibility. Notice that in the Layer Window the layer named "Dark Stucco" is turned off (there is no eye icon next

**Figure 2.7**
Here you can see two examples of how various textures were built up using layers in one file and, furthermore, how layer control allows for the modification and quick output of a texture.

to it like the others), so this layer, though actually in the file, is not visible and is not part of the final texture as a result. Also notice that the layer "Horizontal beams" is on top of the layer "Vertical beams," and these beams have that relationship in the final texture. I output the final texture, which you can see at the lower left of the figure. Layers are critical in texture creation because they allow you to build textures in an easy and effective way and to keep the layers separate so the texture can be adjusted and modified and quickly output again. In Figure 2.7 you can see several examples of how layers are used in Photoshop. Imagine if this layer were flattened and I wanted to remove an element that is part of the final image, such as the horizontal or vertical beams or the cracks. It would be tough: I would essentially have to rebuild the texture instead of clicking a layer on and off.

## The Power of Two and the Grid

Now we will speak a bit about working with 2D images that are meant to be used in a 3D space such as a game world. Most game art books talk a lot about image resolution, and that is an important topic, but for now all you need to know is that you are restricted in most games to a certain image size. When you create a 2D image for a game, you will always have parameters, restrictions, and rules that you must follow, and they can range in number from a few to many. Where you are working, what technology you are using, and even what type of game you are making all contribute to determining those specific parameters and guidelines. The most basic and general requirement for game art is that you must make your textures a power of two in size, which means that the images must be a specific number of pixels in height and width. These sizes are typically as follows:

- $16 \times 16$
- $32 \times 32$
- $64 \times 64$
- $128 \times 128$
- $256 \times 256$
- $512 \times 512$
- $1024 \times 1024$
- $2048 \times 2048$

It is now common to use $2048 \times 2048$ maps and much less common to see anything smaller than 256 in most games.

**Note** A $512 \times 512$ image is four times as large as a $256 \times 256$ image, just as a $256 \times 256$ image is four times larger than a $128 \times 128$ image. Sometimes the fact that the power-of-two numbers are twice as big as the previous number throws some people off. The fact that $256 \times 2 = 512$ makes it seem logical on the surface. But look at Figure 2.8 for a visual representation of this concept. Understanding that concept, you can see that a $512 \times 512$ has four times the pixels of a $256 \times 256$ image. Not long ago, a $512 \times 512$ image was considered a large texture.

We are commonly using $1024 \times 1024$ images as a standard size and frequently go up to $2048 \times 2048$. Add to that hardware and software advances and the jump in visual quality of a game is simply incredible. This may be even more true for those of us who have watched game technology creep along at first, explode, and then keep growing exponentially. The advances are across the board, and most contribute directly to the visual quality of a game: rag doll physics, more complex and refined animation tools, improved artificial intelligence (AI), more complex yet easier-to-use particle systems—the list is very long.

Back to the power of two and the first question that most people ask: "Why must we make our textures a power of two?" The simplified answer is that most computer game engines and 3D cards require a texture to fit certain criteria because they can process and display them faster. Most game engines do not restrict texture size to a perfect square. Rectangular sizes like $256 \times 512$ and $128 \times 1024$ are usually acceptable. I started the list of sizes at $16 \times 16$, but most game engines today don't even use textures smaller than 1024 and when they do it is usually for particles and small decals. Plugging in an asset with the wrong parameters can cause an error message, and

**Figure 2.8**
A 512 × 512 image is four times as large as a 256 × 256 image, not twice as large. The fact that the number 512 is twice as big as 256 sometimes throws people off. I used an image of some tiles so you can see the relationship. The 256 image overlaid takes up one-fourth of the area of the 512 image.

the asset will be ignored and some engines will even crash. Some engines/game tools might even alter the asset so that it will work, changing size, format, color depth, and so on.

The power-of-two limit actually doesn't exist in the code of many 3D graphics engines but is still commonly imposed on game developers for various reasons. I believe that you can already use non–power-of-two textures in certain engines, but I would still stick to the grid for most of the work unless I was in an uncommon situation where I needed to use a non–power-of-two texture. Maybe I am biased and simply used to working on the grid, but I believe that it makes building a game easier for everyone involved, from the texture artist to the level designer. That takes us to the next point about the grid: Aside from technical reasons to use the power of two and a grid, there are productivity issues.

So, your images need to be certain pixel dimensions for technical reasons (currently they won't work in most game engines if they aren't exact), but it also helps in production to work with these standard sizes. Most major game-world editors (the software tool that you use to build the game world) use a grid system based on the same power-of-two dimensions. If you lay out a hall with a floor that is 256 units wide in the world and place a 256-pixel image on that floor, you are going to get a perfect fit. You can also make the texture 512 pixels and scale the UV mapping down by exactly 50%, and once again, you will get a perfect fit. You can use an image of a tile that is only 128 pixels and UV that cross the floor in a repeating pattern and get a perfect fit, too. This way of measuring makes everyone's life easier because you are not guessing, eyeballing, and trying to calculate how to make variously sized images fit in odd-sized spaces.

When working in Photoshop, you can use the grid tool to lay a grid over your workspace to subdivide a power-of-two texture into smaller power-of-two units. We will talk about how to do that later in the book, but for now just know that Photoshop allows for the placing of grids and guidelines over your image that are not part of the art but rather are tools that help you keep things straight. For a game developer this functionality is very useful—you just have to remember to set your grid spaces to the power of two. In the commonly used 3D packages like 3ds Max and Maya, you can also set up a custom grid to these dimensions. The result is that the models, textures, and world space are all built on a standard grid, giving the developer consistent units and sizes. A simple example would be the creation of an object for a game decoration, such as a doorway arch. If the texture artist creates a texture for the arch that is 512 × 1024 and the modeler makes the model of the arch on a grid and creates the arch model 512 × 1024, the image will fit perfectly over it. I left out the third dimension of depth in the model for this example, to keep things simple. That textured model will then fit perfectly in a 512 × 1024 doorway that was built on the grid in the game world. Figure 2.9 shows the visual for this example.

Another reason for creating visual elements within a texture on the grid is so that they line up with each other, even if they are on different textures. For example, in many first-person shooters, the height of a stair is 16 units (a power of two). Therefore, if you make a wall texture with a floor molding 16 units high, it will look much neater when the wall molding runs into the stairs. Even though the real world is often put together in a way that defies these guidelines, that is no excuse to allow those mistakes in a game. In a game those are mistakes and they are noticeable and not looked upon as a faithful recreation of reality. In the real world, you will see wallpaper that wasn't hung correctly, with seams that don't meet up with each other, or a brick wall that was repaired with bricks that don't

**Figure 2.9**
A texture created on a grid will fit perfectly on a model created on the same grid, which in turn will fit perfectly into a game world built on the same grid. In this case, the arch model (left) is 512 × 1024, the texture (middle) is also 512 × 1024, and the boring doorway (right) that we are trying to fill in the game world is of the same dimensions. You can see all the elements together in the image at the bottom.

match in color, grass sod that has been laid down in squares by a landscaper and visually tiled, and other messy real-world examples. In Figure 2.10 you can see a simple texture set applied to a game setting; note how all the various textures fit with each other on the various surfaces of the room.

Although some artists view the grid as a limit, others appreciate it as a tool. And given the fact that we are not bound to it nearly as much as we were just a few years ago, it is more of a tool now than a restraint. Working on the grid helps the world stay consistent and look better, and frankly, you can work much faster. This is called *modular design*. Modular design is very important when you work on a computer game. A computer game requires efficiency and organization. No matter how powerful computers get, you always want to squeeze out every ounce

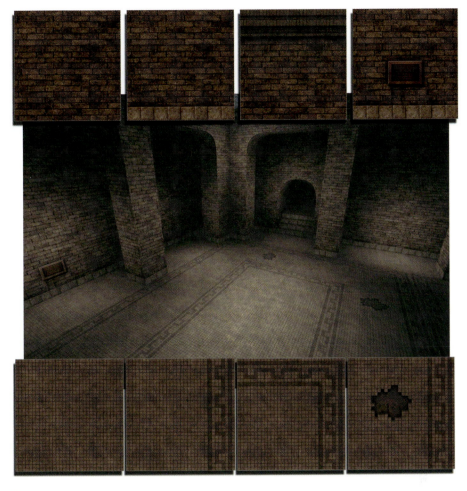

**Figure 2.10**
This texture set of eight textures was built off two base textures: tiles and bricks. Building everything on the grid in Photoshop and 3ds Max allowed for the seamless tiling of the entire set. Notice the pattern that runs through the floor and how it meets at every turn. I was able to rotate the tile with the corner pattern on it and have it still match up to the others. It is pretty easy to tile tiles, I admit, but by making sure they met up properly in Photoshop, I was able to use one corner pattern tile instead of four.

of performance you can. The best way to do that is to use only the textures you need, no more and no less.

## Modular Design

In the context of texture creation, modular design is the art of designing and creating your textures so that they will all fit together. This starts with simple tiling and moves into the next realm of advanced tiling, which we will, of course, cover in Chapter 4, "Prepping for Texture Creation." In the real world, a great example of modular design is office furniture. You can buy the core desk and add hutches, lighted cabinets, bookcase extensions, and on and on. All these parts are designed to fit together, allowing you to create hundreds of combinations, thus ending up with a desk that is unique and fits your office and your needs. Add to that the ability to swap textures … I mean, select the color and finish you want, and you end up with a huge variety of options.

Earlier you saw an example of texture modularity with the set of textures based on a brick and tile with variations that all fit together. The base brick wall covers most of the surface of the game world. To make that space interesting, I added trim, cracks, a baseboard, a vent, and other details. As we progress, you will become very familiar with the concept of modularity. Modularity extends to all aspects of game design, and 3D modelers often create modular chunks of a game world that can be copied and arranged. Typically, modelers start with the large common and repetitive chunks such as floor panels, wall panels, ceiling panels, and other repetitive large-world geometry, then move into decorations such as columns, lamps, and special case meshes. They may even create versions of the large modular chunks with damage such as cracks or holes in them. The power of two and the grid are both limits and tools for creating clean, solid levels. In Figure 2.11 you can see the base 3D parts of a simple level set; in Figure 2.12 the parts are assembled into a room and hall; and in Figure 2.13, the room and hall are textured. In Figure 2.14 you can see an additional example of modular design. The castle wall is actually two pieces: one undamaged and one damaged.

As you create textures on a specific project, you will find that in most instances there are many other parameters to consider besides the grid, but these concern the final output file more than the source file. Although the grid must be considered as you build, things like the largest and smallest file size that the engine can handle, the total texture memory you are allotted, and other technical details are pretty much reserved for after the texture is created and pertain to the output file.

As a side note on technical limits, just because there is a maximum texture size a game engine can handle doesn't mean that you should use a lot of textures at the maximum size. A large image on a small object or one that a player never sees close up is just a waste of resources. In fact, though some game engines demand very specific input parameters, others allow for multiple color depths, variable file

**Figure 2.11**
These are the basic 3D pieces of geometry for building a modular level.

sizes and resolutions, and even differing formats. Knowing your engine is important because you can cut file sizes significantly with little to no loss of visual quality simply by knowing what options you have.

You'll find that limits will always be imposed on you by development technology, game design, target audience, or even genre. Certain texture size is currently just one of those limits. Most important, knowing those limits and what you can do to work around them makes you more valuable than being just a great artist. If you are able to experiment with file size, compression, color depth, and so on and are able to get twice the number of textures into the game, you will not only free yourself up to do more as an artist—you will also be much more valuable as a developer.

**Figure 2.12**
Here the base pieces are assembled into a simple room and hall.

**Figure 2.13**
The simple room and hall, textured.

**Figure 2.14**
Here is an example of a modular piece of geometry. There are two sections of castle wall; one is undamaged and one has a gaping hole in it. They were built on the grid, so they meet up perfectly. The wall here is several normal wall sections lined up with a damaged section in the middle.

## UV Mapping

All the textures that you create will end up being mapped onto a 3D object. *UV mapping* at its simplest is the process of placing a 2D texture on a 3D mesh. We will look at the various ways textures can be placed on a 3D object.

**Note** There is a distinction between a texture and a skin. A *skin* is the art that goes on a more complex model such as a character, monster, or weapon. Skins are generally not tileable and are created for a specific mesh. A *texture* is generally the art that covers the game-world surfaces: grass, floor tiles, walls, and so on. UVing these surfaces is much simpler than skinning an organic model. You will not be applying your textures to any 3D meshes in this book, but you should understand the various UV mapping types, since they can affect the way you create your textures in some cases.

### Mapping Types

#### Planar Mapping

*Planar mapping* works like a projector. The texture is projected onto the 3D surface from one direction. This method can be used on walls and other flat planar surfaces, but it is limited and can't be used

**Figure 2.15**
Planar mapping projects the texture onto the 3D mesh from one direction. This technique can be used on walls and other flat planar surfaces. However, it is limited and can't be used on complex objects. Projecting the texture in one direction creates smearing on the sides of a 3D model that don't face the planar projection directly.

on complex objects, since the process of projecting the texture in one direction also creates smearing on the sides of the 3D model that don't directly face the planar projection. See Figure 2.15 for an illustration of the planar UV mapping type.

## Box Mapping

*Box mapping* projects the texture onto the model from six sides. This method works great on boxes! This mapping scheme can be useful in some varying situations if you plan for it. Obviously you can use it on more complex boxes, and if you design on the grid you can make things work to your benefit. In Figure 2.16 you can see how the box mapping type works in the upper-left corner of the image. At the top

**Figure 2.16**
Upper left: This is how the box-mapping type works. Top right: A rusted box texture and a close-up of the edge of the texture. The edge of the box in the texture is exactly 16 units wide. The box model below has an edge that is exactly 16 units wide as well.

right is a rusted box texture and a close-up of the edge of the texture. I made the edge of the box exactly 16 units wide in the texture. Now look at the box model below that. It has an edge that is exactly 16 units wide as well. I can use box mapping here, and the fact that the texture is projected straight through the model causes that 16-unit edge of the texture to map perfectly on all the edges of the outer and inner rims of the box. The lower-right corner has a close-up of the box, and you can see how the highlights and all the edges meet cleanly.

### Spherical Mapping

*Spherical mapping* surrounds the object and projects the map from all sides in a spherical pattern. You will see where the texture meets along the edge unless you have created a texture that tiles correctly. Furthermore, the texture gets gathered up, or pinched, at the top and bottom of the sphere. Spherical mapping is obviously great for planets and other spherical things. See Figure 2.17.

### Cylindrical Mapping

*Cylindrical mapping* projects the map by wrapping it around in a cylindrical shape. Seams will show if you have not tiled the texture properly. Cylindrical mapping can be used on tree trunks, columns, and the like. See Figure 2.18 for some examples of cylindrical mapping.

Those are the most basic UV mapping types and are the most common ways that we will apply world textures. Actually, world textures are mostly planar- or box-mapped onto the faces of the world. The process of applying these standard UV mapping types is pretty straightforward and usually automatic in the game editor and can be easily changed by the level builder.

## Game Optimizations

To be successful, a computer game must look good and run well. This is a game artist's mantra. Until you have tried to accomplish this goal, you have no idea how much at odds these objectives are. Although the primary focus of this book is the generation of art assets for computer game environments, we can't escape the fact that creating art for a game is more than just making a pretty picture. When you create art for a game, you need to create art that will accomplish several goals, the least of which is that your art must work technically in the game environment and work as efficiently as possible in that environment. This goal requires planning and creating your art to very specific guidelines. Those guidelines may change depending on many variables (I will discuss these later), but they are all essentially the same variables. In any case, you need to be very well aware of what those variables are and build accordingly.

The process of making a game run at its very best is called *optimization*. It is a common belief that this is solely the domain of the programmer—but nothing could be further from the truth. It is, in fact, everyone's job to optimize from day one. The artists have a huge

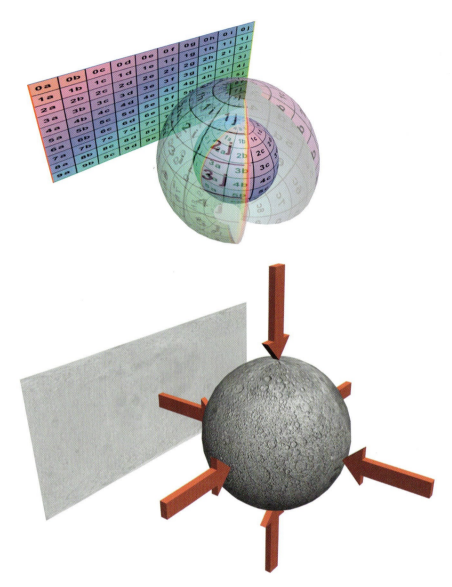

**Figure 2.17**
Spherical mapping surrounds the object and projects the map from all sides in a spherical pattern. You will see where the texture meets along the edge unless you have created a texture that tiles correctly. Spherical mapping is great for planets.

impact on how well a game runs, so we need to know every trick possible to achieve this goal. It cannot be stressed enough that you have to be familiar with the most common methods of game-world optimization because much of what can be done to optimize a game is under your control and takes place during asset creation or the implementation of the asset into the world.

There are many things that can or need to be done during the actual assembly of the game world—tasks that might fall to you. Because the computer game must not only look good but also run well, you

**Figure 2.18**
Cylindrical mapping projects the map by wrapping it around in a cylindrical shape.

will have to use every trick available to you. If you don't, the game world will not run well enough to use or will not look as good as it can. If you fail to make the game look as good as possible due to a lack of optimization, you are wasting an opportunity as valuable as gold in game development.

Game performance is usually expressed as frames per second (fPS). There is a definite limit to what you can do as an artist, programmer, or designer based on fPS—no matter what system specs you are working with. If frame rate is inefficiently used in one place and goes undetected, it is by definition diminishing the available frame rate in other areas of the game. One of my pet peeves is the last-minute gutting of a game to make it run. I have seen entire levels that have taken weeks and months to perfect be gutted at the last minute. Trade-offs are unavoidable, but if you don't look at your game in its totality and track your frame rate (among other resources), you are going to get caught unaware at the end of development as the game comes together and doesn't run as you had hoped (Figure 2.19).

Let me repeat (because this drives me absolutely nuts): You have to track your resources. Just because you can run through your level at 120 fPS doesn't mean that performance is assured. You have to consider several things before celebrating the blistering frame rate: Are you using the target machine, or are you using a high-end machine typical of most development studios? What is left to implement in the game? Are the collision detection and physics in place? What about running AI and game logic? Sometimes the addition of a heads-up display or interface slows things down. As soon as you fire a weapon, you are potentially triggering collision detection, creating hundreds of assets (particles) triggering sound events, displaying decals on walls, and so on. Think about the addition of other players and characters and their weapons. Suddenly you have thousands more polygons on the screen, a few more large textures loading, and other assets and events. In short, can you think of every possible thing the final game will have running and guess what your frame rate target should actually be? You probably can't get a dead-on correct answer early in development, but an educated guess (have lunch with the programmers and question them—they'll love you for it) and the awareness that your actual frame rate will be cut in half when the game is up and running in full will help you hit a more realistic target and prevent the total destruction of a game level at the last minute.

**Figure 2.19**
You can't see it, but is the game engine drawing it and wasting resources?

RADIUS CALCULATING ACTUAL VISIBILITY TO CAMERA

OBJECT NOT VISIBLE TO PLAYER

CONE OF CAMERA VIEW

This section looks at some of the most common tools and techniques accessible to the artist for optimizing a game world. I present them from the artist's point of view, meaning how the tool or technique works and what control the artist generally has over it. Usually you will see that most of these tools and techniques are explored or presented from the programmer's point of view (they are very involved programmatically, to put it mildly), but artists really need to understand these devices, since they are critical to making a level look good and run well.

I personally break optimization into three major areas: asset based, collision based, and occlusion based. In this book we will look only at the asset-based optimizations, because they are in the domain of the texture artist. The other two take place in the modeling and world-building phases. Aside from the things we as artists can do to optimize the game, there are of course many other areas that also need to be optimized. Most of these optimizations are found in the program code. Things like memory management, central processing unit (CPU) and graphics processing unit (GPU) code, AI, collision code, networking, sound, and the game play itself all eat up resources and need to be optimized by the programmers.

*Asset-based optimizations* are simply those optimizations that you can implement and affect during asset production. *Assets* are the art we create, and they present the first opportunity that we have to apply any optimizations. Technically, there are always opportunities from day one to keep optimizations in mind and apply them during the design phase, but often the artist is not present during this time. Our first opportunity is usually when we start to create the assets for the game. Some optimizations are possible in the design and planning of the assets; for example, the design of how a texture is laid out affects the way the UV maps are laid out, and that in turn can affect performance.

**Note** *You!* Yes, you! You the artist are responsible for a great deal of the optimization in a game. In every phase, from planning to create the assets to producing the assets and introducing those assets into the game world, there are opportunities to optimize.

The most common asset-based optimizations are:

- MIP mapping
- Texture pages
- Unlit textures
- Multiple UV channels
- Lightmaps
- Masking and transparency
- Texture size and compression

## MIP Mapping

*MIP mapping*, sometimes called *texture level of detail* (LOD), is usually a programmer-controlled function, but sometimes the artist is given control of this function, too. *MIP* stands for the Latin phrase *multum in parvo*, which means "many things in a small place." The explanation is pretty simple: A large texture seen at a far distance in a game world looks the same as a smaller texture due to the fact that both are being displayed using the same number of pixels on screen; it is therefore a waste of resources to use a large texture on an object that is far away in the game world. In addition, using a larger texture on a small, faraway object usually doesn't look as good as the smaller texture would, due to the fact that the larger texture is being resized on the fly by the game engine. To solve both these problems, programmers usually implement some form of MIP mapping.

MIP mapping is the creation of multiple sizes of a texture for display at various distances in the game (Figure 2.20). Sometimes you can see the MIP maps pop as they change from larger to smaller, especially in older games. MIP mapping allows the texture to be viewed close up and in detail as well as render faster (and look better) from a distance. Figure 2.21 shows the MIP-mapped texture of some jungle vines. Notice that the alpha channel is MIP mapped as well. Fortunately, NVIDIA created several tools to make all this easier for the artist (Figure 2.22). The DXT Compression Plug-in is one of the most useful tools, and I discuss that later in this chapter in the section on texture size and compression. With this tool you can control many variables that affect the visual quality of the image.

**Note** Texture LOD and LOD pertaining to a 3D model in the game engine are both the same concept, but one applies to the use of gradually smaller 2D assets and the other applies to 3D.

### Texture Pages (or T-Pages, Atlas Textures, or Texture Packing)

This section starts with a bit of a disclaimer: It seems that the industry is now moving away from texture atlases. Although atlases

**Figure 2.20**
A texture that has MIP maps associated with it. (Sample image from *Glory of the Roman Empire,* courtesy of Haemimont Games).

will continue to be an effective solution for some hardware, things are shifting over (due to technical reasons that are beyond me) to individual textures. That's great news for me—I find that texture atlases slow things down in the typical artist's workflow.

As you build a game world, you create many textures to cover the many 3D objects in the world. When the game world is loaded and run in the game engine, the game engine has to access (call) each of those textures for each frame it renders. These calls slow everything down, so it is desirable to reduce the number of calls. You can use a technique called *texture packing*, which is creating a texture atlas, that can accomplish this task. Basically, texture packing involves taking a large group of textures that are related in some way (usually geographically close to one another in the game world) and putting

**Figure 2.21**
A texture that has MIP maps associated with it and an alpha channel. Notice that the alpha channel is MIP mapped as well. (Sample image from *Glory of the Roman Empire,* courtesy of Haemimont Games).

**Figure 2.22**
This figure shows the interface and examples of the NVIDIA MIP-mapping tool.

**Figure 2.23**
An example of an atlas texture.

them together to create one large texture. You can see a texture atlas of foliage created for a jungle level in Figure 2.23. You can create an atlas by hand or with a tool. Of course, NVIDIA makes such a tool (Figure 2.24). The primary benefit of a tool like this for the artist is the speed at which atlases can be built and altered. This tool creates the one large texture and with it a file that tells the game engine where each image is placed on the master image.

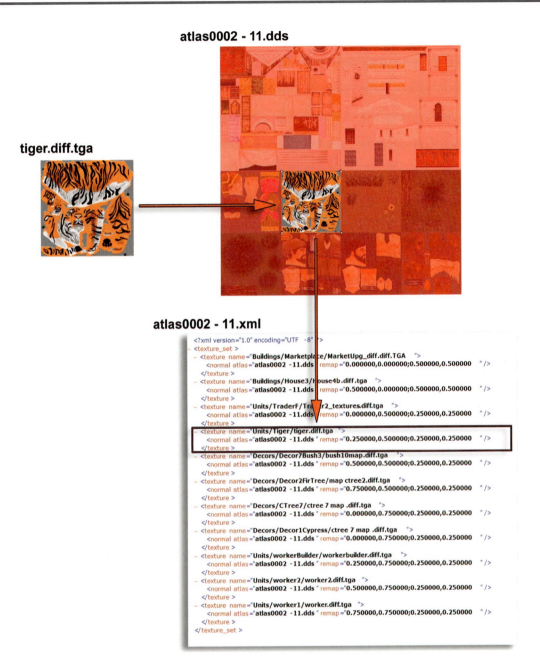

**Figure 2.24**
The texture atlas and accompanying index file.

## Unlit Textures

An *unlit texture* is a texture that is unaffected by lighting and displays at 100% brightness—sometimes called a *full bright* or *self-illuminated texture*. Note that this not the same as a texture that uses an illumination map. When an illumination map is used, it must calculate lighting for a texture and take into account the grayscale illumination map. Because calculating the lighting for a texture can be one of the biggest resource hogs in a game, it can be much more practical to use an unlit texture, which renders much faster.

**Figure 2.25**
An example of a texture that is lit in one scene and unlit in the next.

Using unlit textures is a way to boost performance. This technique is easy with some materials such as water or certain signs, and in some game types or genres you can get away with using large numbers of unlit textures. Large forested outdoor areas can benefit from the use of unlit textures on the foliage. Figure 2.25 shows an example of a texture that is lit in one scene and then unlit in the next. Notice how the sign is at full brightness and remains unchanged by the lighting affecting the walls. Particle systems typically look better unlit and run faster as well (Figure 2.26).

### Multitexturing or Multiple UV Channels

Increasingly often in today's game engines you are not limited to one UV channel. Thus you are allowed to combine textures on a surface in real time. That in turn allows a great degree of variety from a relatively small set of assets. A grayscale image may simply define the dark and light areas of a surface, another map may define color, and another some unique detail. You can see an example of this method in Figure 2.27. The building mesh has a base-colored material applied; on a separate channel I applied dirt, and on another I added details such as posters and cracks. Multiple UV channels are also used to apply bump mapping and other shader effects.

**Figure 2.26**
Particles, lit and unlit.

BASE

**Figure 2.27**
Multitexturing allows you to combine a relatively small set of assets in creating a large variety of surfaces.

## Lightmaps

*Lightmaps* are prerendered images that define the light and shadow on the surfaces of your world. Lightmaps are created before the game runs and are saved as part of a file, which means that the size of that file is increased. There are two things you can do to optimize lightmaps: Lower their resolution or compress them. A smaller lightmap will result in a faster loading and running level, but lowering the resolution also lowers the quality (Figure 2.28).

**Note** For a great article on compressing lightmaps, go to Gamasutra.com and look up "Making Quality Game Textures," by Riccard Linde.

Usually you can opt out of using a lightmap or can determine at what size the lightmap will be created. This step allows you to increase the resolution of the lightmap in those areas where the player can go and lower the resolution for less accessible but visible areas.

**Figure 2.28**
Lightmaps, both large and small, on the same area.

## Masking and Transparency

When possible, it is preferable to use masking instead of transparency because masking renders more quickly. Take a look at Figure 2.29, since these concepts are much easier to grasp pictorially.

*Masking* typically uses a specific color that is designated the "clear" color, and this creates hard, jagged edges (although newer hardware can handle larger-resolution textures and can post-process the images and smooth the edges).

*Transparency* uses a separate additional channel, a grayscale image called the *alpha channel*, to determine the opacity of a pixel. The trade-off is that transparency looks better than masking, but it also requires more file space and more processing power. This is because although masking simply either draws the pixel or not, transparency must look at two pixels (the source image pixel and the on-screen pixel behind it), consider the grayscale pixel of the alpha channel,

**Figure 2.29**
This is the way the three
methods discussed here work
with examples.

and calculate the color of the final on-screen pixel. Technically, what
you are seeing isn't real-world transparency but rather a new image
composed of a blending of two images that gives the illusion of
transparency.

Of course, NVIDIA makes a tool that allows for the rapid adjusting
and viewing of textures before outputting them (Figure 2.30).

## Texture Size and Compression

Make sure to consider the size of each texture you create. A texture
that covers most of the walls and/or floors in your world and has
to tile well while still holding up visually needs to be larger than
a texture that is displayed infrequently and is not subject to the
player's direct examination. The other factor is compression.
A compressed texture file can be significantly smaller than an
uncompressed one yet still maintain visual integrity using the
right combination of compression options. NVIDIA makes a plug-in
(http://developer.nvidia.com) for Photoshop that allows for the rapid
and easy iteration through many compression schemes before final
output of the file (Figure 2.31).

Remember that there are many factors to consider in determining
texture size and compression. How close will the player get to the
asset? How often will the asset appear in the world, and how many
times is it expected to tile or repeat? Can you achieve the same effect
with a more efficient solution? Can you use three small textures
on multiple UV channels as opposed to one enormous texture?
How much can you compress or reduce the resolution of an image
and still maintain visual integrity? One of the most valuable but

**Figure 2.30**
The interface and various
windows of the NVIDIA tool
as applied to masking and
alpha.

underappreciated skills a game artist can acquire is knowing not
only the various ways of implementing game art solutions but what
methods and combination of those methods comprise the best
solution.

## Chapter Exercises

1. Photoshop, with all its powerful tools and options, simply gives
   you an almost unlimited number of ways to do what?
2. Why is working on the grid useful?
3. Explain the difference between a source and an output file.
4. What are the four criteria for choosing a graphic file format?
5. What are the DDS and DXT formats? Explain the features and
   options of these formats.
6. What is the PSD format? List and define at least three features of
   a PSD file.
7. What is the grid? Explain.
8. A 512 × 512 image is how many times as large as a 256 × 256
   image? Explain your answer.
9. What is modular design?
10. What is UV mapping? List and define the most common UV
    mapping types.
11. What is the mantra of a computer game artist?
12. What is optimization and why is it important?
13. Why is it important to track the performance of your game as a
    whole entity?
14. What are the seven optimizations examined in this book and how
    do they speed things up?

**Figure 2.31**
The interface and various windows of the NVIDIA tool as applied to the compression options.

## Conclusion

This chapter presented a quick overview of some vast and complex topics. But the level of coverage of these concepts is enough to help you create textures that will work in a game world. Learning and mastering any one of these concepts will take time, but fear not: good, basic knowledge will allow you to work up to mastering these topics more quickly and more easily.

grayscale

blank

color

norn

**Chapter 3**

ap

normal
map
implemented

# Introduction to Shaders
# and Materials

## Introduction

Shaders allow for a stunning level of realism in games, and the rate at which the hardware is improving is staggering. I purposely wrote this book to address core principles of game art creation that don't change or that change very slowly. Hardware and technology change rapidly, but that doesn't alter the basics of texture, shader and material creation—at least not yet. Figure 3.1 shows some recent screenshots provided by Unigine Corporation of shaders in action. The top scene is from *Tropics*, a benchmark demo that depicts tropical paradise using many shaders: ocean waves stretch off into infinity and undulate, sparkle, refract, and so on. The lagoon islands have sandy beaches with crisp shadows and crawling crabs. There is a ton of detail in this one shot alone as the sun sets on the scene, bathing the huts in color and shadow. The vegetation sways as a gentle ocean breeze passes through. In the animated version of this image (running in real time as a game), you can see the waves crashing on the shore and the clouds moving; there is a lot going on! The two following images show the DirectX 9 version and the DirectX 11 version of the same scene. You can see that the roof and stonework in the building are the places of the most distinction between the two scenes. In the image on the

**Figure 3.1**
Upper image: The *Tropics* benchmark demo from Unigine Corp. Notice the water. It is actually moving in the demo and crashing on the shore and refracting so that the sunken boat is distorted by the waves. Lower image: The two images look almost the same, but the upper one uses DirectX 9 and the lower DirectX 11. With DirectX 11 we can use tessellation, which adds all that detail (protruding stones) in real time.

IMAGES USED WITH PERMISSION OF UNIGINE CORP DEVELOPER OF THE UNIGINE ENGINE TECHNOLOGY 2011

left, the stonework is flat; in the right, it stands out prominently, even casting shadows. This is because DirectX 11 now uses *tessellation*, which is one of the more important DirectX 11 features. Tessellation uses a height map to determine the extent to which a feature should protrude from a surface and actually divides up the mesh and pushes the geometry out from the surface.

DirectX 11, the current version, is beyond amazing to me. I can't go into technical comparisons and discussions without filling a book, but in the last two years alone the graphics card that was top-notch when I bought it runs a game I have at about 10 fPS and the newest cards will run the same game at over 100 fPS. And that is not even a fair comparison because the newer cards are doing so much more in real time. I am purposely vague here because there are so many variables and the technology improves so fast it would be a waste of time to discuss it more at this point.

What this means to you is that although you may create a texture, a shader, and a material in the same manner for one card or the next, the size of the textures, the number of effects and polygons, and so on that you can have in a scene will all go up. This number needs to be assessed when the game you are developing is in the process of being developed.

Simply put, a shader is a mini-program that processes graphic effects in real time. For example, the reflections on a surface can move in real time instead of being "baked," or permanently painted, onto a surface. Shader effects are very powerful visually, even if viewers are unaware of what they are seeing; the average player would have a hard time defining why the game that he or she is playing looks so good. This level of quality may be due to the real-time reflections, normal mapping, or the specular mapping being processed in real time.

Ever since these technologies started rapidly advancing, there has been talk that procedural textures and advanced technologies would one day replace the artist. This will never happen. As amazing as the technology is, it still takes an artist to make these technologies produce the best visual results. In fact, the artist has become more important than ever as technology has become more complex. Although programmers give us incredible new technologies, the artist is still needed to create and control the input and output of those systems.

There are two main types of shader on modern graphics processors (GPUs):

- *Vertex shaders* manipulate geometry (vertices and their attributes) in real time.
- *Pixel shaders* manipulate rendered pixels in real time.

The ability to manipulate an individual pixel or vertex in real time is what makes shaders so powerful; it is also what makes them so processor-intensive. On one hand, we can simulate virtually any condition using shaders; on the other hand, they devour resources. For each frame displayed, all the shader effects for that frame must be processed (or rendered), which takes time. Although each amount of time required is miniscule, it adds up as millions of individual pixels and vertices are processed. Shaders can be used for many complex material appearances and image effects: hair, fire, shadows, water, reflections, and so forth. Shaders are so flexible that the list of possible effects is almost endless—a shader programmer can write almost any imaginable effect. Interestingly, although only very recently has consumer-level hardware been able to handle the intense demand that real-time shaders put on a system, the knowledge of these processes has been around for decades. In fact, many of the techniques that you will read about here are based on algorithms named for well-known mathematical geniuses. For instance, Phong and Blinn are recognizable names if you are a 3D artist.

Remember that the ability to manipulate an individual pixel or vertex in real time is what makes shaders so powerful. Very recently, real-time lighting began being calculated per vertex, not per pixel—that is, lighting is now often calculated for an entire face of a polygon, not for every pixel. This ability is significant because it not only adds a great degree of detail and smoothness, it also allows for shaders such as normal maps to function.

But how does all this work? That brings me to the large fuzzy overlap between programming and art. Granted, these are two very different activities, and there is a line between how much art a programmer needs to understand and how much technology an artist needs to understand. Exactly where that line is, no one can say precisely, but when it comes to shaders, you should understand the basics of how the technology works.

Wait! Don't fling the book across the room just yet. You don't need to know the math behind it all, just a simple explanation of how it works.

## Shader Basics

A shader, from the artist's point of view, is often a bit of a black box. Our involvement usually requires that we generate input for a preexisting shader—set parameters and/or assign textures and then look at the end result. Because the artist's role is mostly confined to creating input and judging the output of the shader, we often have nothing to do with the code. In some cases, shader code is written or edited by an artist, but most newer shader creation tools are more like the material systems in Max and Maya, requiring no programming knowledge. Figure 3.2 shows a couple of examples of how a material shader works from the artist's point of view.

Shaders often require the use of 2D assets as input, and the artist is usually the one tasked with not only creating those assets but also understanding, creating, and implementing the shader to some degree. So, although shaders can perform much of the work that an artist would do on an asset, they may also increase our workload. Already there are effects in games where the artist is no longer painting a texture as an isolated entity but is creating a series of textures that must all work together for a desired effect. Using

TEXTURE MAPS

DIFFUSE (color) MAP

SPECULAR MAP

NORMAL MAP

FINAL

COINS IN COVER SCENE

CANDLES IN COVER SCENE

Texture

Texture

+

Grayscale
Image

=

shaders requires more planning, a different way of thinking about creating the art, and more organization. The artist needs to learn the shader tool, organize more assets (assets that may be linked to one another and are therefore more rigid in their mobility after a shader is in place), and learn the mental discipline of creating assets that are not the end result but component parts of a final result.

We have to get accustomed to painting textures devoid of certain properties that will later be processed in real time. One reason we need to understand the fundamentals of light and shadow or to develop the skill to see the base material of a scene behind all the dirt, reflections, and other surface properties is that we may soon be building textures starting with a very plain surface (even a pattern) and building a complex organizational tree of maps and effects to create a final surface—much as we already do in 3D programs and like the way some texture generators work. For example, the highlights on the armor in Figure 3.3 are controlled by a shader. With no specular highlight, a surface can look flat and dull. With a generic specular highlight applied evenly to the surface, things will often look plastic and fake. Using a map to control the specular highlight, we can make a surface look much more realistic. Although shaders can make our lives easier in some respects and they can definitely make our games look better, they can also be a bit complex to understand at first and require a greater degree of organization.

Some of the most common shaders today require images that are easily created and manipulated in Photoshop. The most common of these are the color map (or diffuse channel), the bump and normal

**Figure 3.2**
Here is a simple flow showing how two shaders work for the artist. The illumination map is applied to the texture of the window to make the proper parts of the window glow with light while leaving the frame dark. The coin, a simple cylinder, is mapped with a diffuse or color map, a specular map, and a normal bump map. You can see the final result at the bottom where the effects of all three maps are combined. In the middle the scene on the front cover uses these techniques on the coins and candles.

**Figure 3.3**
Instead of painting a highlight onto a surface in Photoshop, you can now leave it out and assign a shader. The cover scene uses specularity maps in many places; in the pirate king's throne the carvings are enhanced using a specularity map.

**SPECULAR MAP USED ON COVER SCENE**

**NO SPECULARITY**

**SPECULARITY**

**Figure 3.4**
From right to left: The UV template, the diffuse map created from the template, and the model wrapped with the texture. The left side of the face was left unmapped so that you can see the original mesh.

maps, specularity maps, illumination maps, and opacity maps. In general, a game artist creates textures meant to be tiled over an area or mapped to an object. When the texture is to be mapped to an object, the artist starts the creation of the texture with a template. Whether a complex character skin or a simple prop, this template is generated from the UV coordinates that have been mapped out onto the 3D model. After the basic color information has been put into place, the other shader maps are often created from the initial color map, the 3D model itself, and even some hand painting. The UV map represents the exact way in which the 2D art will be mapped, or wrapped around, the 3D model. In Figure 3.4 you can see how the template was created from the actual face model and the simple prop and then used as a guide to paint the textures. We will be working with templates later in the book.

## Common Shader Effects

Like most issues related to computer game technology, shaders are a vast and complex topic riddled with new vocabulary, concepts, and technological requirements. In addition, each game engine and each game project will have its own vocabulary, process, and subtle nuances in dealing with shaders. But you will always deal with some basic shader effects, and here are some samples of them. You may notice that these shader effects are very similar to filter effects in Photoshop, materials in Max or Maya, and many post-video effects. *Post-video effects* are effects inserted into a film or video during the editing process, after the footage is shot.

In this chapter we look at not only what these shaders can do in a cursory sense, but also some of the ways you can get various effects with these shaders. The following is a list of basic shaders and material types that you will most likely work with in game development:

- Diffuse (color maps or textures)
- Blend
- Detail mapping
- Depth of field
- Heat haze
- Specularity
- Bloom (glow or halo)
- Masking and opacity
- Illumination (emissive)
- Reflection/cube mapping
- Pan/rotate/scale
- Normal, bump, and parallax mapping
- Tessellation

## Diffuse (Color Maps or Textures)

The term *diffuse map* has many meanings, depending on the software you use and your educational background. I will spare you the technical and scientific definition and simply tell you that a diffuse map in the game industry generally means the color map or texture, an image containing only the color information of a surface. This is not to say it is devoid of all detail. Because game engines still don't reproduce the visual world 100% accurately, we still need to fill in the gaps. We can do this with subtle detail in the color map that is supported by the other maps. Areas in the texture where light would be noticeably brighter or darker can be defined to some degree. The spaces between metal panels and wood planks are examples of where some darkness could be painted in with good effect.

In Figure 3.5 you can see the diffuse map for an old pirate. There is probably a bit too much light and shadow information in the texture. The prominent highlights and shadows on the veins and wrinkles are especially noticeable, so I would take them down and replace them with a normal map if this were to be used in real time. There is a normal map on this mesh, but I relied on the color map a bit more because I created this mesh for a specific use at a fixed angle and the normal map didn't need to behave perfectly.

Cracks and seams are places where dirt is most likely to collect, which would further add to the darkness of such parts of the texture. Technically, you can handle these cracks with the normal map and other effects, but I find that relying too heavily on one map type often results in plastic-looking materials.

**Figure 3.5**
The diffuse color map can contain a good deal of information, but currently the use of per-pixel lighting makes this unnecessary and often undesirable.

Originally, game artists had only the diffuse channel to work with, and essentially what you created in Photoshop was what you saw in the game—all shadows, highlights, and details were contained on the color map and were static (or "baked in"). This image was typically of low resolution and color depth and was wrapped around a low-polygon model—presto, you had a game model. This process has changed quite a bit in the last few years. With the advent of new technologies that require a slightly complex separation of visual components into a series of separate assets that are processed together to create the final effect, the color map has become much more simple and subtle. That is, it's simple and subtle in terms of other information aside from the color itself, but it's richer in color detail because we can now use images that have much larger resolutions. In some ways, this method of asset creation is harder to grasp and execute, but in other ways it is actually easier—especially for a trained artist who already understands how the visual world works.

The color map in Figure 3.6 contains the base color of a character's skin. In addition to the skin tone, however, the color map also must convey subtle details that either can't be depicted by the technology or are simply so subtle it may be quicker to paint them into the color map than try to reproduce them technically. Human skin is so subtle yet complex that often the qualities of skin (such as age and condition) and the details of skin (such as small veins, creases, spots, freckles, and pores) are best portrayed on the color map. Human skin is not one smooth color but rather is composed of many colors and interacts with light in a unique way. Such a map can take a long time to produce, since it requires a balance between subtlety and clear detail. Too much contrast, saturation, or other attribute and

**Figure 3.6**
The diffuse color map of human facial skin. Even with complex shaders, the skin on a human face is so full of subtlety and detail that we still need to have some detail in the color map.

the character starts to look diseased; not enough and the character looks like a mannequin.

## Blend

The *blend shader* blends two textures together; depending on what software or game engine you use, it may blend in a default fashion or offer various modes that are very similar to the blending modes in Photoshop. The blending usually occurs between a base texture and one or more textures on top of it. Each layer has its own set of UV coordinates, so you can have one small tileable texture that repeats as your base and blend other textures, such as stains, cracks, and other details, on top. This method not only takes up less texture memory, it also allows for a great deal of variety because there are so many options for blending numerous textures together. The basic blending modes follow and are displayed in Figure 3.7:

- Average
- Additive
- Subtractive

### Average Mode

*Average* blends the colors of the base map and the new map evenly. If you don't want either texture overpowering the other in any way, use the average mode. This mode is appropriate for creating an entirely new texture from two separate textures or, in conjunction with grayscale base maps, for coloring the base map.

### Additive Mode

The *additive* color model brightens the base map. Black becomes completely transparent.

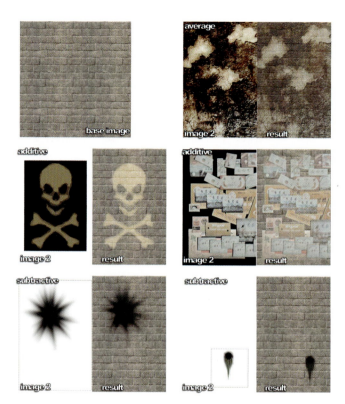

**Figure 3.7**
Various blending effects using the blend shader.

### Subtractive Mode

The *subtractive* color model darkens the base map with the new image. White becomes completely transparent.

## Detail Mapping

A *detail texture* is a layer laid on top of a low-detail color texture. Players can see the detail texture from their point of view, but the detail texture fades in as they move. This allows the texture (the ground, for instance) to look very detailed. Detail textures are usually grayscale images that add detail to the color map below it, using one of the blending modes discussed previously. Detail textures can be used to add detail to stone, metal, wood—any surface in the world (Figure 3.8).

## Depth of Field

*Depth of field* in photography is the distance in front of and beyond the subject being focused on and photographed. A shader can create the illusion that objects in the background are far off by blurring them, thus causing a depth-of-field effect. You can adjust the depth of field, just as you can in photography, so that the area in focus can range from infinite to very narrow or shallow. A shallow depth of field means that objects are in focus only in a very small area. Depth of field can be so shallow that a very close-up picture of a coin can have

**Figure 3.8**
Players can see the detail texture from their point of view, but the detail texture fades in as they move.

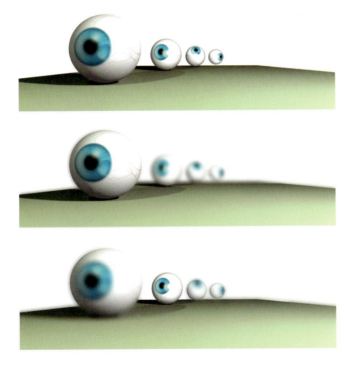

**Figure 3.9**
This shader creates the illusion that objects in the background are far off by blurring them, thus causing a depth-of-field effect.

one side of the coin in focus and the other totally blurry. Figure 3.9 shows an example of depth of field.

### Heat Haze

*Heat haze* creates the shimmering effect you can see emanating from very hot objects or the ground on hot days. Figure 3.10 shows the effect applied to the exhaust pipe of a vehicle.

### Specular Highlights and Glossiness

A *specular highlight* is that bright spot that appears on most surfaces when light hits. That spot can be small and bright or large and barely noticeable, depending on the quality of the material the light is hitting. A specularity map allows you to control this effect, and you can even use a mask to control how various parts of the same surface display the specular light differently. A good example is beaten-up metal armor. You may have a layer of old paint and dirt

**Figure 3.10**
The bottom muzzle blast has the heat effect present.

**Figure 3.11**
A specularity map and examples of specular basics.

that will not be highly reflective and areas where this coating has been worn away to reveal reflective metal, which is metal that has been polished by constant wear and tear (Figure 3.11). Sometimes glossiness is separated from the specular highlight; the distinction is that *glossiness* determines the size of the specular highlight, and *specularity* controls the intensity of the highlight.

A specularity map controls what parts of the surface are shiny or dull based on the grayscale value of the specularity map. You can see that the armor has no specular control on the left, and the

**Figure 3.12**
Specularity map.

middle and right have two different specularity maps. Specularity maps are generally created from the color map. In Photoshop you simply desaturate a copy of the color map and adjust from there. You can see the exact spot where the grayscale image is affecting the specularity on the model (Figure 3.12).

## Bloom (Glow or Halo)

*Blooming* makes a light source appear brighter than it really is by spreading the light source out over the edges of the object it is on. A bright light will appear to bleed over onto objects around it, both in front of and behind the object. Usually this effect is achieved by creating a glow around the light source that is blended with its surroundings, but sometimes the engine actually processes the entire screen. Using several render passes, it will multiply the frame (like the Photoshop blending mode, this lightens the lighter areas and darkens the darker areas), blurs the image, and then draws it on top of the original screen. Blooming helps create the illusion that a light source is brighter than it can actually be displayed by the monitor. See Figure 3.13.

## Masking and Opacity

*Masking* typically uses a specific color that is designated as the "clear" color and is more efficient than transparency. *Transparency* uses a separate channel or grayscale image to determine the opacity of a pixel. The trade-off is that transparency looks better, but it requires more file space and more processing power. Masking can significantly speed up a huge scene that has tons of overlapping elements with transparency on them, such as a forest or jungle. In Figure 3.14 you can see examples of masking and transparency.

**Figure 3.13**
Bloom shots. Light glow, with
full-frame processing.

Figure 3.15 shows the interface of the NVIDIA tool that allows for the rapid adjusting and viewing of textures before outputting them.

*Opacity maps* determine whether an image is solid, transparent, or somewhere in between. Opacity is generally best used when there is a need for transparency, as on windows, and/or subtle ranges in opacity, such as seen in smoke and fire. Although masking can do the job for tree leaves, fences, and grates, opacity is better for in-game effects such as explosions, fire, bullet holes, smoke, and particles such as rain and magic sparks. In Figure 3.16 you can see various examples of such effects.

## Illumination and Unlit Textures

An unlit texture and a texture with an illumination map applied to it are two different things. An *unlit texture* is simply a texture that is unaffected by lighting and displays at 100% brightness under all conditions. An unlit texture can be known by other names, such as a *full bright* or a *self-illuminated texture* (Figure 3.17). In Figure 3.18 you can see an example of an unlit texture on a particle that looks better unlit and also runs faster. An *illumination mapped texture*, sometimes known as an *emissive texture*, uses an additional image

**Figure 3.14**
The upper portion of this figure shows an image of some grass with an alpha channel; the lower shows a color mask. Notice that the images look virtually identical from afar. It isn't until we are very close that we can see the jagged edge.

**Figure 3.15**
The interface of the NVIDIA tool. The three most common masking and alpha formats have been highlighted.

(typically a grayscale image) to control the portions of the texture that are lit and to what degree. When you use an illumination map, additional calculations must be done and additional resources used for controlling the lighting on a texture this way. So, whereas the fully bright texture can make things run faster, the addition of the illumination map to a texture creates more processing demands and

**Figure 3.16**
Particle examples.

**Figure 3.17**
Image 1 is the control panel texture, and to the right is its illumination map; image 2 is a version of the control panel where the lit parts are slightly blurred, as are the corresponding bright parts on the illumination map. In image 3 you can see the control panel in a darkened setting and the control panel unlit (or full bright), and in image 4 you see the illumination-mapped versions. By blurring the portion to be lit in the color map and the illumination map, a glow effect is simulated.

**Figure 3.18**
Magic particle unlit and lit.

requires more memory to hold the additional map and can therefore slow things down.

## Reflection

The reflective nature of a surface can be like a mirror (100% reflective) or completely matte; a rough wood may have no reflection at all. Real-time reflections can be very draining on the computer, so there are ways to fake reflections using environment or cube mapping.

There are many ways to generate reflections in a game, but the most common and easiest to implement is the *cube map*. A cube map is a series of images that the environment map uses to fake the reflection on the surface of an object. Cube maps are so named because the reflections you see are actually six images arranged in a cube and projected back onto the reflective object. These images are rendered from the location of the reflective object so that the cube map reflects the objects' surroundings accurately. These six images cover all directions: up, down, front, back, left, and right. Ideally they all line up, meaning that the images meet at the edges so that the reflection is seamless. The images of the cube map are most commonly static, meaning that they are always the same. If you are looking into a reflection created by a static cube map, you won't see yourself (or your in-game character). This is the most efficient way to handle cube mapping, but there are also other techniques for generating real-time reflections. One of those techniques is called *dynamic cube mapping*. This method redraws the six images in the cube map every frame. If the object mapped with the environment map moves or something in the environment around it moves, the cube maps are updated to render an accurate reflection in real time.

Figure 3.19 shows how the (static) cube map was created for the pitcher. Notice the maps arranged as though the cube were folded open like a box. The six images that form the cube map were rendered from the location of the pitcher, so the metal looks as though it is reflecting its surroundings from the proper position. You can even use a simple cloud image as a cube map and get some great results (Figure 3.20). I did nothing more than use cloud images for each face of the cube map, and the armor looks like it is made of silver. The neat

**Figure 3.19**
This cube map was created for the pitcher. The metal looks as though it is reflecting its surroundings from the proper position.

**Figure 3.20**
With a simple cloud image as a cube map, this armor looks as though it were made of silver.

thing is that in a game, those reflections would move with the armor and look so much more convincing than a static image of a reflection.

### Pan/Rotate/Scale

Often shader systems give the artist the ability to pan, rotate, scale, and otherwise move a texture in real time, which can be useful to convey the movement of elements on a computer screen or fluid through pipes or to create a moving walkway. This capability has been used to animate waterfalls and rotating fans. In Figure 3.21 you can see the simple concepts of *panning* (moving vertically or horizontally), *rotating* (turning), and *scaling* (making larger or smaller). You can also see that to make a wheel look like it is turning, we must pan and rotate the texture. You should be aware that although this figure illustrates the concept, chances are that in a 3D game the mesh the

**Figure 3.21**
Pan (moving vertically or horizontally), rotating (turning), and scaling (larger or smaller).

**Figure 3.22**
Scrolling and panning smoke texture over a simple laser light texture for a "dust in the laser beams" effect.

texture is on, not the texture itself, would turn and move. I have used a scrolling and panning smoke texture over a simple laser light texture with a great "dust in the laser beams" effect (Figure 3.22).

## Bump, Normal, and Parallax Occlusion Mapping

The bump, normal, and parallax occlusion mapping shaders add 3D depth to an otherwise flat surface. *Bump maps* are grayscale and

polygon normal

low polygon surface

low polygon surface

high polygon surfaces

normal map
low polygon surface

**Figure 3.23**
A simple visual
demonstration of how the
shader operates.

display the most limited 3D effect; the others add depth using a color
map with lighting information encoded in it. These shaders are all
similar in what they accomplish, but depending on the exact code of
the shader and the supporting hardware, the effect can range from
really cool to absolutely awesome. A basic *normal map* adds a level of
depth deeper than the bump map, but more advanced forms of these
shaders add details and behaviors such as self-occlusion, silhouetting,
and self-shadowing. Figure 3.23 is a simple visual demonstration of
how the shader operates. Because we can calculate the light of the
surface for every pixel, we don't need to include geometry to create
shadows and highlights as we did when we lit per polygon. We can
now tell the 3D application to treat each and every pixel as if it were
reacting to light, as it did when it was on the high-polygon model.

Have you ever seen a mural or painting that looked real, but when
you changed your viewing angle, you could suddenly see that it
was fake—a flat, 2D image? The light and shadow didn't move. The
artist painted it to be viewed from that one angle, so it only looks
good from that one angle. Imagine if you could create a painting that
quickly repainted itself every time you moved, so it looked as though
you were seeing a real three-dimensional scene. That is essentially
what a normal map is doing as it calculates light and shadow in
real time. We still need to maintain the silhouette of the model as

grayscale

blank

color

normal map

normal
map
implemented

**Figure 3.24**
A surface built up using
images created in Photoshop.

best we can. Using a present-day "vanilla" normal map allows us to focus more polygons on the silhouette of the model, which is a benefit. But there is also a drawback: It means that the normal map cannot change the silhouette. Back to the painting analogy: Even if a painting can be repainted so quickly it looks real, there is a limit to the effect. When you move too far off on an angle, you will see that it is just a flat 2D painting that is updating in real time. That is how a basic normal map works. But more complex versions of normal maps can actually move the pixels in real time and change the silhouette when viewed from the side; this would be like the canvas of the painting actually pushing out to form the detail painted on it.

In short, a normal map is an RGB image that records all the light and shadow detail from a high-polygon model. When this map is applied to a low-resolution model, the light and shadow are calculated as though the light were hitting the high-resolution version of the model. The idea is actually simple to understand. (Of course, my standard disclaimer of how tricky this is for a programmer goes here, but seriously, we artists have the fun part of the development process).

Although the best normal maps are typically generated from very highly detailed 3D models, you can get a free Photoshop plug-in from NVIDIA (http://developer.nvidia.com) that will generate a normal map for you from a 2D image. There are many other tricks for creating normal maps entirely in Photoshop, and we will use them later in the book. This method is especially easy when we're creating environmental art, since the surfaces we work with tend to be much simpler than the surface of a character. In Figure 3.24 the surface was built up using images created in Photoshop; even the normal map was created as a black-and-white map and exported as a normal map. You can see the grayscale image used to create the normal map and the surface with nothing applied to it. Then you see the color map only, and the normal map only, and finally the surface with all the maps applied. We look at normal mapping in much greater depth later in the book and actually create normal maps using a few different methods.

## Tessellation

One of the coolest new features of DirectX 11 is tessellation. The process of tessellation is straightforward: You take a polygon and chop it into many smaller parts. DirectX 11 and the newest hardware

IMAGES USED WITH PERMISSION OF UNIGINE CORP DEVELOPER OF THE UNIGINE ENGINE TECHNOLOGY 2011

**Figure 3.25**
A tessellated surface with a displacement map can make a surface take on very impressive detail. The top two images are the wireframe and the scene before tessellation was applied. Notice the detail in the bottom images after tessellation was applied, specifically the stairs and the cobblestones.

can do this in real time. This is cool when you combine the newly tessellated surface with a black-and-white displacement map. When these tools are used together, a surface can take on very impressive detail; see Figure 3.25.

With DirectX 11 we can finally use displacement mapping to its fullest potential because we can also perform tessellation in real time. Tessellation doesn't suffer from the limits of bump and even normal mapping; those are illusions of detail whereas tessellation is actual geometric detail. The need to no longer create normal maps is a huge boon. Now you can paint a highly detailed model in 3D and export a displacement map to use on a low poly version of the model.

Tessellation also allows for a much easier and much, much smoother transition in level of detail. Tessellation can alter the level of detail continuously on the fly so the artist doesn't need to create and juggle multiple versions of the model and the model won't pop as it is swapped when a player moves closer to it. For example, a distant building may be rendered with only 10 triangles, but as you move closer its prominent features will emerge as extra triangles are added to the mesh. As you continue closer still, you will see finer details. When you are right up on the building you might be staring at only the door, so thousands of triangles will be devoted to rendering that door. It can be as detailed as you like.

I mentioned this a few times already, but one of the greatest benefits of tessellation is behind the scenes of the workflow and workload of the game artist. We can now build one asset that allows us to scale from film quality to very low poly model for use in-game.

## Node-Based Shader Systems

*Node-based shader systems* are fairly common and well worth the effort to understand. They are powerful and, I find, easy to work with.

**Figure 3.26**
The node-based material system from Poser 7.

They are very visual by nature and are literally movable nodes that you can connect to each other. You can create new nodes, delete, cut, copy, and paste them. They contain all the functions that we've discussed and more. You can connect nodes to each other in many combinations and see the results in real time. The most basic feature of a node is the input and output of data. By linking nodes, you can exercise almost infinite control over the final behavior of the material. Each node will have different options based on what the node does. The node-based material system from Poser 7 is shown in Figure 3.26.

**Note** Although there is no theoretical limit to the number of nodes, or connections, in a material, there is a practical limit; this is an area where you can optimize your work. Make sure that you are not creating a material that's too complex for where it will be used and don't create a material with 10 nodes when 3 will do.

## Basic Node Operations

*Basic node operations* consist of the process of moving and connecting the nodes. Figure 3.27 shows a basic node tree. You can see that nodes can be created, selected, connected, and moved as well as cut, copied, and pasted. You usually can expand and collapse both the node itself and the node tree branches. Most nodes will have many fields for the input of data variables from numbers, files, colors, and more. These values are dictated by what the node does and should be looked at on a case-by-case basis. An example is that a 2D image node will simply contain a place to input the image and other variables pertaining to 2D images such as UV information, and so on. This node can then be plugged into a node requiring the input of an image map such as a specular map. It all starts with the root node.

**Figure 3.27**
A basic root node.

## Root Node

The *root node* is a complete shader that contains the most common inputs for a material. You can plug into this a complex combination of nodes that will allow you to achieve almost any effect imaginable.

Poser has a very robust node-based material system. The root node usually contains the following fields, at the very least:

- Diffuse Color
- Specular
- Highlight Size
- Illumination
- Pan Rotate Scale
- Ambient Color
- Transparency
- Translucence
- Reflection
- Refraction
- Bump/Normal
- Displacement

## Common Node Setups

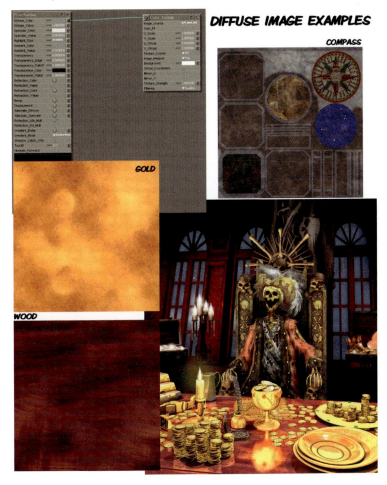

**Figure 3.28**
Many of the diffuse materials in the scene on the cover of this book are very simple tiling images. The shader effects make the surfaces look so good. The simple tiling gold and wood are made to look polished and reflective using shaders.

## Conclusion

This chapter gave you a quick look at what shaders can do. We will implement all of them in the coming exercises to create various effects. Our implementation will be generic, meaning that we will create the assets for a shader based on the most basic parameters. If you are using Max, Maya, Blender, or any other shader system, these basics will translate easily into those systems.

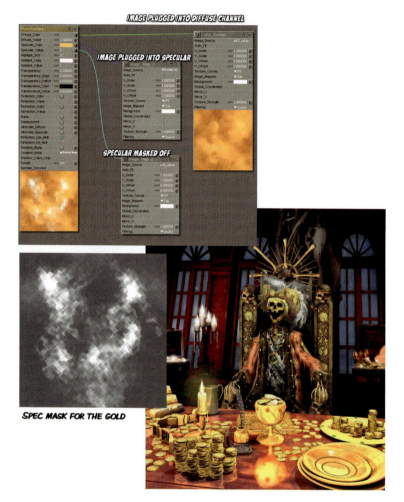

**Figure 3.29**
All the gold in the scene (except for the coins) is covered in the same tiling image. Using various shaders and their settings I am able to get a wide range of effects. Here you can see a simple specularity mask used on the gold.

## Chapter Exercises

1. Give a simple explanation of what a shader is.
2. Give an example of a common shader.
3. Diagram and explain the workflow of a simple shader.
4. Explain how shaders can both increase and decrease the workload of the texture artist.
5. List and explain the common shaders discussed in this book.
6. What is a node-based shader system? Sketch a simple material using the material from this chapter in node form.
7. Using the image in Figure 3.33, match the shader name with the image.

**Figure 3.30**
The candles' flames are fully lit, but the image is also masked off so the flame has a faded edge to it and the rest of the square image is removed. The mask also makes the wick look solid when the viewer is close to it. The candle wax also was illuminated and masked so that the wax glows at the top, where the flame is, and fades to the bottom like a real lit candle.

Answers:
- Diffuse map only
- Reflection only
- No material
- Bump map only
- The diffuse map
- The bump map
- The specularity map
- All shaders applied

**Figure 3.31**
A complex node system used to create an animated fire.

**Figure 3.32**
Even a simple one-node material system can create this beautiful hammered metal.

THE SPECULARITY MAP ☐    NO MATERIAL ☐    BUMP MAP ONLY ☐

REFLECTION ONLY ☐ THE DIFFUSE MAP ☐ THE BUMP MAP ☐

ALL SHADERS APPLIED ☐    DIFFUSE MAP ONLY ☐

**Figure 3.33**
Match the shader name with the correct image.

# Chapter 4

# Prepping for Texture Creation

*Do, or do not. There is no "try."*

—Yoda (Jedi Master)

## Introduction

In this chapter we will take the next step in creating the best game textures possible, which is to use the best texture resources possible. We will look at the various sources of digital resources for texture creation and each of the steps in the process of gathering, preparing, and storing your assets.

Although the focus of this book is the creation of textures using Photoshop so that you develop strong Photoshop skills, in reality it is more common, easier, and more effective to use photo references in texture creation. We will be using a little photo reference in the book, and the CD contains a good collection of the kinds of images that I find to be the hardest to create in Photoshop without actually hand-painting them. Cracks, splats, drips, wood grains, and other organic random stuff, though they can be created in Photoshop, simply look more genuine when taken from a good source photo.

Typically, a texture is built with layers containing various sources of imagery, and photo reference plays a big part in this process. Layers are "composited" together using the various tools in Photoshop, such as layer-blending modes. (If you are unfamiliar with the concept of layers and layer-blending modes, see Chapter 2. For additional information, see the appendix on Photoshop.) We will be using compositing throughout the book. Even if all the elements of a texture are created entirely in Photoshop, we will still be using layers and blending modes to composite the various parts together. No matter what source you get the image from, you always end up using Photoshop to combine and manipulate the various sources to create the imagery that fits your needs. You will almost always use Photoshop in the creation and final output of a texture.

A resource, in the context of this book, is any digital image from any source that helps you create your art. Therefore, a small checkered pattern made in Photoshop that can be tiled across a canvas in Photoshop and used as the base of a tiled floor is a resource. A high-resolution digital photograph of a dirty surface that you might overlay to make the tiled pattern look dirty is another resource. And so is any other image that can be used to get the effect you desire (Figure 4.1).

The examples are as endless as your imagination and limited only to the number of digital images you can collect. There are no cut-and-dried rules here. A resource that might seem useless to some artists might be just what you need. In general, you will want to avoid wasting space and dealing with the clutter of low-resolution, poor-quality, and just plain bad images. But if you come across an image that you have a specific use for, keep it! Keep in mind that although it is easy to make a texture like the previously mentioned

**Figure 4.1**
A resource is any image that can be used to create art. Here, a simple checkered pattern was used to create a tile floor by combining it with other images.

plain-and-simple checkered texture, it takes time to create. Why not have one on hand that you can drop into an image when needed?

If possible, save everything you can. You never know when you will need a high-resolution image of a penny, a close-up of rotting meat, or 101 highway signs from South America. Naturally, my first recommendation to you as a game artist is to buy a very large hard drive—the biggest you can afford. This makes the process of sharing, backing up, and switching to a new computer much easier. In addition to a large external hard drive, I also have a redundant array of independent disks (RAID) in my system that mirrors several hard drives, so if one crashes I don't lose any work—even my most recent work. It has also provided me with peace of mind, in that when I'm out of town I can leave my external drive in a safe location away from my house. If my computer is stolen, the house burns down, or my system is damaged in any way, I will still have my external drive. I could more easily replace the system than the data stored on it.

It is also a good idea to crop, resize, and otherwise manipulate your images to make them as size-efficient and user-ready as possible without degrading their quality. An image that tiles nicely and is already a power of two will not slow your inspired workflow, since you can simply drop it into your work and not stop to crop, clean, tile, and otherwise make it useful.

In the process of greedily obtaining and hoarding digital images, you will discover that whatever time you spend up front to make them easier to find and use in the long run will be worth every second. You need to categorize your assets by type (terrain, liquid, doors) as well as keep track of where you got them. Some texture collections have copyrights and "use restrictions" attached to them. Therefore, you might not be able to store all your images in one neat structure, instead of having them in various folders according to many criteria. We will look at that process later in this chapter in some detail.

First, let's look at the process of gathering the raw images for your collection. There are many ways to collect images for your collection; all have their pros and cons.

## Gathering Textures

There are many sources for textures and digital imagery, including creating them in Photoshop, taking digital photographs, scanning them in, buying texture collections, surfing the Internet for useful images, and using 3D applications to model and render images.

### Creating Textures in Photoshop

Although there are many ways to create a texture, for this book I wanted to focus on using pure Photoshop as much as possible. I believe that if you are able to create anything you want in Photoshop, when you have the other resources at your disposal you will be much better and faster at creating textures. I briefly introduce this method here, and we will spend the rest of the book creating textures using Photoshop. Technically, every game texture you create will pass through Photoshop and become a "Photoshopped" image to some degree. This is especially true in the age of shaders/materials. You will spend more time in Photoshop creating, adjusting, and altering the other images often used in shaders to control the various effects.

Many people are intimidated by the prospect of a blank slate in Photoshop when they're creating a texture, or they may be critical of this method based on low-quality work that they have seen. Creating basic materials and even objects in Photoshop is not that hard and does not require special painting skills. In fact, you can create materials and objects with a greater degree of control and thus create an image that might be better than a digital image of the same thing in some cases; see Figure 4.2.

In the end, no matter what source you obtain your raw assets from, you will always use Photoshop (or a similar 2D image editor) to manipulate and assemble your textures in their final state. For example, you may create a frame for a window in Photoshop based on a photograph, create the glass panes from scratch, and use an actual image of a wood grain to add detail to the window frame and overlay a grime layer, too (see Figure 4.3).

There are some cons to this method. It does take some time to start from a blank slate and use all the proper filters and tools to create a realistic texture or material from scratch. If you are not patient and understand the methods, the textures will look Photoshopped, which is not a negative term pertaining to Photoshop but is a comment on a lack of quality in the image itself. Not adjusting any Photoshop default values or taking the time to tweak and test the texture will result in substandard work. One positive is that this method allows you to create an image that is uniquely yours. You will never be stuck without the texture you need. If you can imagine it, you can create it in Photoshop. Just because you can't find a picture to manipulate, you don't have to stop working.

**Figure 4.2**
The image on the left is a
digital photograph; the one
on the right was created
entirely in Photoshop.

Even if you don't need to create from a blank slate in Photoshop, you
will still need to use Photoshop to manipulate your images to make
them useful to you. The better you know how to use Photoshop and
its many tools, the better your work will be—no matter what method
you use.

Finally, there is consistency. Knowing how to use Photoshop to its
fullest extent will allow you to achieve consistency with your texture
sets, and that is very important. No matter how great your textures
look, if they don't visually mesh together in a game world, all the
good you have accomplished in your texture work will be diminished.

### Digital Cameras

Using a digital camera to collect images is very common and
becoming easier as the prices of digital cameras drop and their
quality increases. The only real cons of this method are that people
don't like it when you take pictures of their front doors and they will
often call the police (true story). Art gallery owners don't like it when
you take pictures of the paintings hanging on their walls (true again).
And the government hates it when you take pictures of their secret
alien storage facilities and will try to take your camera away from you
(can't talk about this one).

In all seriousness, there are no drawbacks to this method other than
the cost of the camera. Depending on what camera you purchase,

**Figure 4.3**
This window was created in Photoshop using a mixture of photographic and Photoshop elements.

you may be stuck with limited storage and resolution, odd formats, and slow data transfer times. But this should not be a problem with a fairly recent purchase. Decent digital cameras are now very inexpensive, and you can get one that will do the job well and make data transfer easy via memory cards or a direct connection to the computer from the camera. With a decent digital camera, you can take pictures of anything and everything. The images will be yours (unless you are taking pictures of copyrighted artwork, people, and so on) and you can set up shoots for specific items. I have taken pictures of dirty dishes and fake blood smears on paper, and I have stood in the highway for the right angle on a sign—all for the sake of textures. Be warned that since September 11, 2001, taking pictures of most places will be at least noticed and you need to be more careful. Before September 11, no one would think much of it if you were taking a picture of the rusted door of a power station or warehouse, but now you may be watched or even reported. I have been pulled over and questioned by the police after taking pictures around a warehouse. Someone thought it suspicious, wrote down my car's license plate number, and reported it.

Digital images are versatile, too. Don't be limited to the original context or scale of the asset. Use the texture where it works. A rock can be the side of a mountain, a small crack in a sidewalk can be a large crack in a wall, the vent opening on a hairdryer can be a large sewer grate, and so on (Figure 4.4). This applies not just to scale but to context as well. A really great source for some of the most disgusting textures I have ever seen were simply close-ups of the pots and pans in the kitchen after dinner. Grease drippings from a roast, congealed butter after the vegetables have been removed, and dried ketchup can make for some great imagery. We have included some on the CD, of course. Figure 4.5 shows some of the sick images in my collection.

**Figure 4.4**
Don't be limited to the original context or scale of an asset. Use the texture where it works. A rock can be the side of a mountain, a small crack in a sidewalk can be a large crack in a wall, and in this case the vent opening on a hairdryer is a large sewer grate.

The possibilities are as endless as your imagination with a digital camera. Another benefit is the ease and extremely low cost of experimentation with a digital camera. You are not limited by factors such as the number of prints on a roll or the cost of film and developing. You can shoot and delete 1,000 images for the price of 10.

**Tips on Taking Digital Photographs**

Taking digital photographs for use as texture resource takes a different mindset than traditional photography. Most likely, the first images you take will have aspects that will make them hard to use in a texture. You won't be able to see these problems right off; in fact, you will have to go home and look at the images up close on your computer and try to work on them before the problems pop up.

**Figure 4.5**
Guess what these are.

But there is no substitute for this process, and going through it a few times is the only way to develop an eye for potential problems before taking a picture. Even so, here are some general tips for using a digital camera to capture texture resources that will help speed up that process.

### Image Resolution

This first tip is an obvious one. The higher you set the resolution on your camera, the higher the detail will be in the image. It also eats up memory, but a higher-resolution image makes for a better resource.

### Diminish Image Tilt

This is a rather simple tip. When you take a picture, look closely in the viewfinder. You will see some marks (Figure 4.6); whether they are lines, squares, or circles doesn't matter. These marks may be there for a number of reasons, but primarily they are there to help you line up your shot. These are very useful and easy to use when you are taking a picture of a surface with straight lines, such as a brick wall or the frame of a window. Unfortunately many newer cameras don't have viewfinders anymore; rather, they have a small screen on the back of the camera. This screen may or may not have any marks at all. If you have such a camera and want to line up your shots, you can carefully draw a set of your own lines using a very fine-point water-soluble marker. If you do this, be very careful not to scratch the screen, don't use a permanent marker unless you want the marks to be permanent, and do this at your own risk. Take your time measuring out the lines so they are perfectly straight across the screen horizontally, vertically, and centered.

### Watch the Auto Settings

Many digital cameras come with preprogrammed image control modes. These are various presets for the camera for taking various types of pictures: close-ups, portraits, sports, and nighttime pictures, to name a few. The danger here is that some of the presets have a

**Figure 4.6**
Save yourself some work; use the marks in the viewfinder to line up your shot. These marks are very useful and easy to use when you are taking a picture of a surface with straight lines, such as a brick wall or the frame of a window.

shallow depth of field and other settings that can distort or affect the image in an undesirable way. Depth of field refers to the area of the image that is in focus from the camera lens to infinity. You can have a shallow depth of field so that items that are only within a few feet or inches are in focus and objects that are farther from the camera are blurry. In Figure 4.7, you can see a few examples of depth of field.

A shallow depth of field can be bad when it is so shallow that when you are photographing a surface, parts of the surface are out of focus and blurry and other parts are crisp. This can easily happen if you are taking a picture at an angle—looking up at a window, for example— and using a shallow depth of field. The part of the window closest to you will be in focus and the farthest parts will be blurry.

### Diminish Lens Distortion (Fisheye)

When purchasing a digital camera, make sure that you get a decent lens. Cheaper lenses tend to give you a fisheye effect (Figure 4.8), spherically distorting the image, which can make it much harder to clean up your images for use. You can get a 5-megapixel camera the size of a pack of cigarettes and a lens the size of a drop of water, which will give you bad distortion. There are cheaper cameras with lower pixel resolution and better lenses, and those are the ones I would buy over the ones with poor lenses.

If you have a camera with a lens prone to fisheye, you can counter the effect by getting as far back as you can from the surface you are

**Figure 4.7**
Many digital cameras come with preprogrammed image control modes. Be careful of the presets that have a shallow depth of field and other settings that can affect the image in an undesirable way. Depth of field is the area of the image that is in focus from the camera lens to infinity. You can have a shallow depth of field so that items that are only within a few feet or inches are in focus and objects that are farther from the camera are blurry. To the left you can see that the bird and the background are both in focus; in the middle the bird is in focus, but the sky is not; and on the right is an image where the foreground object is in focus but the background is not.

photographing and zooming in. See Figure 4.9 for an example of a surface that was photographed close up and zoomed all the way out and then farther away and zoomed in as far as possible. The effect is not very pronounced, but the bulge in the lines of the bricks would be very noticeable if you tried to tile this image.

### Diminish Angle Distortion (Position)

Distortion also comes from the position of the camera in relation to the subject. This issue relates to perspective, which we discussed in Chapter 1. When you take a picture standing above, below, or to the left or right of whatever you are photographing, you are creating perspective in the image. You will not have straight lines and therefore will need to make corrections in Photoshop. The Photoshop work is not too time-consuming when you're correcting straight lines that are at an angle using the Free Transform or Crop tool (we look at that later in this chapter). Correcting a bulged-out image might be harder, but what's bad about skewed angles as opposed to the bulge is that dramatically changing the perspective and angles in an image will cause it to fall apart visually. Even if the lines are perfectly straight, an object with any kind of depth, such as

**Figure 4.8**
When you're buying a digital camera, try to get a decent lens. Even high-megapixel cameras often have cheap lenses that distort the image, creating a fisheye, or spherical, effect. This makes using the image as a texture more difficult because it takes more time to correct such errors and does more damage to the image when doing so. This image is very distorted due to the cheap lens on the camera and would be very hard to correct (not even worth it, in my opinion). Notice the blue lines that are straight compared to the edges of the window frame.

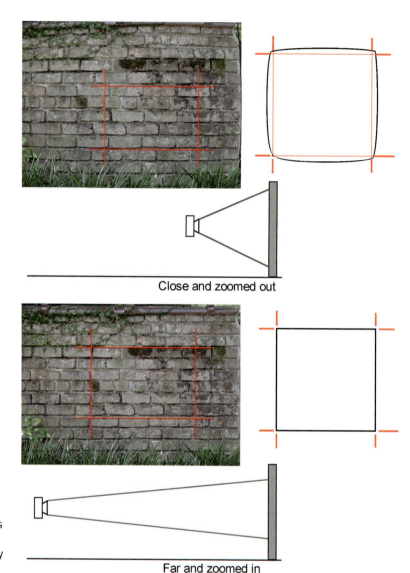

Close and zoomed out

Far and zoomed in

**Figure 4.9**
Distortion from a cheap lens can be countered somewhat by getting as far back from the surface you are photographing as you can and zooming in. This is an example of a surface that was photographed close up and zoomed all the way out and then farther away and zoomed in as much as possible. The effect may not look that pronounced, but later, when you try to use this image to tile across a wall surface, the effect will be very noticeable.

windows and doors that have protruding frames around them, retains visual information about the angle at which the object was captured (this relates to Chapter 1's discussion, too—particularly light and shadow). The human eye will detect those differences and the image will look off. There are ways to correct those errors, but they are time-consuming, since you are basically rebuilding the image—so it's best to avoid them if possible. So, even if you get all the lines in the image straight in Photoshop, the shadows will simply not look right. Things that are flat like signs can be more easily compensated for in Photoshop. You can see some examples in Figure 4.10 and in an illustration on how to position yourself in Figure 4.11.

**Figure 4.10**
Distortion also comes from the position of the camera in relation to the subject. When you take a picture standing above, below, or to the left or right of whatever you are photographing, you are creating perspective angles in the image that will have to be corrected in Photoshop. The windows on the upper left are okay, but the windows on the upper right are at too dramatic an angle. The second row shows some windows all taken at a good straight-on angle. The third row shows a sign that was taken at a skewed angle but that can be easily fixed because it is flat and lacks a lot of depth. These windows on the bottom left are at a very extreme angle. Bottom right, even after straightening the lines, the protruding frame retains visual information about the angle at which the window was captured and the image doesn't work.

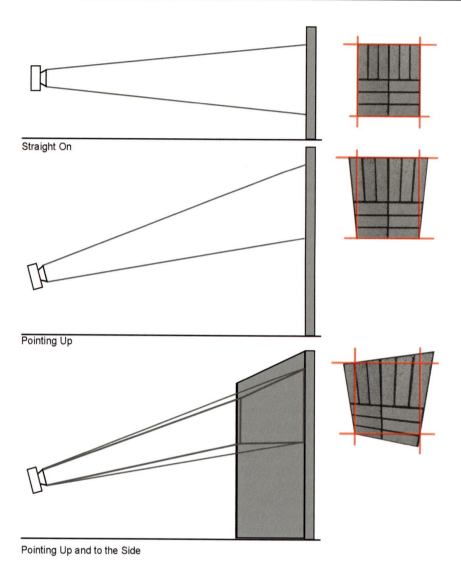

Straight On

Pointing Up

Pointing Up and to the Side

**Figure 4.11**
Ideally, you want to take a picture straight on to minimize angle distortion, but even if you can't get into
an optimal position, you can still minimize angle distortion by positioning yourself as straight vertically or
horizontally as you can. Top, ideally the camera should be pointing straight at the subject. If this is possible,
the image will be mostly square and easier to fix in Photoshop. The illustration in the middle is of the camera
looking up, like at a window or a sign high on a wall. In this scenario the image will come out wider at the top
than the bottom. At the bottom you can see that taking a picture from an angle that is both horizontally and
vertically off will create a very distorted image.

### Diminish Lighting Problems

Lighting is a big concern, too. If you have studied photography
or film, you may be familiar with the term *golden hour*. For
photographers, the best light for photography occurs one hour after
sunrise and one hour before sunset. During this time, the light is

**Figure 4.12**
Although we have a lot of control over our images in Photoshop, harsh shadows are almost impossible to remove. Here are images of two wooden shutters, one shot on an overcast day and one on a sunny day.

diffuse. For a texture hunter, this is not always the best time to take pictures, because the light tends to be saturated with blues and oranges and is changing rapidly. But during the day, light is of very high contrast and harsh when the sun is overhead. When the sun is low in the sky, the shadows can be equally harsh but longer. During these hours, when the sun is low in the sky, you are also faced with the problem that anything you are trying to photograph might be facing away from the sun and therefore silhouetted. These images generally come out really dark. This is not a good time to take texture source images, either.

So, what does that leave us? If possible, wait for a cloudy or overcast day. Although many photographers don't go out on overcast days, it is the best time for game artists to go out and shoot. Light is plentiful, it is just diffused by the clouds. There are no harsh shadows because the light is more evenly distributed. On overcast days, plants and trees in particular are more saturated. Although we have a lot of control over our image in Photoshop, harsh shadows are almost impossible to remove. Figure 4.12 shows two wooden shutters, one shot on an overcast day and one on a sunny day.

### Don't Use the Flash If at All Possible

Another problem is flash burn. Avoid using flash if possible. A professional photographer knows how to use a flash so that it casts just the right amount of controlled light, and maybe you can learn that, too, but in general if you take a picture using a flash, you will get harsh light and shadow and a large flash burn in the image. Even surfaces that don't seem highly reflective will be burned by a flash. In fact, even if you are photographing a very matte (nonreflective) surface, you will still get a large overlit area in the middle of the image and the edges will recede into darkness. This is just as bad as a burn for texture work. You can remove a mild flash burn in Photoshop, but usually doing so requires you to clone and paint the flashed part of the image to remove it. I would opt to take another path if possible. Figure 4.13 shows a flash-burned image and how poorly it tiles.

### Plan for Alpha Channels

We talked about alpha channels in Chapter 2 (making parts of the image transparent) and later we will look at various ways to create alpha channels. Many of the techniques for removing backgrounds to create alpha channels rely on the separation and deletion of the background colors from the foreground objects. Knowing this, if it is at all possible try to make sure that the objects you are capturing have a contrasting color behind them. Figure 4.14 depicts a plant that was photographed so that the background could easily be removed and an alpha channel created. There is also an example of an image of grass that is too full of grass; there is no clear delineation between grass and background.

### Plan for Tiling

If you know that you will be tiling the surface you are photographing, then try and capture all the edges and boundaries you will need to make the tiling easier. If you clip off part of the image, the tiling of that surface will be much harder. If you are photographing a surface, such as a brick or stone wall that you intend to tile, try to pick a section of the wall that has as few repeatable aspects as possible.

## Scanners

Scanners are another way to capture digital images. Not only can you scan documents, you can also scan small 3D objects such as knives,

**Figure 4.13**
Avoid using a flash if possible. In general, if you take a picture using flash, you will get harsh light and shadow and a large flash burn in the image. Even surfaces that don't seem highly reflective will be burned by a flash. The top image shows a flash burn and the bottom shows how poorly it tiles.

**Figure 4.14**
Plan for creating alpha channels if possible. If it is at all possible, try to make sure that the objects you are capturing have a contrasting color behind them so that the background is easier to remove. The image on the left is an example of a plant that was photographed so that the background could easily be removed and an alpha channel created. The one on the right is an image in which there is no clear delineation between grass and background.

**Figure 4.15**
You can scan small 3D objects such as knives, leaves, or feathers. Just be careful not to scratch the glass or spill damaging liquids into your scanner.

leaves, or feathers (Figure 4.15). Just be careful not to scratch the glass or spill damaging liquids into your scanner. Keep in mind that even though scanners have dropped in price and increased in quality, it is often easier to simply take a picture of an object with a digital camera rather than scan it. Also keep in mind that most existing images you would like to scan may be copyrighted.

Scanners are great for artists who actually do their work on paper, but once again a digital camera would be better, considering the fact that artwork can easily be too big for a scanner and the paint or ink may rub off on the scanner glass.

## Texture Collections

There are some terrific texture collections for sale that anyone can buy, and they fall into three general categories:

- The finished game texture
- The digital photograph collection
- The digital image of a surface or thing

The problem with the finished game texture is that anyone and everyone will recognize those purchased textures. They can almost never be used "as is" and will need to be modified, so it is generally better to get a good set of base images and build your own textures. But if you can get your hands on these texture collections, they are very useful for learning. You can also use these "as is" in certain circumstances. If you are prototyping or building a walkthrough that will not be sold on artistic merits, these sets can be very useful and can save you time.

The digital photograph collection is the sort that features a kid holding balloons, a shot of the Chrysler building, the Statue of Liberty, and a sunset. These are editorial shots, and though they may have their uses, they aren't generally useful to the texture artist. Give me a good image of a rusted dumpster panel, cracked stucco, or a wall of wooden planks. The digital photograph is sold mostly as clip art for Web sites and newsletters. Only a texture artist would love a high-resolution image of a pile of rotten meat swarming with maggots. Most people would prefer the kid holding the balloons.

Finally, we have the digital image of the rusted dumpster panel, the side of the dead seal, the close-up of pork drippings, and dried vomit (see Figure 4.16). These are the images the texture artist lives for—the ones we find most useful. These are the images you will composite over other images in Photoshop using the layer-blending modes to create some incredible textures. These images are best when you swap them with your fellow artists.

## The Internet

The Internet is a great source of images. Of course, you will run into copyright restrictions and low-resolution images, among other problems, but quite often the images you will find by going to the image search on Google will be surprisingly good (Figure 4.17). Even just for a source of reference, the Internet can be invaluable. Type in a few keywords and you can see pirate gold, maps, Persian rugs— almost anything you can imagine that someone took a picture of and uploaded somewhere on the Internet.

## Using 3D Applications

Another method for creating 2D textures is to model them in 3D. This method is great for modeling things that you can't get a picture of

**Figure 4.16**
From left to right, an image of a digital photograph from a clip-art collection and a digital image of—ugh, that's sick. Which image would you prefer in your collection? (By the way, it's ketchup and bacon fat.)

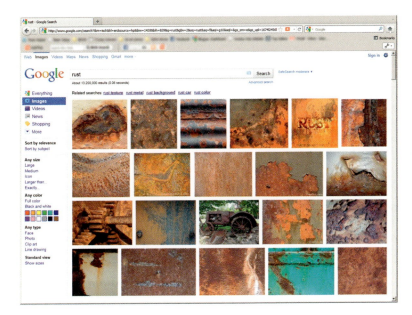

**Figure 4.17**
Type a few keywords into the Google image search and you can see pirate gold, maps, Persian rugs—almost anything you can imagine that someone took a picture of and uploaded to the Internet. Searching for the word *rust* netted me 13,200,000 images (it was 178,000 images in 2009). (Google image search screen used with permission.)

and that would lack the depth you need in Photoshop. This method also allows you to create a surface using all the lights, materials, and shaders the 3D package has to offer. You can render an image from a 3D application, process it in Photoshop, and then apply it to a lower-poly-count game model. The big drawback to this method is that it relies on the assumptions that you (1) are a 3D modeler and (2) own the necessary software. It is obviously a major drawback if you don't own and know how to use the software to create the 3D model, apply the texture to it, and light the scene it is in. This method can also be time-consuming and must be weighed against other options.

## Cleaning Your Textures

The process of cleaning up your textures is an important one. Time spent at this stage will save you a good deal of time later on. When an image is cropped, it saves space; when it is named and saved appropriately, it is much easier to find when you need it; and when an image tiles nicely, it can be used "as is"; you won't have to stop your creativity to clean up the image. Also, the process of working for a few minutes with each texture helps you become familiar with the images you have on your hard drive. This will speed up your workflow and allow you to create better textures because you will be aware of the many options you have when building your texture. Of all the things you can do to manipulate an image when you're cleaning it up, the first thing you will most likely do is crop it.

## Cropping

*Cropping* an image is simply the process of cutting off unwanted portions of it. Cropping literally chops away the portions of the image outside the crop box (see Figure 4.18). The Crop tool in Photoshop can, however, do much more than merely cut your image down to size. Some of the features of the Crop tool can be very useful and save you time.

As you are cropping your images, keep in mind that although power-of-two textures (discussed in Chapter 2) are often your final goal, a perfect square of any size will be fine as long as you remember to start your texture work in the power of two, resizing the source to fit. Some resource images defy the perfect-square rule, so don't stress about it. If the image is a panoramic scene of the horizon or is to be used as an overlay for stains and weathering, leave it as complete as you like.

Cropping an image can save file space, as can resizing it, but I don't resize and I crop as little as possible. I like to keep the entire image, and I always use a copy of the image and never alter the original. Increasing the image size doesn't buy you anything but a larger file size; sizing it down or cropping it only degrades quality and/or removes portions of the image you can't get back later if you need them. I do crop a lot when I am working on windows, doors, and things like that as I straighten them, especially if all there is around the window is a boring wall that looks like all the other walls I have.

**Figure 4.18**
Cropping chops the image down to the size of the crop box and removes what's outside it.

**Warning** Cropping is permanent unless you change the Delete option to "Hide" in the option bar in Photoshop. Once you do that, the canvas size will be scaled down, but the image will still be the same size and is simply hidden because it is outside the canvas area. If you use the Delete option and save and close your file, you can never get the cropped portion back. You cannot use the Hide option on an image that only has a background layer. You need to either convert the background to a layer, duplicate it, or create a new layer.

**Note** You can make the canvas size larger using the Crop tool. You can drag the crop box handles outside the canvas.

Here are some helpful tips for cropping an image in Photoshop. Using the Crop tool, you can:

- Hold down **Shift** and it will make the selection perfectly square.
- Hold down **Alt** and you can drag and size the crop box from its center point.
- Hold down the **Shift** and **Alt** keys and make the selection perfectly square as well as drag and size from the center point of the crop box.
- Press the **Caps Lock** key and your cursor will change to the small crosshairs instead of the thick Crop icon that can get in the way of the image you are trying to crop.
- Enter a height and width in the options bar. After you drag out the crop box and press **Enter**, the image crops and resizes. You will notice that you can size the crop box but not change the proportions. The height and width stay proportional to the values you entered.
- You can also hold down the **Ctrl** and **Alt** keys after you start dragging out the crop box to make the crop box selection the exact size of the dimensions you entered, so the image will not resize after you press **Enter**.
- You can rotate the crop box and it will crop and rotate the image to match the selection.

See Figure 4.19.

**Figure 4.19**
You can rotate the crop box and it will crop and rotate the image to match the selection. From left to right: The original image, the crop box dragged out, the crop box rotated, and the final result after you press Enter.

## Fixing Perspective (Bad Angles) with the Crop Tool

Using the Crop tool in Photoshop, you are also able to instantly fix perspective problems. I find this feature particularly useful. All you have to do is drag out a crop box on your canvas (doesn't matter how big it is; you can adjust it later) and make sure that the **Perspective** box is checked in the options bar. Then you can drag each individual handle to the corners of the thing you want to crop and fix. When you press **Enter**, *bam!* The image is cropped and the perspective fixed. See Figure 4.20 for a visual of the Crop tool fixing perspective in an image. This works best on images with straight lines. I mentioned earlier that a bulged-out image is harder to work with than one with straight lines. This is one of the reasons. The lines connecting the crop box handles are straight, but if the area of the image you are trying to crop is bulged, the lines will be curved and you won't get a clean result when you crop.

## Resampling an Image Using Crop

*Resampling* means resizing your image to change the pixel height and width of the image. The Crop tool allows you to crop your image based on the dimensions and resolution of another image. You must first open the image you want to take the information from and then select the Crop tool. Click **Front Image** in the options bar and then click on the image you want to crop. Drag the crop box out (it will maintain the proportions of the sampled image), and when you crop your image it will also resize it.

**Figure 4.20**
The Crop tool allows you to instantly fix perspective problems. The image at the upper left is the source. The upper right shows the extent of the perspective problem with red lines. The lower left image is the crop box on the canvas after each handle has been dragged to the corners of the part of the image I want to retain and fix. Lower right: after you press Enter, the image is cropped and the perspective fixed.

You can also change the color and opacity of the shading shield and turn it off and on (see Figure 4.21). The shading shield is the area outside the crop box that will be cropped.

### Crop Using the Trim Command

The Trim command (**Image** > **Trim**) crops an image by cropping away the parts of the image that have transparent pixels; therefore, Trim will have no effect on a full layer (see Figure 4.22).

**Figure 4.21**
You can change the color and opacity of the shading shield and turn it off and on. The shield is the area outside the crop box. Here you can see various settings applied to the shield.

**Figure 4.22**
The Trim command crops an image by cropping away the parts of the image that have transparent pixels.

## The Free Transform Tool

The Free Transform tool allows you to size and distort the layer or selection in many ways. This tool is particularly useful for cleaning up textures and in texture creation. The Free Transform tool allows you to scale, rotate, skew, distort, and change the perspective of an image as well as other options for quickly rotating or flipping the image (see Figure 4.23). You can choose to flip the image horizontally or vertically or rotate the image exactly 90° clockwise or counterclockwise as well as 180°. All of this manipulation of an image is really useful for creating textures. Manipulating one visual element to fit convincingly into another is a good deal of what you will be doing during texture creation. Not all digital resources will come to you at the same resolution, angle, and so on. You might want to

**Figure 4.23**
Use the Free Transform tool to scale, rotate, skew, distort, and change the perspective of an image as well as other options for quickly rotating or flipping the image.

overlay a crack from one image on a wall texture and might need to scale, rotate, or even distort it to make it look the way you want it to.

You will use the Free Transform tool frequently in texture creation. As you are creating a texture, you will be bringing images together from various sources, and those images will be of various sizes. You may be working on an image that is one size, say 1024 × 1024, and paste in an image to use in the texture as an overlay or detail that is larger or smaller and will need to be fit into the texture.

**Note** Once an image is in the computer, the maximum detail is set and cannot be increased. The Free Transform tool is one way to make an image larger, but the amount of detail doesn't increase; only the number of pixels is increased by a mathematical process called *interpolation*. This process does not increase the detail; it simply adds extra pixels to smooth the transition between the original pixels.

**Warning** Be careful doing any severe manipulation to an image, because you could degrade the image quality. Resizing, for example, does a lot of damage to an image. If you reduce a large image and later reenlarge it, you will seriously degrade its quality. Once you shrink an image and save it, you lose the resolution of the original image.

## Texture Tiling

A *tiling texture* is an image that can repeat over a surface and still look good. Although it is easy to remove the seams in an image in most cases, it is more art than science to create a texture that can tile across a large surface, not have a pattern to it, and still look good (not being a blurry mess in order to tile). I purposely didn't discuss how to tile a texture until after I discussed the best way to collect and prepare your resources, because some images are just not worth working with if you can help it. If the lighting is so bad, the resolution so low, or the image so distorted that you are looking at some serious reworking of the image, I would wager that it would probably be quicker to get a new base image than to try to rebuild a bad one. There are so many sources of digital imagery it just doesn't make sense to perform major surgery on a bad base image. Some images are literally tiles—like floor tiles—and are easy to make repeat across a surface, but others can be complex manmade or organic patterns that are more challenging to work with. With these types of images the challenge is not only to make them tile but also to create an interesting texture without high contrast or unique details that make the tiling noticeable (see Figure 4.24). These errors are often called *banding* and *hot spots*.

Tiling a texture is arguably the most discussed aspect of texture creation, but there is more to tiling than just using the offset Filter and cloning away the seams. That method doesn't always work when you're tiling various surfaces. The approach you use to tile an image will depend on the image you start with, where the texture will be used, and even the technology you use.

**Figure 4.24**
At the top are examples of organic and inorganic images that do not tile well. The organic water image has severe banding; you can see harsh, dark stripes running vertically in the tiled image. The inorganic white bricks have a very severe hot spot; there is a clearly identifiable spot on the texture that you can see repeating. The bottom two examples are a set of organic and inorganic images that tile much more nicely.

## The Base Image

The condition of the base image and what the final outcome must be will determine what you will have to do to the image to make it usable. At this point in the chapter, you are well aware of the things you can do: cropping, fixing angles, smoothing the lighting, and others. If you are starting with an image that was shot dead-on straight, you might not need to fix the angles. If it was perfectly lit, you will not need to spend time adjusting the lighting. You get the idea.

## The Context of the Texture

Where will this texture be used? The answer to this question has a lot to do with the tiling techniques we'll discuss shortly. But context also has to do with how close the player gets to the image and how many times the image will tile across a surface. You need to know this information because you can spend a lot of time making a texture tile a thousand times across a large terrain and find out that the image will be used in a place where it will only tile four times or that you took too much detail out of the image trying to make it work where it was not intended to.

## The Technology Used

If you are developing for a platform or technology that is limited to low-color 128 × 128 images or a cutting-edge game engine using a high-end system that allows for high-color 1024 × 1024 images, you will obviously approach the processing and creation of the image differently. A larger image will allow for more detail and be a bit easier to tile due to the larger area it covers. But image size is not the only technological consideration when you're determining the final appearance of your texture. What you can do with those textures in the game engine makes a huge difference in the final form that your texture will take.

Some game engines allow combining of multiple layers of textures on terrain (just like Photoshop layers), and this allows the texture artist to make a number of textures that are predominantly one material. Textures composed of one material are much simpler to tile. It used to be that terrain was covered in one texture and if you wanted something like a road or dirt patch, you had to create various versions of that one texture to place on the terrain polygon on which you wanted the road to run or the dirt patch to appear. This was limiting, to say the least; roads ran in straight lines and right angles, and you had to create a separate texture for any unique terrain detail. Now we can create a few versions of the terrain textures—packed dirt, grassy dirt, dried dirt, grass, dead grass, and other single-themed textures—and paint them onto the terrain. We can make our base layer grass and paint on darker grass, dirt patches, or a dirt road with a dirt-to-grass border. This is easier, and the results are far more pleasing. This approach also makes dealing with texture tiling much easier. See Figure 4.25 for an example of a terrain built using the layer system.

Some engines allow for random swapping of textures across a surface. You can create a texture and various versions of it and apply the main image to a surface, and the game engine will randomly assign the textures to various polygons. This method usually relies on a naming convention so that the engine will know that when Wall_Texture_001_a (for example) is present and Wall_Texture_001_b is also present, and more in the sequence, it should use those other textures in the random tile.

These random tiles are usually more subtle in their differences than the textures in a texture set, as shown in Chapter 2. In a texture set, you may have a very noticeable detail in the various textures: vents, large cracks, and so on. But a random tile is meant to break up the pattern produced by a tiling texture and not add specific detail (Figure 4.26). Four vents showing up at random spots on a wall would look weird, whereas subtle variances in the pattern of a brick—and even gradual light shifts, in this case—could work well. This is another technology that would allow for smaller textures. Four 128 × 128 versions of a randomly tiled texture would look better than one 256 × 256 tiled texture and would take up the same texture memory. (If this doesn't make sense, look at Chapter 2, in which I discussed the power of two.)

**Figure 4.25**
Not too long ago (top), terrain was textured by covering it in one texture. Roads, dirt patches, and any unique area had to be created as a separate version of the base texture and placed on the terrain polygon where the detail appeared. Roads ran in straight lines and right angles. Nowadays (bottom), most commercial game engines allow for the layering of textures on terrain, like Photoshop layers. These textures can be composed of predominantly one material. Using base dirt, grass, and other single-type textures, you can paint them onto the terrain. This method allows for a much more organic terrain with more variety using the same number of textures. Not only are the results far more pleasing, but this approach also makes dealing with texture tiling much easier.

But this newer approach is being supplanted by an even newer technology. With shaders and projected textures, or *decals*, you can make the wall texture simple and add detail in other ways. Figure 4.27 shows an example of how a projected texture works. Shaders (discussed at length in Chapter 2 as well, with visual examples) can use even simpler textures and process varied detail in real time.

### Fixing Light Variations Across an Image

You will notice that when you are tiling a digital image (right after you run the offset filter for the first time), there are often variations in the lighting across the surface. This is almost unavoidable and

**Figure 4.26**
Some engines allow for random swapping of various textures across a surface. This method usually relies on a naming convention so that the engine will know to include all textures of a certain naming pattern in the process. These random tiles are usually more subtle in their differences than the textures in a texture set. In a texture set you have noticeable detail, but a random tile is meant to be subtle, to break up the pattern produced by a tiling texture and not add specific detail. In the left image, you can see a repeating pattern. On the right, three versions of the tile have been randomly applied to the surface. Some of the bricks are actually more pronounced, lighter or darker, but still work because of the random tiling.

**Figure 4.27**
A projected texture works the way it sounds. You can project a texture onto a surface in the game world. Here you can see the image of a crack with an alpha channel projected onto a wall texture, and the result is a wall with a crack in it.

why I spent some time earlier saying, "Diffuse light good, flash bad." Probably the first thing you should correct in an image you plan to tile is the lighting. There are several ways to do this. Most commonly you can use the High Pass filter or use the image itself to manually adjust the lighting (or a bit of both).

**Figure 4.28**
On the top left is an image
of dirt and to the right the
image is offset, so you can
see the lighting variance.
Below are three versions of
the image from the same PSD
file. Playing with the blending
modes and other variables
will give you various results.

The High Pass filter basically "reduces brightness differences, it also reduces the contrast of the image, paling the colors." The use of the High Pass filter is detailed in an excellent article on Gamasutra, "The Power of the High Pass Filter," by Peter Hajba (www.gamasutra.com/features/20010523/hajba_01.htm).

I try many things in conjunction with the High Pass filter. For one, I copy the image I am repairing on a new layer (**Ctrl+A, Ctrl+C, Ctrl+N,** and **Ctrl+V**), blur the copy using the highest setting of Gaussian Blur (this makes the layer a solid color), or just use an adjustment layer (explained in Chapter 3) and fill it with a desired color. Then I use the High Pass filter on the original layer. Tweaking the High Pass filter is a balancing act between the smaller radius (gray and flat) and a higher radius (little to no effect on the image) to even out the lighting. Then I play with the blending modes (also explained in the last chapter) and levels and other settings on the color layer. Sometimes I even use a copy of the high pass layer, invert it, blur it a little, and play with the blending modes and opacity to further adjust the lighting.

New to Photoshop CS is the Shadow/Highlights command (**Image** > **Adjustments** > **Shadow/Highlights**). This tool allows you to control the shadows and highlights in an image, especially silhouetted and flash-burned images. The Shadow/Highlights

**Figure 4.29**
Upper left, the wall texture was designed to tile only one way: horizontally. Right, the vertically stacked textures show how the texture was not designed to tile. Below, the texture is horizontally tiled. At the bottom, the texture is used in a scene where it is horizontally tiled.

command goes beyond levels and does not merely darken or lighten the image. It treats the shadow and highlight areas separately from each other and enables their independent control. Because the default settings are designed for images that have bad backlighting, you will have to play with the adjustments if your image doesn't look just right when you first open the tool.

Each image you process will be different from the last. There is no one perfect way to fix the lighting in an image. At first you might have to experiment with several ways, but after a while, you will begin to have a more immediate sense of the best approach for each particular image.

## One-Way Tiling (Horizontal and Vertical)

Making an image tile on only one axis, horizontal or vertical, is much easier than making an image that must tile across a larger surface in all four directions. See Figure 4.29 for a visual of one-way tiling. One-way tiling is usually used on a wall where the texture only needs to tile across the wall, not up and down it.

## Three- and Four-Way Tiling

Three-way tiling is used in the case of a wall set where the sides of the texture are designed to tile with each other and the top edge with another texture; the bottom edge doesn't tile at all. The top of the wall texture will tile with itself side to side and with another texture on the bottom (see Figures 4.30 and 4.31). The center tile must tile in all four directions (with itself) and the top of the bottom texture and the bottom of the top texture. This is easy to understand when it's presented visually. Four-way tiling can be easy if you are working with clean and simple textures such as clean blocks and bricks. In the figures, the center of the brick wall tiles with itself, is clean, and is not a huge challenge. It gets a bit more challenging when you are working with stone walls and odd-sized bricks with dirt and weathering thrown in.

## Organic vs. Inorganic Tiling

Inorganic surfaces are manmade and generally more easily tiled along seams. Things like walls, bricks, cut wooden planks, metal plates, windows, and so on are pretty easy to tile. Organic surfaces can be easy, too. Things like grass and dirt are fairly easy to tweak and blend into a seamless tile. The challenge comes when you try to tile things with obvious and complex patterns, such as cobblestones and other

**Figure 4.30**
Three- and four-way tiling is used in this wall texture set. The top texture tiles only in three directions; with itself, side to side, and with the base wall texture below it. The base wall texture in the center tiles in all four directions, and the bottom texture tiles in three directions, side to side and with the base above it.

assembled stone surfaces that aren't on a grid. Organic surfaces with pronounced segments—pine bark, dirt, or rock with striations, or even certain grasses—can be challenging to tile. Because of the randomness with which the objects or materials are laid out, they don't tile in the real world and are harder to capture and tile on the computer. This leads us into the next section on the various tiling techniques.

**Texture Tiling in Practice**

There are several ways to tile a texture, and like most other aspects of computer art, you will most likely use a bit of each technique to get the job done. Of course, most texture tiling starts with the classic offset filter. The simple steps are:

1. Copy the layer you want to tile.
2. Run the offset filter.
3. Enter half the height and width of your image (or with CS, you can use the slider bars to move the image in real time).
4. Erase the hard line in the texture that appears in the vertical and horizontal centers of the offset image with a soft brush.

. . . and voilà, you have removed the seams.

This is the first technique you will learn. If you are new to texture creation and have tried to find any information on the topic, you most likely didn't find much beyond the use of the offset filter. In four lines or less, you can be taught to tile anything, right? Or maybe you need the deluxe version of the tutorial that tells you to use the Clone tool to remove conspicuous detail that could be noticeable when the texture tiles. Unfortunately, making a texture tile usually involves more work than this. Even if the texture looks flawless by itself, when it is repeated over a surface several times it might be painfully obvious that your texture is tiling (Figure 4.32).

**Figure 4.31**
Here are the three- and four-way tiling texture sets used in a scene.

**Figure 4.32**
The offset filter is the first tiling technique you will learn, but making a texture tile usually involves more work than simply removing the noticeable seams. Even if the texture looks flawless by itself, when it is repeated over a surface several times it might be painfully obvious that your texture is tiling. The top left image is the original, the top middle is the offset image, and the top right is the image with no seams. The large image at the bottom is the seamless tile tiling, but it's not doing it very well. Notice the very repetitive patterns and the diagonal banding, too.

### Edge Copy

Other than using the offset filter, you can also use a different technique. The Edge Copy method involves starting with an image larger than you intend the final texture to be and copying some of the outer portions of the image from one side and moving them over to the other side. You don't flip or rotate this piece. By selecting a piece of the image outside the portion of the image you want to tile and moving it over, you are creating a seamless transition between the left and right sides of the image. The seam you need to deal with now exists on the inside edge of the pasted portion and is easier to work with than an offset image. This process is detailed in this section.

You will still need to clean and clone, but I prefer this method when I'm trying to tile an image with large irregular elements, such as stones. With this method you are working with one edge, whereas with the offset filter you are trying to blend two edges at once.

## Project: Tiling Stones Using Edge Copy

One problem with tiling stonework is that often there are wide variations of color, contrast, size, and even the positions of the stones. Unlike bricks, wooden planks, and other manmade materials, stones are not uniform in length and width and as a result don't fit together in a perfect pattern. There is another, simpler, way than this to make stones in Photoshop that are more uniform and easier to tile. I prefer that method and use it in the chapter on fantasy textures. But you should know this method in the event that you need to tile a specific image that fits these criteria. The following project illustrates edge tiling as well as a few tricks to make natural stones more uniform.

**Setting Up the Image**

1. Open the source image from the CD for this project. Note that this image is larger than 1024 and not a power of two. That is preferred in this instance.
2. Set your grid to 128 (**Edit** > **Preferences** > **Guides, Grid**).
3. Choose a square portion of the image you want to tile. Use the grid and make sure your selection is a power of two. I selected the portion you can see outlined in red in Figure 4.33. The square I chose is a 1024 × 1024 section, with some of the image to the left and the bottom of the selection.
4. Drag out some guidelines to mark the four edges of your selection. These will help you later on. You might even want to zoom in and make sure your guides are snapped precisely on the edge of the selection.

**Cleaning Up the Image**

The very first thing I do when working on an image like this is to make all the stones more uniform. I don't just mean adjusting the lighting, but actually resizing and moving stones just a bit to get them closer in size. I find this practice makes tiling easier later on. You can see the original image and the corrected image where the stones are more similar in Figure 4.34. I resized and moved stones by cloning some stones over others, using various parts of several stones to create, or fix, another. That technique is explained next. You can also play with the High Pass filter, the Highlights and Shadows command, and other methods for adjusting the lighting and consistency at this point. In this case I simply used the High Pass filter.

**Figure 4.33**
Setting the grid and choosing the portion of the source image you want to tile.

**Figure 4.34**
Making all the stones more consistent before working on the image makes tiling easier later on. The original image is on the left and the corrected image on the right. By cloning some stones over others, using various parts of several stones to create or fix another, the stone can be made to look more uniform.

### Copy and Crop Parts

1. Now select the left part of the image on the outside of your square selection. This is the 128 × 1024 column marked in blue in Figure 4.33 and you can see it in Figure 4.35.
2. Copy the selection and paste it, creating a new layer (**Ctrl+C** and **Ctrl+V**) and move the new layer with the copied part of the image over to the right side of your selected area. Make sure you have snap turned on, so it will snap in place and look like Figure 4.35.

I turned off the grid so you could see the part of the image pasted over the right side and how obvious the inner seam is that needs to be cleaned up. You can also see that by moving the outer piece we just moved to where it is inside the image, the edges will now tile. The small arrows point out a spot where it is easy to see how the two halves of the stone will line up.

3. Repeat these steps for the horizontal portion of the image below your selection. Don't worry if this piece is not exactly 1024 × 128. This image was not a power of two to begin with, so the part at the

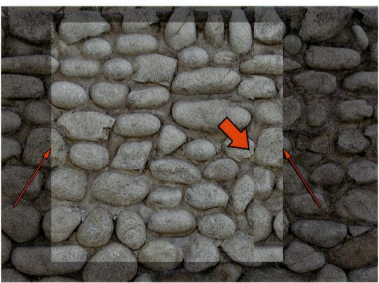

**Figure 4.35**
By selecting an area outside the part of the image you want to tile and moving it over, you are creating a seamless transition between the left and right sides of the image. The seam now exists on the inside edge of the pasted portion and is easier to work with than an offset image.

bottom will not be 128 pixels high. Just make sure that the top of your selection is aligned with the bottom of the selected portion of the image we are going to tile.
4. Copy and paste this horizontal section into its own layer, drag it up to the top of the image, and hide the layer for later.

### Removing the Seams

To remove the seams, I don't use the eraser. I find it so much easier, and faster, to create a layer mask and paint the edges away. If I make a mistake, I don't need to lose any work with the Undo command; I can just press the **X** key and switch the brush color from black to white and paint back what I want.

1. Press the **D** key to set your colors to black and white.
2. Select the layer with the vertical portion of the image on it that we first created.
3. Create a layer mask for this layer by clicking the **mask** icon on the bottom of the **Layers** palette.
4. Start painting away the seams. Use the **X** key to switch from black to white. You will find that some areas miraculously work and others simply will not. Just do your best on this first pass and don't try for perfection just yet. Figure 4.36 shows what I ended up with, good and bad.
5. Unhide the vertical layer and do the same.
6. Flatten the image.
7. Crop the image to a 1024 × 1024 image (**Image** > **Crop**). Use the grid to set your crop area precisely.
8. **Filter** > **other** > **offset**. Because this is a 1024 × 1024 image, the offset values in both directions should be 512. You will see that although there are no hard seams, we still have work to do.

### Build/Rebuild Stones Using Clone

To get stones to tile involves a few tricks to make all the seams between the stones look good. Simply copying the stones won't work because they are not all the same size or shape or at the same angle. Usually you will never get a copy of a stone from one part of an image to fit with the other stones in different parts of the image.

You want the stones to all look different (but not too different), and many copies of the same stone would stand out. The answer is to build and rebuild stones using parts of other stones.

Where two stones have blurred over each other, you can find edges and corners from other stones to clone over these stones. Figure 4.37 shows the few steps it took to restore the space between the stones. You will also need to use the Clone tool lightly in some cases to retouch the main surface of the stone, as in Figure 4.37.

This process may take some time, so be patient and get those edges clean. I said earlier that you probably can't copy and paste a stone into your image and have it fit neatly, but you can copy small portions of a stone (a bottom edge or corner) and paste them in if they need to be rotated to fit. You can also use parts from other images. If you

**Figure 4.36**
After you create a layer mask
and paint away the seams,
you will find that some areas
work and others don't. Just
do your best on this first pass
and don't try for perfection
just yet.

took several pictures of the same stone wall, you can use stone parts
from all the images to build one clean texture.

### Testing a Tiling Texture

After you have rebuilt and repaired the stones to your liking, you
can test the tiling of the texture. This is easy to do using the Define
Pattern option in Photoshop. Note that there is a difference between
defining a pattern and the Pattern Maker. We are defining a pattern
to later fill in an area; this does not alter the image. Pattern Maker
attempts to create a tiling pattern using a selection. Pattern Maker
gives me mixed results, sometimes good and sometimes bad. Even
the good results will require some touchup.

1. To get the best result, you might want to first look at your image
   size. If you are working on a large image (and you should be),
   you might want to create a copy of the image and reduce it

**Figure 4.37**
You can use edges and corners from other stones to restore or build the space between stones. You will also need to use the Clone tool lightly in some cases to retouch the main surface of the stone. On the upper left are the blurred stone and the three places from which I determined I could take detail using the Clone tool. The lower right is the result of the repair.

to 256 × 256 so you can tile it across a larger canvas without creating a super-huge image.

2. Select your entire image (**Ctrl+A**). You can select an unflattened Photoshop file, which will create a pattern using all layers that are visible.
3. Go to **Edit** > **Define Pattern**. These steps are illustrated in Figure 4.38.
4. The Pattern Name dialog box will appear and you will see a small thumbnail image of your pattern and have the option to name it.
5. Select **OK**. Nothing will seem to happen, but your pattern is now in the Pattern Preset Library.
6. Create a new image (**Ctrl+N**) and make it at least four times the size of your texture. If your image is 256 × 256, make the new image at least 1024 × 1024.
7. Select the entire surface of the new image (**Ctrl+A**).
8. Right-mouse-click inside the selection and choose **Fill...**.
9. When the Fill dialog box comes up, you will be able to choose what to use to fill the selection. You can also drop down the Custom Pattern list below that and your new pattern will be at the end of the list.
10. After you select the pattern, click **OK** and the image will be filled with the pattern.

**Figure 4.38**
The basic steps to define a pattern to test the tiling of your image. The upper left is the beginning image and the lower right the tiled result.

You can now get a much better idea of how your image will tile over a large surface. It is still preferable to put the image into the game engine it will be used in and see it tile there. The size of the pattern you create and the size of the test image you create to tile it in also depend on the final use of the texture. If you are creating a horizontally tiling wall texture, you can make the pattern larger, say, 512 × 512, and make the new fill image 512 pixels high but 1024 pixels or more wide.

After a few times doing this, your Pattern Preset Library will begin to get pretty full. You can delete patterns by going back to step 9 in the previous list, and when you have access to the pattern library, simply right-click and select **Delete** or hold down **Alt**. The cursor turns into a cute little pair of scissors and you can left-click to delete the pattern.

**Note** You can't undo or cancel the deletion of a pattern from the preset library!

## Storing Your Textures

The way you store your textures is important. The names you give your images, where you save them, the resolution and file format you save them in, and other decisions will directly affect how well you can work with your resources. As mentioned earlier in this chapter, you might need to store image assets according to several criteria in your personal collection, such as ownership, image size, and usefulness. Here we will discuss how you should name those images and save them in a directory structure so that you can find and use them later on.

If you buy a texture set and want to save all those files on your hard drive so you have easy access to them, you should simply name a folder after the company and copy all the files into it. If you are surfing the Internet and you download a hundred images from various sources on a theme, name a folder "Internet Images of Dogs" (or whatever you were researching) and save them there so you know where they came from. When you start snapping your own digital images and creating your own textures, you will want to have a folder for raw assets and finished work for each project.

When you name a folder or individual file, choose a naming convention and use it. A *naming convention* is a set of rules for naming the files in an organized fashion. Keep in mind that it is simple to create a naming convention and far harder to stick with it. One key is to create a text file or document with the legend to your naming convention and folder structure in it and place it in your art drive. Print it out and keep it nearby until you get used to the convention. Although we can use long filenames now, it is always advisable to keep filenames as short and consistent as possible. This makes it easier to skim through them and sort them. In some cases, computer applications still don't like long filenames.

### Tips for Good Naming Conventions

Use underscores (_), not dashes (-), in your filenames because the computer will see the dash as a minus sign and that affects the sorting of filenames.

Underscores are good separators for data; they make content easier to read. Consider grndrtrghv2.tga versus grn_drt_rgh_v2.tga. Using this example, here is a sample naming convention for a set of images. grn_drt_rgh_v2.tga, which might mean:

grn = Ground
drt = Dirt
rgh = Rough
v2 = Version 2

That convention might be for finished textures. For 150 raw images of pinecones, you may want to use numbering at the end, like so:

fol_pine_con_001.tga fol_pine_con_002.tga

and so on. The naming convention for this raw asset is:

fol = foliage
pine = pine trees
con = cone
### = the number of the many images you took of pinecones

Some artists like to include the file size in the naming convention, such as "lrg" or "sml" for large or small, or even the resolution, say, 256 or 512. Naming conventions, like so many other aspects of game development, are often dictated by the project, the technology, and the company you are working for. A certain company might have strict naming conventions or might leave you in charge of creating your own. A certain game technology might need certain naming conventions such as "_a" appearing at the end of a texture that uses an alpha channel. A large outdoor game might have a complex naming convention for foliage, and an indoor game with a few trees might simply have the trees stored as decorations or props.

No matter what, you need to be consistent and persistent with naming and organization. Writing the naming convention down and making sure that everyone understands and uses it is a good idea.

## Conclusion

This chapter looked at the important aspects of collecting, preparing, and storing your textures and resources. Next we will start creating textures—and we will start with the Sci-Fi setting.

## Chapter Exercises

1. What are some good sources for gathering textures?
2. List at least five tips for taking digital photographs.
3. What are the basic types of texture collections?
4. What are the most common functions used to clean up a texture?
5. What is tiling? Are there different types of tiling?

# Chapter 5

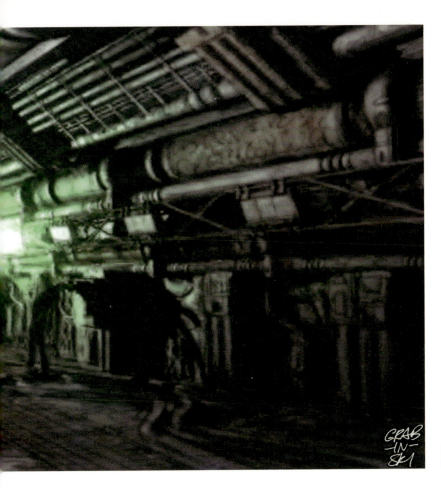

Sci-Fi Hall Concept, 2005, by Brian Grabinski

# The Sci-Fi Setting

## Introduction

For this first tutorial chapter, I chose a scene that looks complex due to the geometry and effects but that in actuality involves a very simple texture set. In this particular example, shown in Figure 5.1, we have some leeway to create a close approximation of the scene because, although this concept art is beautiful, it lacks close-up, hard detail that would dictate what we need to create for the scene. Some game companies will dump a load of concept art and textual descriptions on you, but others might give you a loose image like this one and let you fill in the gaps (because you are that good!).

We will start by taking from the concept sketch ideas for the materials that we want to create for this scene. As texture artists, we need to create a simple and versatile set of textures for the 3D modelers to use as they create/make up the finer details in the scene using geometry. In a real-life situation, you would ask several questions about this, or any, scene before creating textures for it: How old is this structure? What is it made of? What is it used for? What is the atmosphere like here? For this exercise, we will make assumptions about the exact materials the hall is made of and their condition.

Concept art and production issues aside, the method for creating these textures relies on a few smaller and simpler textures, so it is a good place to start. It also requires some fudging on the specific details present in the concept art due to the limited set of textures we are working with, which is perfect for this example. Although some texture creation demands a focus on high detail, those textures tend to have limited uses. This method produces textures that can be used in various ways and are designed to be used with shader technology (like bump and normal mapping, and so on). These textures can be

**Figure 5.1**
This concept art is beautiful, but it lacks hard detail that would dictate exactly what textures we should create for the scene.

mapped in different ways, but because this method is designed for a more advanced game technology, we can also use lighting and other effects to help further contribute to the visual diversity of the scene.

This type of setting lends itself to a general approach to texture creation. A structure such as this one that is industrial or military in nature would actually be built in such a logical and modular fashion. This method can also be used in more traditional settings where shaders will be adding more detail and the artist needs mostly to apply base materials and few detailed textures. I have built Gothic settings using this method and, rather than corroded metal, created various wood and iron trims and fills.

## The Concept Sketch

The front plate shows the concept art for the space hallway. Like warehouses full of crates, the space station hallway full of pipes is a game staple. I figured I would stick to the archetypes of game environments so that (after you master these base settings) you can expand outward to your own unique and complex settings that stem from these roots.

## Determining Texture Needs

Looking past the colored lights, glow effects, and the light suggestion of dirt and wear, we see metal—and lots of it. In fact, this place looks like it is composed entirely of the same type of metal with some specific detail in only a few places. The only textures that need to be created that are not a metal variant are the black and yellow caution stripes and a few minor detail textures.

We will start with the base metal texture and build our set from that. Even the caution stripes are painted over this metal, so they are part of that texture as well. The trick to this method, in which a few textures are used in many ways in a scene, is to build a set of textures that contain a selection of common parts that the environmental modeler will repeatedly use on high-poly-count geometry—things like a grate with an alpha channel, a larger wall piece, a metal fill, and some textures with parts that can be used as trim that will all add rich detail to complex geometry.

Our set will contain the following elements, as described in the next few sections:

- Base metal
- Metal fill
- Wall panel
- Floor panel with (alpha-channeled) grate
- Detail texture: Vent/panel/bracket/hose
- Pipe
- Caution stripes

*Base Metal*

The metal in this scene appears to be an industrial-type metal used for mass fabrication. It wasn't created to look pretty. I am sure the bureaucrats who had to handle this large job wanted something durable that met their specs and was cheap. No money was wasted on fancy finishes or fresh lemon scent. This metal might have been loaded and unloaded many times before it reached its final destination. Then it was manhandled (or robot-handled) in the construction of this outpost. So we will start by creating a flat, mottled, and less-than-perfect tiling sheet of metal (with no lemon scent).

**Note:** Throughout this book I use a simple convention to tell you what to do in Photoshop; this convention is centered around the menu commands for clarity's sake. I do suggest you use the hotkeys if at all possible.

1. Open Photoshop and create a new file: **File** > **new**.... We work from big to small, so make this image **1024×1024** pixels. Name this image **sci_fi_metal_base** and save it.
2. Create a new layer (**Layer** > **new** > **Layer**).
3. Press the **D** key to reset your colors to black and white.
4. Press the **G** key to activate the Paint Bucket (make sure that the Paint Bucket and not the Gradient Fill is selected in the toolbar) and fill this layer.
5. **Filter** > **Render** > **Clouds**.
6. **Filter** > **Render** > **Difference Clouds**. Use **Ctrl+F** and run this filter five times. I chose five times because the difference (although subtle) just looks right to me after five applications of the filter.
7. **Filter** > **noise** > **Add noise** > **7.5%**. Change your noise settings in the dialog box to **Monochromatic** and **Gaussian**.
8. **Image** > **Adjustments** > **Brightness/Contrast** > **Contrast −70**. In newer versions of Photoshop, check the **Use Legacy** box.
9. **Filter** > **Artistic** > **Colored Pencil**: Pencil Width **6**, Stroke Pressure **8**, Paper Brightness **20**.
10. **Filter** > **Artistic** > **Fresco**: Brush Size **2**, Brush Detail **8**, Texture **1**.
11. Fade **Fresco (Ctrl+Shift+F) 50%** > **Blending Mode: Multiply**.
12. **Filter** > **Render** > **Lighting Effects**. Match the following settings:
    Light Type: Spotlight
    Intensity: 18
    Focus: 63
    Gloss: 68
    Material: 25
    Exposure: −16
    Ambience: 32
    Texture Channel: Blue
    Height: 71
13. **Filter** > **Artistic** > **Plastic Wrap** > Highlight Strength **4**, Detail **7**, Smoothness **3**.
14. **Filter** > **Sketch** > **Chrome** > Detail **5**, Smoothness **5**.
15. **Fade Chrome 50%** > Blending Mode: **Exclusion**.

16. **Image** > **Adjustments** > Brightness **10**, Contrast **−20**.
17. **Filter** > **Brush Strokes** > **Accent Edges** > Edge Width **2**, Edge Brightness **18**, Smoothness **7**.
18. **Fade Accent Edges 60%**.
19. **Filter** > **Render** > **Lighting Effects**. Use the same settings as before. They should still be set the same, but double-check. Also, there seems to be a bug in the Render Lighting Effects filter. Move the light around a bit to reset it. If Photoshop crashes when you run this filter, you can find the solution via Google. I hesitate to tell you here because I don't want you messing up your install of Photoshop on my advice.
20. **Fade Lightening Effects 40%** > Blending Mode: **Exclusion**.
21. Tweak the contrast and resolution. I set the brightness to **−18** and the contrast to **47**.
22. Copy the layer and offset it, then erase the seams so that you end up with a tileable image. Your image should look like the finished metal at the bottom right of Figure 5.2.

## Metal Fill

The metal fill texture doesn't need to be as big as the base metal. The base metal is used to create the larger textures such as wall and floor panels. The fill needs to be just a small texture created from the base that is much lower in contrast so that it can tile over surfaces you want filled with metal. It is small for memory efficiency, too. I simply copied a 256×256 portion of the base metal into a new image and lowered the contrast a lot. You can make lighter and darker versions of the fill based on your needs. I only needed a darker one. You can see the metal fill in Figure 5.3 and how it would be used.

## Wall Panel

Now that we have a base metal, the rest is easy. Making this tiling wall panel will also be easy because (1) they are supposed to be modular and logically we can get away with repeating parts, and (2) these wall panels can be pretty simple, since they are hidden behind all the pipes.

1. Open a copy of the base metal we created and save it as **sci_fi_metal_wall**.
2. You will be applying a layer style to this image and you can't apply layer effects and layer styles to a background, locked layer, or layer set. You need to duplicate the layer so you can apply effects to it. Name this layer base.
3. Apply the **Inner Glow** layer style with the following settings:
   **Structure:**
   Blend Mode: Vivid Light
   Opacity: 65%
   Noise: 19%
   Color: RBG: 216,216,216
   **Elements:**
   Size: 16 px
   **Quality:**
   Range: 50%

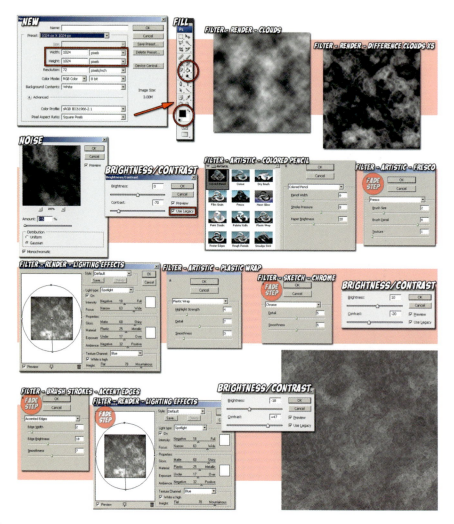

**Figure 5.2**
The steps to create the base metal for our scene.

4. Apply the **Bevel Emboss** layer style with the following settings:
   **Structure:**
   Style: Inner Bevel
   Technique: Chisel Hard
   Depth: 81%
   Direction: Up
   Size: 2
   **Shading:**
   Highlight Mode: Screen
   Opacity: 51%
   Shadow Mode: Multiply
   Opacity: 75%
5. Create a new **Layer (Ctrl+Shift+N)** and name it **Panel**.
6. Set your **Grid** to **32** units (**Edit** > **Preferences** > **Guides Grid**…).
7. Using the **Polygonal Lasso**, outline the shape shown in Figure 5.4. You can do whatever you like here, but the pattern I used was designed so that I could use it in a few places—specifically, the trimmed edges and the crossbar.

**Figure 5.3**
Metal fill is used to fill in areas that don't need a lot of detail. Here is our metal fill in the scene.

8. Fill the selection with any color.
9. Set the **Fill** of this layer to **0**.
10. Apply the **Drop Shadow** layer style with the following settings:
    **Structure:**
    Blend Mode: Multiply
    Opacity: 23%
    Distance: 15 px
    Size: 73 px
11. Apply the **Outer Glow** layer style with the following settings:
    **Structure:**
    Blend Mode: Color Burn
    Opacity: 25%
    Noise: 15%
    Color: black
    **Elements:**
    Technique: Softer
    Size: 46 px
    **Quality:**
    Range: 50%
12. A white inner glow with some noise and the right blending mode can make the edges of the metal look scratched and worn. Apply the **Inner Glow** layer style with the following settings:
    **Structure:**
    Blend Mode: Vivid Light
    Opacity: 92%
    Noise: 19%
    Color: RBG: 190,190,190
    **Elements:**
    Size: 54 px
    **Quality:**
    Range: 40%

**Figure 5.4**
The pattern for the wall panel.

13. Apply the **Bevel Emboss** layer style with the following settings:
    **Structure:**
    Style: Inner Bevel
    Technique: Smooth
    Depth: 131%
    Direction: Up
    Size: 6
    **Shading:**
    Highlight Mode: Screen
    Opacity: 75%
    Shadow Mode: Multiply
    Opacity: 75%
    At this point, I turned my grid back on and used a very hard, small brush (3 pixels) and erased a small gap in the panel horizontally across the canvas. Do the same on your image, which should look like Figure 5.5. Take note of where the gaps are.

14. Create another layer and paste the layer style from the panel layer into it. You will have to go into the layer style and make the **Bevel and Emboss** depth deeper. On this layer, you can add the

**Figure 5.5**
The wall panel with frame. Notice the gaps in the frames. This allows us to use this texture as trim in various places. The image at the right is a variation of the wall panel.

little squares on the edges. They are 64 pixels wide and 22 pixels high. I offset the left and right columns of these shapes vertically by one shape, so when the texture tiles, the shapes look like they are interlocking.

To create another version of the wall panel reminiscent of sheet metal:

1. Copy the **Panel** layer and delete the contents of the layer using **Ctrl+A** and **Ctrl+X**.
2. You will be left with an empty layer that still has the same layer effects applied to it.
3. Create new panels. I used the grid again and created those simple panels. I did tweak the Bevel and Emboss style.

## Floor Panel with Grate

The floor panel is very similar to the wall panel; in fact, you can use a copy of the wall panel to create it. Make sure that you are using a *copy!*

The floor is more complex and involves creating an alpha channel for the grate and creating a diamond plate pattern. We will also put a little wear and tear on the floor:

1. Name your new image **sci_fi_metal_floor.**
2. Go to the **Panel** layer and **Select All** (**Ctrl+A**) and press **Delete**. The layer is still there with the layer styles; it is just now empty. Fill the layer with any color.
3. Select the layer the **Base metal** is on (it should be below the panel).
4. **Filter** > **Brush Strokes** > **Crosshatch** > Stroke Length **33**, Sharpness **12**, Strength **1**.
5. **Fade 50%** > **Blending Mode: Overlay**. This makes the metal look duller and scratched.
6. **Image** > **Adjustments** > **Brightness/Contrast** > Brightness **5**, Contrast **50**.
7. Drag out a vertical guideline. Make sure you have "snap" on so this line will snap to the center of the image (**View** > **Snap To** > **All**).
8. Go back to the **Panel** layer and erase a line down the middle using a hard 9-pixel brush.
9. **Select All** and **Select** > **Modify** > **Border: 8 pixels.**

10. Press the **Delete** key to remove the very edges of the image. **Deselect** your image.
11. You can turn the Drop Shadow and Outer Glow effects off the Panel layer. Make sure the Fill is set to **0**.
12. On the base metal you can use the **Dodge** tool and a soft 45-pixel brush to subtly augment the Inner Glow, making the corners and a few random spots give a bit more wear to the metal than the rest.
13. Duplicate the **Panel** layer and delete the contents. Turn off the **Inner Glow** effect and, using the Polygonal Lasso, make a shape for a frame on the left side of the image that is only two grid units wide (64 pixels) and is only on the two vertical sides of the image. The inside edges of this frame need to be straight. See Figure 5.6 for reference.

I also made another layer that added some complexity to my frame. There are seams where parts fit tightly together on the frame; these are just another frame layer with fitting pieces. You could also accomplish this by using the eraser with a small, hard brush on the same layer.

1. Duplicate the Layer Style of the **Frame** layer.
2. Copy the base metal layer and paste it, creating a new layer under the **Frame** layer. Name this layer **Grid1**. We can't set the Fill to **0** for the grid, because the parts of the grid overlap each other, so we need to use some of the metal.
3. Use the **Marquee** selection tool on the grid to create one-unit-wide vertical bars that are one unit apart and fit between the frames. Invert the selection and delete the metal outside the selection.
4. Paste the **Layer** style and make sure that the **Inner Glow** is not too big and that there is a subtle drop shadow and faint darkish **Outer Glow**. Even though we will be creating an alpha channel for the grid, you will still see the areas where the bars overlap and the shadows will be noticeable.
5. Create a horizontal version of these bars on a layer underneath the vertical bars. Your image should look like Figure 5.7.

Now we will create diamond plate. You will recognize it when you see it if you aren't familiar with the term. It is a common texture, but like most things, if I can make it in Photoshop and have it tile perfectly and be totally flexible, I will do it. Spending the time up front to make an image or pattern that I can completely and quickly alter will speed up my work considerably in the long term.

Now look at Figure 5.8. To make diamond plate, make the first diamond. This is nothing more than the space where two circles intersect. Fill a circular selection, move it over, invert it, and use it to delete the portion of the circle outside the diamond. Creating this pattern can be accomplished in many ways; there are numerous patterns for diamond plate, or you can even create your own.

Diamond plate is usually seen as a diagonal pattern, but I just tiled them straight up and down on a canvas larger than I needed, rotated it 45 degrees, and cropped the image down to 512 pixels. This pattern can be made into a diamond plate texture or dropped into an image with Fill at 0 and Layer Styles applied. In this case the pattern

**Figure 5.6**
The floor panel, more beat up. The beginnings of the frame are in place.

**Figure 5.7**
The floor panel with the grid in place.

was pasted into its own layer, the layer style copied from the Frame layer, and the Fill set to 0. I also dropped the opacity down to 25%. See Figure 5.9.

To finish this texture, I pasted a copy of the base metal at the very top of the layer stack and set the opacity to 50%, the blending mode to Overlay, and Colorized (**Ctrl+U**) the layer to a desaturated orange-brown. This gives the metal a nice light swathe of rust, as though it has been in place a while and is used enough to keep the rust worn away but not cared for so much that it shines. This also makes the entire texture look consistent and blends the elements together visually.

## Alpha Channel

Finally, we must make the alpha channel for the grate:

1. Create a new layer on the top of the stack (**Ctrl+Shift+N**).
2. Fill this layer with white: Press **D** to reset your colors, press **X** to swap them, and press **G** to use the fill bucket.
3. Hold down the **Ctrl+Shift** keys and click on the icons for the grates and frames layers.

**Figure 5.8**
The diamond plate pattern starts with one diamond duplicated and rotated on the grid. There are numerous patterns you can use to create diamond plate.

**Figure 5.9**
The floor panel with diamond plate added. We don't want our space marines to slip and fall.

4. Hold **Ctrl** and press the **I** key to invert the white to black.
5. Select the white half of this image with the **Marquee** tool and fill it with black.
6. The grate holes should be the only white that you see. Figure 5.10 shows the alpha image for this texture.

## Detail Texture: Vent/Panel/Bracket/Hose

Now we will create a texture that contains various areas of detail, such as a vent, a panel, and two strips for a bracket and a hose that are able to tile horizontally. These small detail pieces can be mapped in various places to add a lot of visual variety.

1. Open a copy of **sci_fi_metal_wall** and save it as **sci_fi_metal_details**.
2. Remove all but the **Base** and **Panel** layers.
3. Delete the contents of the **Panel** layer by selecting it all and pressing **Delete**.
4. Set the Fill to **100%**.
5. Use guidelines to divide this texture evenly in half vertically and horizontally. Make sure that snap is on. The lines should be at the 512-pixel point on a 1024 image.
6. Create a new **Layer Set** and name it **Vent**.
7. Put the **Panel** layer in this new set and rename it **Vent Frame**.
8. Copy the base metal and paste it into the new **Vent Frame** layer.
9. Set the grid to **32**.

**Figure 5.10**
The alpha image for the floor panel grate.

10. Use the **Marquee** selection tool with the grid and delete the metal, leaving only a square in the upper-right side of the image.
11. Use the **Marquee** and the grid again to delete the center of the square, leaving a one-unit (32-pixel) frame.
12. Change the following settings in the **Layers** styles:
    **Drop Shadow:**
    Distance: 8
    Size: 10
    **Inner Glow:**
    Choke: 10
    Size: 18
    **Bevel and Emboss:**
    Highlight Mode: Soft Light
13. Duplicate the **Vent Frame** layer and place it below the **Frame** layer.
14. Name this new layer **Vent Louvers** and delete all the content from the layer.
15. Set the Fill to **0**.
16. Use the **Marquee** to select the empty space inside the vent frame and fill it with a color.
17. Use a small, hard eraser (3 pixels) and erase lines every two units on the grid.
18. On the **Frame** layer, you can play with the **Outer Glow** size and opacity to get the vent to look more dirty around the louvers underneath. Your image should look like Figure 5.11.

You will notice that this next part of the texture is created in the same way as the previous part. Here you will create a simple panel with some detail on it.

1. Duplicate the vent layer set and name it **Panel**.
2. Delete the **Louver** layer from the new layer set.
3. Delete the contents of the **Vent Frame** layer and rename it **Panel**.
4. Set the **Fill** to **0**.
5. Fill this new layer with a color.
6. Using the **Marquee** selection tool and the grid, **Delete** all but the upper-left square of this image. I erased some lines down the center of this panel to create a few smaller panels.
7. Duplicate the layer again and place it above the panel layer. Name it **Panel2**.
8. Change the **Outer Glow** settings. Take the **Choke** down to zero and lower the size to **29** px.
9. Add a **Gradient Overlay**. Set the Blending Mode to **Color Dodge** and the Opacity to **20%**.
10. Using the grid and selection **Marquee**, create a few random shapes and invert the selection, then delete the metal around your shapes. Your image should look like Figure 5.12.

**Note:** At this point, you will notice that the layer styles from the various layer sets overlap each other. You can create a layer mask for an entire layer set and mask the section off.

1. Duplicate the **Panel** layer set and name it **Bracket**.
2. Delete the **Panel** layer.
3. Delete the contents of the **Panel2** layer and rename it **Bracket**.

**Figure 5.11**
The vent on the detail texture.

4. Adjust your layer set mask so that it only reveals the 1024×256 rectangle below the middle of the image.
5. Open the **Layer Styles** and turn off the **Gradient Overlay** and apply a Color **Overlay**. Set the Opacity to **25%** and the color to **RGB: 84,68,39**.
6. Select the 1024×256 area of this layer and fill it with a color. Keep this region selected.
7. Because the **Layer Fill** is set to **0**, we are seeing the layer style and effects of the bracket layer and the texture of metal is from the base layer. Go to the **base** layer.
8. **Filter** > **Brush Strokes** > **Angled Strokes**: Direction Balance **50**, Stroke Length **23**, Sharpness **4**.
9. Set Fade Angled Strokes (**Ctrl+Shift+F**) to **70%**.
10. Go back to the **Bracket** layer and delete some sections of the rectangle to look like Figure 5.13.
11. To make this image useful, I selected the area and copied all layers (**Ctrl+Shift+C**).
12. Then I pasted this into a new top layer and offset it so that I could clean it up and make it tileable.

Now do the following:

1. Create a new layer set and name it **hose**.
2. Create a new layer and name it **hose**.
3. Adjust your layer set mask so that it reveals only the 1024×256 rectangle at the very bottom of the image.
4. Copy a 1024×512 section of the base metal layer and paste it into the hose layer. Make sure that it is snapped in place along the bottom.
5. **Filter** > **Brush Strokes** > **Accent Edges**: Edge Width **2**, Edge Brightness **18**, Smoothness **7**.

**Figure 5.12**
The panel details. The layer effects of each layer set have been masked.

**Figure 5.13**
The horizontally tileable bracket.

6. Use the **grid**, the **Dodge** tool, and a soft **65**-pixel brush to put vertical highlights evenly spaced along the hose. Do this again with a smaller brush (**27** pixels).
7. Create shadows between the highlights with the **Burn** tool.
8. Create a new layer and name it **ridges**. Set the Fill to **0**.
9. Use a small, hard brush (**13** pixels) and draw the vertical ridge lines on the light part of the hose. You can use the Offset Filter horizontally to make sure that the ridges are consistent across the hose.

**Figure 5.14**
The horizontally tileable hose and the final texture.

10. Apply the following layer effects:
    Drop shadow: **Default settings**.
    Outer Glow: Change the color to **black**, the Blending Mode to
        **normal**, and the size to **18**.
    Bevel and Emboss: Change the Technique to **Chisel Soft** and the
        Size to **3** pixels.

Your image should look like Figure 5.14.

## Pipe

We need to make a tileable strip of shiny metal for the hydraulic
pipes on the door. We can also use this technique to make a few
of the pipes in the hall shiny, as though they were just installed or
repaired.

1. Open a copy of the **Metal Fill** and save it as **sci_fi_metal_pipes**.
2. Crop this image down to a one-to-four ratio: 512×128 or 256×64,
   depending on the file size you are working with.
3. Lighten the metal using **Levels (Ctrl+L)**.
4. Lower the contrast.
5. Run the **Spatter** filter on this.
6. Use the **Burn** and **Dodge** tools to put horizontal highlights down
   the center of the pipe and shadows below and slightly on the top of
   the pipe. Figure 5.15 shows the pipe texture and the texture in use.

## Caution Stripes

The caution stripes start as nothing more than black and yellow
alternating strips. You can create them vertically, and the artists can
later rotate them 45 degrees on the model. The work is in making the
stripes look painted on the metal.

1. Open your **base metal** and save a copy as **sci_fi_caution**.
2. Create a new layer and name it **stripes**. Fill the layer with dark
   gray **RGB: 66,66,66**.

3. Turn on the **grid** and make the yellow stripes **3** units (96 pixels) wide. Use a yellow **RGB: 234,219,111.**
4. **Filter** > **noise** > Add noise **6%.**
5. **Filter** > **Artistic** > **Colored Pencil** > Pencil Width **10,** Stroke Pressure **6,** Paper Brightness **21.**
6. **Filter** > **Blur** > **Gaussian Blur:** **3** pixels.
7. **Filter** > **Sketch** > **Torn Edges** > Image Balance **25,** Smoothness **12,** Contrast **12.**
8. Set Layer Blending Mode: Soft Light, Opacity 75%.
9. Use various erasers and make some subtle worn spots and scratches in the paint.
10. You will have to offset the stripes and remove a hard edge. See Figure 5.16.

## The Complete Scene

Here is the complete scene using the textures we just created (Figure 5.17).

## Building It Up Using Overlays

In this exercise, I attempted to emulate the concept art as closely as possible, but I also did a variation that took me only a few minutes.

I put a rust overlay on the textures and changed the lighting in the scene. Because the lights are no longer glowing so brightly in this darker scene, I made a little yellowish dirty texture for the glass. See Figure 5.18 for the rusted texture set. In reality, you would use various types of assets to create a texture. Even if you do everything in Photoshop, nothing replaces the look of adding an overlay of a quality digital image. Several overlays are often used in texture creation. The overlay for this exercise is on the CD that accompanies this book. Try other overlays for various effects.

## Tearing It Down for Shaders

There are a couple of shaders used in the final scene that add a great deal of visual richness to the scene: illumination, opacity, and bloom. Although bloom is often a shader assigned to a material that doesn't require any special work on the part of the texture artist, illumination maps can be created in several ways for various effects.

**Figure 5.15**
The pipe texture and the texture in use.

The simplest way is to start with a solid black layer in the source file of your texture and paint in the areas you want lit with white. In the case of this scene, look at the texture set. We actually created an opacity mask for the grate, so let's make a quick and easy specularity map for the metal—the metal wall, specifically, because it has lots of edges for wear and tear and it is everywhere in the scene.

**Figure 5.16**
The caution stripes.

**Figure 5.17**
The final scene with the textures that we just created.

1. Open the file for the image that you created for the wall texture. You should have named it **sci_fi_metal_wall**.
2. You can create a copy of this image or create a new layer by selecting all (**Ctrl+A**), copying all layers (**Ctrl+Shift+C**), and pasting the result on top of the stack of layers. Name this layer **specularity**.
3. Using the brightness and contrast, do the following: **Image** > **Adjust** > **Brightness/Contrast** > Use Legacy, Brightness **−39**, Contrast **77**).

**Figure 5.18**
The texture set with a rusted overlay: a quick and simple step that changes the scene dramatically.

**Figure 5.19**
A variation with a simple rust overlay and lower lighting.

4. I ran the **Crosshatch** filter on this: **Crosshatch** > Stroke Length **7**, Sharpness **3**, Strength **1**. This helps make the wear look more scratchy. In Figure 5.20, you can see the texture with and without the specularity map applied.

## Chapter Exercises

Go back through this chapter and create a texture set that is uniquely yours by altering the following:

1. The roughness of the base metal and/or the color of the base and fill.
2. The pattern used to cut the wall panel.
3. The pattern used to cut the floor panel. Try the floor without a grate or using all grate.
4. Change the pattern on the diamond plate.
5. Create your own details for the detail texture. Keep in mind how this texture is used in the scene in this instance.
6. Create a set of overlays to achieve a moldy look, a rusty look, a dusty look, and/or a cold look.

**Figure 5.20**
The wall texture with and without the specularity map applied.

# Chapter 6

Warehouse Concept, 2005, by Jose Vazquez

# The Urban Setting

## Introduction

In this chapter, you will learn to work more faithfully to the detail in a concept sketch or any reference material that is given to you. When you need to create textures for a game environment, you are usually creating them for a world that has been thought out, detailed, and developed to the point that showcasing your creativity is not the primary goal of your work. You are showcasing your talent and ability to recreate what you see in the materials in front of you.

As discussed earlier in the book, textures traditionally come in sets: base, wall, floor, and ceiling variants as well as fill, trim, and so on. This chapter focuses on breaking out the materials that need to be created for a scene and then the details that also need textures created for them. Even though this approach is changing somewhat with technological advances, it is still a skill that is applicable to many games and applications and a good skill to have when you are required to work with more advanced technology. We always start with the basics to build a material (shape, color, texture) and build detail on top of that. What you end up with is a full texture set that is easily altered and built on. By the end of the chapter, you will have created all the textures needed for the urban environment concept sketch on the facing page. We will use the standard urban environment so popular in many military, sci-fi, driving, and other game genres in this chapter, since it offers a good variety of materials and objects.

Unlike the last chapter, in which we used fewer and simpler textures on a high-polygon-count scene, here we will be putting more detail into the textures and using fewer polygons. In the last chapter, we mostly made simple variants of one texture, as opposed to the full texture set composed of materials and images for specific uses (such as signs or a door). In the fantasy chapter we will go all-out on polygon and texture usage to create a high-detail world.

## The Concept Sketch

The front plate of the chapter shows the concept sketch for our urban area—a warehouse interior. To create a set of textures for a scene, you need information that is often not yet known to you or anyone else on the project. If you are in the early stages of development and are helping to test and prototype, you will be creating many variations of the assets needed for a scene. This is one reason to work large to small and in an organized/modular fashion. Even if all the specifications are in place, you will still mostly likely be producing many variations on the textures you are creating.

Technical questions aside (these were addressed in the earlier chapters), you will also have to ask some questions pertaining to the fiction of the game world and the space for which you are creating textures in particular. Some concept sketches are fuzzy in nature and often don't come with accompanying verbal descriptions. Usually you will be given a thorough briefing on the game and the world space, but something that looks like one material to you in the sketch might be something else.

The scene we will be working with is pretty straightforward. We can assume that the walls are bricks, the floor is concrete, and so on. But look at the windows (not the skylights). They don't look right for windows in a warehouse; I had the artists draw them that way on purpose and promised that I would say so in the book. The windows are also different from the skylight windows. As a texture artist, you might see the opportunity to save on texture space (memory) by making one texture that is applied to both surfaces. You should probably check this out with your boss, but he or she will either tell you to go for it or explain why the windows are the way they are. In any case, you can demonstrate that you are on the ball with this texture thing.

## Breaking Out the Materials in the Scene

Look at the concept sketch again and let's start identifying the materials in the scene. We have to look beyond the details, decorations, light and shadow, and effects to determine what basic materials compose this scene. Look at Figure 6.1 and the subtle clues that I left to help you identify the base materials.

### Brick

Looking at the walls, you can see that the structure is obviously made of bricks. We will make our own bricks in Photoshop. Bricks are a common texture that you can easily get on the Internet or simply photograph in the real world. Making your own bricks is not only faster in many cases—they also often look better in a game since they are more visually consistent and easier to tile. Plus, if you build

**Figure 6.1**
To determine what base materials compose a scene or environment, we have to look beyond the details, decorations, light and shadow, and effects.

them up in layers, you have more control over the speed and variety of changes you can make to the texture.

### Windows

I identify the windows next only because my eye is drawn to them. Looking closer, I see that they will be easy to tile, since they are made in sections (panes) that can be easily tiled, but how do you get them to glow like that? And what about those shafts of light?

### Wood

I then notice that the ceiling is made of dark wooden planks. There are also other places where wood is used: the crates and the wall of the little office. These are all variations of wood and can be made from a base wood-grain material.

### Concrete

The floor is made of concrete. There are subtle cracks and details on this floor, but it is mainly a big gray plane. We will experiment with two versions: a smoothly poured floor with no seams and a floor with seams that looks as though it had been poured in sections.

### Metal

Finally, there is the metal. There are three types of metal that must tile in this scene. There are the beams, which are rusted; the grayish rolling garage doors; and the pipes on the wall. Unlike the wood, these textures are different enough that I will start with a different base texture to create two of them.

You will also notice that there are many other details for which art will need to be created. We will break those out after we create the base materials.

## Creating Bricks

Creating bricks is easy. They are rectangles and are composed of two substances: bricks and mortar (mortar is the cement between the bricks). There are many styles of brick and many types of mortar, too. There are also variations of the patterns in which the bricks are laid out, their length and width, the space between them—even the mortar can be very different. An interior warehouse brick may have mortar that was put down sloppily and squishes from between the bricks, whereas the exterior of a house would have neat mortar that was scraped away to make the mortar indented and smooth.

Tiling bricks, when you first start doing it, can be a challenge. Bricks are various sizes and not always a neat fit for a power of two. In this exercise we will make our warehouse bricks—they're a standard red brick—and lay out the bricks using the grid so that they tile perfectly. After this, you will have a pretty flexible template for creating other types of bricks and even rough stones (as you will later see in the fantasy chapter).

Way back in Chapter 1, we covered some of the basic elements of art. They were:

- Shape (2D) and form (3D)
- Light and shadow
- Texture: tactile vs. visual
- Color
- Perspective

To create a texture from a blank slate in Photoshop, you start with shape, choose a color, start creating the visual texture, and work in the light and shadow toward the middle/end of things. You can approach the creation of a texture from many angles, but starting with shape seems to be the most logical progression to me. I like to lay the groundwork and make sure that things all tile and line up properly. It is a terrible thing to have worked on a texture for a long time only to find that it doesn't tile. Bricks are especially tricky if you don't do some math and consider brick and mortar heights and widths as they relate to the grid.

Then I choose a color that is at least close to the object or surface I am creating (the great thing about Photoshop is that you can recolor things fairly easily later on). I start to tackle the visual texture of the object immediately; this step takes the most time and experimentation. Although what follows is a linear exercise, meaning I take you through the creation of the bricks in steps from beginning to end, in reality, as you create your own textures, you will go back and forth, changing the color and light and shadow several times. You will need to tweak and change and even redo things until the texture is right.

## Tiling Brick Pattern

The first issue is shape. A brick is basically a rectangle. To make a brick pattern that tiles on the power of two, do the following:

1. Create a new image that is 1024×1024 and name it **brick_pattern.**
2. Set the grid to 32 and give it two subdivisions.
3. Create a new layer (**Ctrl+Shift+n**) and name it **Brick Shape**.
4. On this new layer, we will create our first brick shape. Look at Figure 6.2 to see the shape and size of the brick. Notice how the selection is one unit away from each major gridline. The units are 16 pixels and the bricks 496×112.
5. You can copy and paste the brick until it looks like Figure 6.3.

   You will have to push some of the bricks off the canvas edge to make them fill the half-brick spaces. Double-check your mortar spacing! Copying and pasting creates a new layer each time you paste a brick, so alternatively you can choose Select All (**Ctrl+A**) and hold down the Ctrl and Alt keys and click and drag a copy of the brick on the same layer. This is faster but a little trickier.

**Figure 6.2**
Bricks! There are many shapes and sizes. Lower right: The brick shape close up as it is built on the grid.

**Figure 6.3**
The brick pattern is the basis for the entire texture. Make sure it tiles right.

Every time you let up on the mouse the shape is pasted at that spot. You have to position exactly before placing a brick or you will spend a lot of time undoing your work.

6. Crop the image. Make sure the **Delete** option is on and drag the **Crop** tool over the canvas so that it will not change the canvas size but will crop off the half-bricks hanging out of the canvas space.

7. Check the **Image Size** to make sure it is still **1024×1024**. I am including all these little steps to begin with because they are good habits to pick up. Checking things now and fixing them when you can still use Undo is much easier than discovering a mistake when the texture is complete.

8. Now use the **Offset Filter** and enter **512** for both the horizontal and vertical values. If you see any gaps or misalignments in the bricks, fix them now. Redo the exercise or, in the case of one brick being messed up, cut the brick out, copy another, and paste and position it in the empty spot. If you create a new layer, make sure that you merge the two layers together. You can simply link the two layers and use **Ctrl+E** to merge linked.

**Note:** Merging layers creates a new layer that inherits the name from the layer that is selected when you merge. If you have the named layer selected when you merge layers, it will save you typing the name again.

9. Save your file. You now have a tiling brick pattern. Before you make a texture out of this, you might want to save a copy in your image collection.

## Brick Texture

We will create the texture for the bricks and mortar separately.

1. We will start by selecting a color for the bricks. I used **RGB 131,85,67**. There are many ways to change the colors of the bricks; I simply used the Paint Bucket and filled them in.
2. **Noise** > **Add noise 8%**.
3. **Brush Strokes** > **Sumi-e**: Stroke Width **10**, Stroke Pressure **4**, Contrast **29**.
4. Fade this filter (**Ctrl+Shift+F**) to about **10%**.
5. **Filter** > **Brush Strokes** > **Spatter**: Spray Radius **20**, Smoothness **5**.
6. **Filter** > **Artistic** > **Dry Brush**: Brush size **4**, Brush Detail **10**, Texture **2**.
7. **Filter** > **Artistic** > **Paint Daubs**: Brush Size **12**, Sharpness **5**, Brush Type **Simple**.
8. Fade by **50%** and change the Blending Mode to **Lighten**. Your image should look like Figure 6.4.
9. Here is where you have to do a little handiwork. The edges of the bricks are still too uniform. We need to chisel them down, so press the **E** key to activate the Eraser.
10. Right-click and select a hard brush, size **13** (see Figure 6.5).
11. You might want to copy the layer and hide it in case you want to go back to this step later.
12. Start whittling down the edges and knocking some chips in the bricks. Take your time and be subtle. Remember that these bricks have to tile, and from far away subtlety doesn't pop, but when the player gets close, the subtle chips and imperfections will look good. Work at 100% zoom or even 125% so that you can control your brush. I rounded off the corners to help the bricks look older. When we put the mortar in, it will have the same interesting shape because it will follow the space between the bricks.

1. COLOR FOR THE BRICKS - RGB 131,85,67.

2. NOISE > ADD NOISE - 8%.

3. BRUSH STROKES > SUMI-E - WIDTH 10, PRESSURE 4, CONTRAST 29.

4. FADE (CTRL + SHIFT + F) TO 10%.

5. FILTER > BRUSH STROKES > SPATTER - SPRAY RADIUS 20, SMOOTHNESS 5.

6. FILTER > ARTISTIC > DRY BRUSH - BRUSH SIZE 4, BRUSH DETAIL 10, TEXTURE 2.

7. FILTER > ARTISTIC > PAINT DAUBS - SIZE 12, SHARPNESS 5, TYPE SIMPLE.

8. FADE 50% BLENDING MODE - LIGHTEN.

**Figure 6.4**
This is what the bricks should look like so far after running a few filters.

## Mortar Texture

Creating mortar is easy—it is simply the space between the bricks.

1. Create a new layer (**Ctrl+Shift+n**) and name it **Mortar**.
2. Select the layer with the bricks on it and use the **Magic Wand** tool to select the empty space between the bricks.
3. Select the new **Mortar** layer and fill the selection with a very pale yellow. I used **RGB: 200,200,175**.
4. Deselect the selection.
5. **Filter** > **noise** > **Add noise 10%**.
6. **Filter** > **Artistic** > **Dry Brush**: Brush Size **4**, Brush Detail **7**, Texture **1**.

Your mortar should now look like Figure 6.6. The colors are still off, but we will fix that toward the end, after we add some depth and merge the two layers.

## Brick and Mortar Depth

Giving the bricks depth simply requires the Bevel Emboss layer style with the following settings:

**Structure:**
Style: Inner Bevel
Technique: Smooth
Depth: 61%
Direction: Up
Size: 13
Soften: 5
**Shading:**
Highlight Mode: Linear Light
Opacity: 62%

**Figure 6.5**
Knocking the edges down slightly with the eraser helps make them look older and more natural.

**Figure 6.6**
The bricks with the mortar added. The colors are off, but that will be fixed as we progress.

Shadow Mode: Multiply
Opacity: 63%

Adding depth to the mortar begins with an inner shadow. Note that as you apply filters you might notice they affect the edges of the image. Don't worry about that; we will fix it later.

Change the following:

Inner Shadow settings:
Opacity: 57%
Distance: 13 px
Size: 13 px

Add an Inner Glow:

**Structure:**
Blending Mode: normal
Opacity: 60%
Noise: 20%
Color: Pure black
**Elements:**
Size: 22

Apply Bevel and Emboss:

**Structure:**
Style: Inner Bevel
Technique: Chisel Soft
Depth: 101%
Direction: Up
Size: 10
Soften: 6
**Shading:**
Highlight Mode: Screen
Opacity: 42%
Shadow Mode: Multiply
Opacity: 35%

If your background layer is white or a light color, you may notice that the bricks and mortar have some of the bright color showing through. To fix this, simply fill the background layer with black or a very dark color. Your image should now look like Figure 6.7.

## Brick Completion

We are going to merge the bricks, mortar, and background together, so make a copy of the unflattened Photoshop file so that you can change things later if you like. You can also copy the layers and work in one file. Put the layers in their own layer set and hide the set.

1. Link the bricks, mortar, and background image together and merge them (**Ctrl+E**).
2. **Filter** > **Artistic** > **Dry Brush**: Brush Size **2**, Brush Detail **10**, Texture **2**.
3. Fade this (**Ctrl+Shift+F**) and take the opacity down to **50%**.

4. **Filter** > **Brush Strokes** > **Spatter**; Spray Radius **3**, Smoothness **10**.
5. **Filter** > **Texture** > **Craquelure**: Crack Spacing **52**, Crack Depth **3**, Crack Brightness **4**.
6. Fade by **45%** (**Ctrl+Shift+F**).
7. I found the bricks to be too saturated for the warehouse scene, so I made a copy of the layer and adjusted the brightness up +16 and the contrast down −29. I could have gone back and changed the steps of this exercise to end up with the results I wanted, but I had you do what I did because that's how it really happens. Now we have two versions of the bricks instead of one.
8. Offset the image by **512×512** both ways and clone out the seams with a soft brush.

## Top of the Wall

Having trim pieces, even subtle drip stains, around the top of a wall helps make the wall feel more real and the scene more solid. This is easy to do now that you have your base brick texture. You can experiment a lot, but always keep in mind these tips:

- Don't move or alter the base texture.
- Keep a sharp eye on the edges that are supposed to tile.

MORTAR
1. CREATE A NEW LAYER (CTRL + SHIFT + N) AND NAME IT MORTAR.
2. SELECT THE EMPTY SPACE BETWEEN THE BRICKS.
3. FILL THE SELECTION WITH A VERY PALE YELLOW.
4. DESELECT THE SELECTION.
5. FILTER > NOISE > ADD NOISE –10%.
6. FILTER > ARTISTIC > DRY BRUSH – SIZE 4 DETAIL 7 TEXTURE 1.

MORTAR DEPTH
INNER SHADOW
OPACITY – 57%
DISTANCE – 13 PX
SIZE – 13 PX

BEVEL AND EMBOSS
STRUCTURE
TECHNIQUE – CHISEL SOFT
SIZE – 10
SOFTEN – 6

INNER GLOW
STRUCTURE
BLENDING MODE – NORMAL
OPACITY – 60%
NOISE – 20%
COLOR – PURE BLACK
ELEMENTS
SIZE – 22

SHADING
HIGHLIGHT MODE – SCREEN
OPACITY – 42%
SHADOW MODE – MULTIPLY
OPACITY – 35%

BRICK DEPTH
BEVEL AND EMBOSS
STRUCTURE
DEPTH – 61%
SIZE – 13
SOFTEN – 5

SHADING
HIGHLIGHT MODE – LINEAR LIGHT
OPACITY – 62%
SHADOW MODE – MULTIPLY
OPACITY – 63%

**Figure 6.7**
The bricks are starting to take shape as we add depth to them.

**Figure 6.8**
Now that we have a strong base that tiles well, we can make many variations of brick.

Remember that the base texture must still tile with itself. If this is confusing, flip back to Chapter 4, Figure 4.30, and look at the figure that explains three-way tiling using this very example. I usually completely clean the tiling edge of my texture, the edge that needs to seamlessly tile with itself, just to be sure. Even a slight change in brightness from a glow or airbrush stroke on the tiling edge of the texture (that your eye can't even detect) will look like a hard line running around the room when you put the texture in the world. Simply use a hard eraser, or even the selection tool, to make sure that no pixels are in the top few rows of your texture. You can even mask a few pixels at the top so that if there is a slight line, you can see it while you are still working on the texture.

We can add subtle drip stains or a general haze of dirt that may have accumulated in the corners in this old warehouse. Because we create drip stains on the windows in the next section, let's do the haze of dirt here.

1. Start by opening a copy of your **base brick** texture.
2. Our base brick texture has too few bricks on it to make a detailed tile set. I reduced the image to a 512×512 image and made the canvas size 1024×1024 and tiled it four times.
3. Name the new image **Brick_Warehouse_Base**. Now you have a base brick texture and a new base texture for your warehouse. I further darkened, desaturated, and lowered the contrast to get an old-brick feel.
4. Make a new layer and name it **Dirt**.
5. Make **Black** your foreground color and use the **Gradient** tool with the **Foreground to Transparent** preset selected.
6. Drag from the top to the bottom of your image about halfway. Hold **Shift** so the gradient is straight.
7. **Filter** > noise > **Add noise 50%**.
8. **Filter** > **Blur** > **Motion Blur**: Angle **90**, Distance **100**.
9. **Filter** > **Artistic** > **Dry Brush**: Brush Size **2**, Brush Detail **10**, Texture **2**.
10. **Filter** > **Artistic** > **Fresco**: Brush Size **2**, Brush Detail **8**, Texture **1**.
11. **Filter** > **Blur** > **Gaussian Blur: 1.5 pixels**.
12. Set the layer's Blending Mode to **Multiply** and the Opacity to **67%**. Your image should look like Figure 6.9.

NEW LAYER NAMED DIRT
FOREGROUND COLOR BLACK
USE THE GRADIENT TOOL
    FOREGROUND TRANSPARENT
DRAG FROM THE TOP TO THE BOTTOM
    OF YOUR IMAGE ABOUT HALFWAY
HOLD SHIFT SO THE GRADIENT IS STRAIGHT

FILTER > NOISE > ADD NOISE – 50%
FILTER > BLUR > MOTION BLUR – ANGLE 90, DISTANCE 100.
FILTER > ARTISTIC > DRY BRUSH – SIZE 2, DETAIL 10, TEXTURE 2.
FILTER > ARTISTIC > FRESCO – SIZE 2, DETAIL 8, TEXTURE 1.
FILTER > BLUR > GAUSSIAN BLUR – 1.5 PIXELS.
LAYER BLENDING MODE TO MULTIPLY
OPACITY 67%

**Figure 6.9**
Trim pieces and subtle drip stains around the top of a wall help make the wall feel more real and the scene more solid. You might notice the trim at the top of the texture. After creating the bottom of the wall texture (which we will do after the top of the wall), I took that trim from the bottom of the wall and added it to this texture, scaling and darkening it.

*Bottom of the Wall*

This is a warehouse, so we don't have to get too fancy with the trim that runs around the floor. Most likely it would just be a beat-up piece of wood or metal. We create wood and metal in more detail later in the chapter. Here we will make a plain and simple metal strip.

1. Create a new layer and name it **metal strip**.
2. Turn on the **grid** and set the grid size to **128** with **1** subdivision.
3. Drag out a selection that is **128** pixels high and **1024** wide.
4. Fill this selection with a dark gray, such as **RGB: 105,105,105**.
5. Lock the layer transparency.
6. **Filter > noise > Add noise 7%**.
7. **Filter > Blur > Gaussian Blur 1.5 pixels**.
8. Set your foreground color to black and use the **Gradient** tool (while holding **Shift**) and start from the bottom and go halfway up the strip. You could also use a large, soft brush to paint this black strip on.
9. Fade the gradient (**Ctrl+Shift+F**) to 25% and set the Blending Mode to **Color Burn**.
10. **Filter > Artistic > Fresco**: Brush Size **2**, Brush Detail **8**, Texture **1**.
11. Fade to **24%** and set the Blending Mode to **Overlay**.
12. Apply the following layer styles:
    **Outer Glow:**
    **Structure:**
    Blending Mode: normal
    Opacity: 45%
    Noise: 36%
    Color: Pure black
    **Elements:**
    Spread: 9
    Size: 174
    **Bevel and Emboss:**
    **Structure:**
    Style: Inner Bevel
    Technique: Smooth
    Depth: 150%
    Direction:Up
    Size: 7
    Soften: 0
    **Shading:**
    Highlight Mode: Overlay
    Opacity: 60%
    Shadow Mode: normal
    Opacity: 50%

Your image should look like Figure 6.10. You can take a few extra steps to add some detail and interest. I copied the dirt from the top image and flipped it vertically using the Free Transform tool and lowered the opacity of the dirt. I colorized the metal strip (**Ctrl+U**) a desaturated orange to make it look more rusted. Finally, I created a new layer, set the Fill to 0, and copied the Metal Strip layer style and pasted it to the new layer. I added those little vertical strips with a small, hard brush.

You will need to offset this image horizontally and fix the edges. To do that, you will have to merge the layers so that the layer styles are no longer editable. You will want to copy all the layers in a layer set so that you can change them later. Then merge the copies of the layers.

## Windows

I mentioned earlier that the windows were purposely drawn wrong in the concept sketch. They don't look like actual warehouse windows. I went to a nearby warehouse and took the reference photo shown in Figure 6.11. You can see that these windows are basically destroyed, but their construction can be seen in the reference photo and their color and texture taken from the actual concept sketch. In this section we look at variations of these window panes and create a version with an alpha channel.

### *The Frame*

Windows are easy—just like bricks! A window consists of a metal frame with panes of glass in them. We start with the metal frame and work down to the panes, similarly to the way we created bricks and created the mortar around them. Then we can control the amount of weathering on the windows to our liking.

1. Open a new file, make it **1024×1024,** and name it **Windows_ Warehouse_Base**. If your computer is having difficulties handling the larger files, you can work at 512×512 and simply adjust the effects and other parameters down by 50%.
2. Set your grid to **256** with **one** subdivision.
3. Create a new layer set and name it **Frame**.
4. Create a new layer in the set and name it **Outer Frame**.
5. Set your foreground color to a very **dark brown**. I used **RGB: 69,59,54**.
6. Select the entire empty layer using **Ctrl+A**, then right-click and select **Stroke**. Set the Width to **18** pixels, Location **inside**.

**Figure 6.10**
Like the top, the bottom looks better with trim and some dirtying up.

7. I like to create the outer frame separate from the inner frame that holds the panes of glass, since it adds more depth to the texture. Create a new layer and name it **Inner Frame**. Make sure that this layer is underneath the outer frame layer.

8. Use the same color to draw lines along the grid. Use a hard **13**-pixel brush.

9. Add the **Layer Style Drop Shadow** to the Outer Frame layer and change the following settings:
   Blend Mode: normal
   Distance: 8 px
   Size: 16 px

10. Add noise; **Filter** > **noise** > **Add noise**: Amount **0.75**.

11. Copy and paste the layer style from the **Outer Frame** layer to the **Inner Frame** layer and change the size to **6**.

12. Apply the noise filter again. **Ctrl+F** will reapply the last filter you ran using the same settings. Your frame should look like Figure 6.12.

**Figure 6.11**
Warehouse window reference.

**Figure 6.12**
The base window frame.

## The Glass

The process of creating the glass panes is similar to the way we created the brick mortar. We will make the glass and then delete the portions of the glass where the frame covers it. This gives us additional flexibility in using layer styles, because many of them operate on the edge of an image.

1. Create a new layer set and name it **Glass**. You can turn the **Frame** layer set off for this part of the exercise so that it will be easier to see the canvas and speed up the computer's response time.
2. Select a muddy yellowish amber (I used **RGB:127,106,48**) and fill this layer using the paint bucket. Or **Ctrl+A** to select all, then **Right-click** > **Fill** > **foreground color**.
3. Add noise: **Filter** > **noise** > **Add noise**: Amount **7%**.
4. **Filter** > **Artistic** > **Dry Brush**: Brush Size **10**, Brush Detail **4**, Texture **1**.
5. **Filter** > **Distort** > **Glass**: Distortion **8**, Smoothness **3**, Texture **Frosted**, Scaling **166%**.
6. Press the **D** key so your foreground and background colors are black and white.
7. **Filter** > **Render** > **Clouds**: Fade this filter to **25%** (**Ctrl+Shift+F**).
8. **Filter** > **Blur** > **Gaussian Blur**: 1.5 pixels.
9. **Filter** > **Artistic** > **Fresco**: Set all the settings to their **max**.
10. Fade the filter to **15%** and set the Blending Mode to **Multiply**.
11. Now we'll cut out the panes. Turn the **Inner Frame** layer on and select an empty pane. **Right-click** and **Select Similar**. **Right-click** again and **Select Invert**. Go to the **Glass** layer and press the **Delete** key to remove the portion of the glass behind the frame.
12. Do the same for the **Outer Frame**. Turn both frame layers off and your image should look like Figure 6.13.

**Figure 6.13**
The glass panes without the frame.

### Pane Variations

Creating multiple variations of the panes is easy and makes this texture very flexible. See Figure 6.13. Remember to create copies of the pane layer as you alter them. Some of the layer effects I applied to the panes that you might want to try are:

- Subtle Dirt: Inner Glow, Black—play with the size, opacity, noise, and blending modes.
- Subtle Dust: Change the Inner Glow color to a very light gray, Blending Mode: Dodge, Opacity 65%, noise 16%, Size 40 pixels.
- Subtle Highlight: Bevel and Emboss, try changing the settings to a large, low depth, highlight and soften it. This can give nice even highlights to the panes; just be careful they don't look bulged out.
- Inside Light Source: For a large tiling texture, you want to keep things even, but in case this window might be used in one instance with no tiling, you can add a subtle gradient using a layer style and experiment with the blending modes and gradient types to get the appearance that there is a stationary light source in the room beyond the window.

You can also play with colorization (**Ctrl+U**), desaturation, and other filters and effects for panes of various appearances. What you are trying to achieve may depend on the concept art, condition of the building around the window, and other environmental factors.

### Weathering and Dirt

Various types of weathering and dirt can be applied to a surface, depending on the location and the material the surface is made of. The concept sketch shows indoor windows that do not need any dirt or weathering (maybe a bit of rust on the frames and a hint of dirt on the glass). In fact, you might have noticed that the windows in the concept sketch are glowing a white-blue. That effect is a combination of making the texture the same color, using a shader to make the panes bright, and a special effect for the light beams. A more advanced shader called *bloom* can also be used for the glow to actually go outside the frames themselves. The light beams are

**Figure 6.14**
Window pane variations from left to right are subtle dirt, subtle dust, and subtle highlights/inner light source. They have also been colorized and the saturation and brightness adjusted.

easy, but we don't create them here. These types of effects were covered in Chapter 3.

But what if these windows were outside? The metal frame might be rusted. The panes might be streaked with rain and dirt. Depending on the location of the building and the condition it is in, this weathering could be mild to heavy. First, we can rust the frame.

1. Duplicate the layer set **Frame** and name it **Frame Overlay**.
2. Make sure the new Frame Overlay set is on top of the Frame set in the layer stack.
3. Open the new layers set and turn off the layer effects, link the two layers, and merge them together (**Ctrl+E**). You now have a solid copy of the entire frame.
4. Lock the **Transparency** on this layer.
5. **Filter** > **noise** > **Add noise 10%**.
6. **Filter** > **Artistic** > **Dry Brush**: Brush Size **2**, Brush Detail **8**, Texture **1**.
7. Colorize: **Ctrl+U**, Hue **14**, Saturation **30**.
8. Change the Blending Mode to **Darken** and experiment with the opacity. Around 30% to 45% is light rust and 50% to 75% is heavy.
9. Changing the Blending Mode to **Lighten** will give you a brighter, drier-looking rust. Figure 6.15 shows a few variations of the rusted pane.

The panes can be weathered as well.

1. Start by duplicating the **Glass** layer set and naming it **Outside Glass**.
2. Desaturate the **Glass** layer (**Ctrl+Shift+U**).
3. Fade this by about **50%** (**Ctrl+Shift+F**). Now the panes look faded, as though they have been outside a long time.
4. To create a general dirt layer, create a new layer on top of the stack and name it **smog**.
5. **Filter** > **Render** > **Clouds**.
6. Change the Blending Mode to **Multiply** and set the Opacity to **50%**.
7. **Filter** > **noise** > Add noise: **50%**.
8. **Filter** > **Blur** > **Motion Blur**: **90** degrees and about **30** pixels of blur.

**Figure 6.15**
Variations of the rusted pane, easily created because of the power of layers and blending modes.

**Figure 6.16**
The image is small and the canvas large. This makes it easier to vary the length of brush strokes on the canvas without having to change brushes, because you can start drawing anywhere you want outside the canvas.

## Rain Streaks

1. To create rain streaks, turn off the smog layer (you can turn it on later if you like) and create a new layer named **Rain Streaks**.
2. Select a medium gray as your foreground color (**RGB: 157,157,157**).
3. Zoom way out so that your image is pretty small and the canvas fills most of the workspace; see Figure 6.16. This makes it easier to create various streak lengths.
4. Select a brush of medium size and softness. Go to the **Brushes** palette and under **Shape Dynamic**, change the control to **Fade**. Set the pixel fade to **128**. This is the window to the right of the fade selection.
5. Now drag a few lines down your window. Hold **Shift** to keep the lines straight. Vary the length by starting to draw higher above the canvas and vary the width using the **[** and **]** keys. Be subtle.
6. **Filter** > **Blur** > **Motion Blur 90** degrees and about **30** pixels of blur.
7. Set the Blending Mode of this layer to **Overlay** and set the Opacity between **50% and 75%**. I ended up at **63%** in Figure 6.16. You can, of course, experiment with the color of the streaks, the blending modes, and opacity. You can even add some noise and run the Motion Blur filter again with a lower pixel blur for streaks with a little more body.

**Figure 6.17**
Rain streaks on the window.

## Window Alpha

An alpha channel is a grayscale image used in various ways to achieve many effects on a texture in a game engine. (For more information, see Chapter 2.) We will make an alpha image for this window and use it in various ways.

1. Duplicate your **window** image. We will be merging layers and it is safer to work from a copy.
2. Duplicate the **Frame** layer set and name it **Alpha**. Make sure this new layer is on top of the layer stack.
3. Open the new set and turn off the layer effects, link the two layers, and merge them together (**Ctrl+E**). You now have a solid copy of the entire frame.
4. Use the **D** key to reset your colors.
5. Select an empty pane, **right-click**, and select **Similar**, and then **Invert** the selection and switch to the rectangular marquee. **Right-click** and fill the selection with **white**. We want this frame solid white because in the alpha channel white is solid and no light will pass through the frame or reflect off it.
6. Hide the new **Frame Alpha** layer set.
7. The windows should already be the way you want them in the texture. If they're not, go back and change them before making the alpha so they match. When you are ready, **Merge Visible**. The white frame should be a separate layer on top of your merged panes.
8. Desaturate the panes (**Ctrl+Shift+U**).
9. Using **Levels,** drag the middle arrow a little to the right to darken this image.
10. Using **Brightness/Contrast**, take the brightness down **20** and the contrast up **20.**
11. Your image should look like Figure 6.18. If you keep the frame separate from the panes, you can adjust and alter the panes

**Figure 6.18**
In most applications the white in an alpha channel is solid, so the frame is white and kept as a separate layer (it is red here only so that you can see it). It always stays solid white if you adjust the panes on their own layer.

while keeping the frame solid white. With the panes this dark, they are almost completely transparent, so you will want to experiment with light/dark and contrast settings.

This alpha image can go into an alpha channel in Photoshop or an image format that supports alpha, or it can be used as a separate image. Some game engines use a separate grayscale image as the alpha; others will recognize the alpha channel of an image. Some can do both, so you can use one grayscale image to define the opacity and illumination of the window and another to define the bump. In the case of a bump map for a window, you would want the panes smooth, unless there were mud splatters that would stand off the glass and the frame would protrude. In Figure 6.19 you can see the window texture with various effects on it that use the alpha channel. Notice that in the image with opacity there are broken panes. This effect was easily created by making the broken and missing portions solid black with hard edges.

The size of the texture and the number of panes will fluctuate depending on your parameters. One approach is to make more panes in the same texture space; another is to make one pane, if the panes are all the same. This would allow a smaller image size but more detail per pane. You can even have a polygon for every pane in the window and make an image with several pane variations—normal and several broken in various ways. Then the environmental artists can cover most of the panes with the normal pane and randomly place the broken ones.

**Figure 6.19**
The top image is simply the texture as it is. The middle image has an illumination shader on it. It is hard to see in this image, but if you were on a dark street, these windows would be bright, as though there were a light inside. The bottom image has an alpha channel used for opacity. White is solid, so black is clear. The broken panes are just solid black shapes on the alpha channel.

**Note:** Some game engines and 3D applications use black as solid and white as transparent, and some use the opposite. If this is the case, you can simply invert your image using the invert command (**Ctrl+I**).

## Wood

Our next material is wood. There are several places where wood is used in this warehouse, so we will start with a wood grain and create various versions of wood from there. One of the new features of Photoshop CS is the Fibers filter, and that comes in handy when making wood grain.

### Basic Wood Fill

1. Open a new file and make it **512×512**. Name it **Wood_Fill_001** (you might want to create more than one version, so using a number helps).
2. Create a new layer and name it **Wood Grain**.
3. Fill the layer with a brownish color (**RGB: 85,80,70**). I chose this washed-out brown, since this is older wood. Normally I would have made a more saturated version and simply copied it to a

**Figure 6.20**
Basic wood fill. Subtle, understated, and oh-so-useful.

new layer, then desaturated it. This way I would begin building up different versions of the wood grain.

4. Make sure your foreground color is the brownish color and the background color is just a darker version of it (**RGB: 61,58,50**).
5. **Filter** > **Render** > **Fibers**: Variance **16**, Strength **4**.
6. This filter doesn't create a tiling image, so you need to copy this layer and offset it by **256** in both directions.
7. Use a big, soft brush and erase most of the top layer except for the edges. Keep an eye open for any hotspots you might want to remove.
8. Use the **Offset Filter** again (**Ctrl+F**) and look for any seams or corners you might have missed and hit them with the **Clone** brush. You should have an image like Figure 6.20.

This is a basic wood fill. As you use it in various places, you might need to desaturate it, make it smaller and tile it, blur it—whatever works in the context where you are using the texture. Our first variation of this basic wood grain will be to create the wooden panels that compose the ceiling of the warehouse.

### Wooden Planks

The ceiling of this warehouse is composed of dark wooden planks. The steps to create planks are easy.

1. Open a copy of the wood fill and name it **Wood_Planks_001**. Create a new layer and name it **seams**.
2. Set your grid to **128**.
3. Use a small medium brush (**5** pixels) and draw vertical lines along the gridlines using the darker background color from the last exercise. Remember to get the edges of the image, too, or you will have one wide plank when you tile this image.
4. Use the **Bevel and Emboss** layer style with the following settings:
   Style: Outer Bevel
   Depth: 50%
   Size: 6 px
   Highlight Mode: Vivid Light
   Opacity: 100%
   Shadow Mode: Overlay
   Opacity: 87%
5. Make a copy of the **Wood Grain** layer and link it to the **seams** layer. Merge them (**Ctrl+E**).
6. When you merge these layers, the formerly adjustable layer styles are now permanent and the image is fixed. As a result, there are pixels outside the canvas area, so you need to use the **Crop** tool to remove them. Simply drag the tool completely across the image and press **Enter**. Check your image size and make sure it is still 512×512.
7. Now you can use the **Offset Filter** and offset the image by **256** both ways. If you haven't used the Offset Filter since the last section, you can use **Ctrl+F**. You might have some small edge imperfections, so you can fix those now. Your image should look like Figure 6.21.

**Figure 6.21**
Basic wood planks. I can't think of anything else to say, but they're cool.

**Figure 6.22**
Some quick adjustments and
our wood planks are ready for
the office structure. Here they
are on the office structure.

## Wooden Planks, Office

The small office is also made of wooden planks. These are nothing
more than a copy of your current planks altered.

1. Copy and paste the **plank** layer and name the new resulting layer
   **Office Planks**.
2. **Desaturate** this layer.
3. Take both the **Brightness/Contrast** settings up **+30**.
4. Set your foreground color to **RGB: 120,118,131**. This is the
   washed-out blue of the office boards.
5. Use **Hue/Saturation (Ctrl+U)** and check the **Colorize** box. The
   saturation will be way too high, so take it all the way down to **3**.

## Wood, Crate

The crates are yet another variation, only this time we need to give
the wood grain more detail, add knotholes, build the frame around
the crate, and create seams.

1. Open and duplicate the **Wood Grain** image. Name it
   **Crates_Wood_001**.
2. We will first add knots and detail to the wood that would be
   undesirable for a tiling texture, but for the face of a crate they
   will look great. Use the **Liquify** tool (**Ctrl+Shift+X**).

**Figure 6.23**
Wood grain made in minutes with the Liquify and Bloat tools.

3. Start with the **Bloat** tool with a large brush between **100** and **200** pixels and drag it a little in a few places to create the knots.
4. Then use the **Forward Nudge** tool with a **200** brush and subtly push the grain around. You don't have to do too much here. You can maybe make the grain contour to the knotholes. Your image should look similar to Figure 6.23.
5. Set the grid to **128**. Before we start making planks, we are going to flip and rotate sections of the wood around so that the planks look like they are cut from different boards. Turn on the **grid**, then select the **first and third columns** of wood. Use the **Free Transform** tool (**Ctrl+T**) and **right-click** and flip this selection vertically and horizontally. You can select and flip or rotate the boards more later as well.
6. Add seams just as you did for the wooden planks by creating a new layer named **seams** and drawing lines down the gridlines. This time use a **3**-pixel brush and change the following settings in the **Bevel and Emboss** layer style:
Style: Outer Bevel
Depth: 97%
Size: 1 px
Highlight Mode: Vivid Light
Opacity: 75%
Shadow Mode: Overlay
Opacity: 75%
7. The wood needs to be colorized as well to match the crates. Set your foreground color to **RGB: 167,140,82**. Use the **Hue/Saturation** tool and **Ctrl+U** to move the saturation up to **37** and the brightness to **17**.
8. Now we can make the frame. Set the grid to **64**.
9. Use the **Polygonal Lasso** tool and make a selection like the one in Figure 6.24. These sections are simply copied and pasted into their own layer and can be copied from any section of the wood grain. A vertical selection tends to work best.

**Figure 6.24**
The shape you need to make with the Polygon Lasso for the crate edges.

10. Make four different sections and arrange them like a picture frame by flipping or rotating them.
11. Make sure that the **frame** layer is above the **seams** layer. Turn the background **wood** layer off so that you can see the four pieces. If there are small gaps, it's okay. Link the four layers and merge them together.
12. Zoom in with the **grid** on and use a **1**-pixel brush to erase a small gap between the corners of the image and the inner corner where the boards meet. Remember that you can click once in the corner to start a line and hold **Shift** and click where you want the line to end. This will give a quick and perfectly straight line.
13. Add the **Layer Style Outer Glow** with the following settings:
    Blend Mode: Normal
    Opacity: 40%
    Size: 35
14. Add the **Layer Style Bevel and Emboss** with the following settings:
    Style: Inner Bevel
    Technique: Chisel Soft
    Depth: 90%
    Size: 1 px.

At this point your image should look like Figure 6.25.

**Figure 6.25**
The crate base is a starting place for many variations.

You can add a lot of detail to crates in addition to variations of the wood (Figure 6.26). You can weather them and add decals and even a stencil, as in the concept sketch. The stenciled letters FRAGILE across some of the boxes are simply a text layer. Add a text layer, size and position it using the Free Transform tool, rasterize it (right-click), and add a little noise. Set your background color to black and run the Spatter Filter. Zoom in and select the black splotches on the edge of the letters (then right-click and select similar) and delete them. Set the Blending Mode to Color Burn and take the opacity down a bit. Now they look painted on.

These crate textures are the one texture in this scene that would benefit the most from the use of a reference photo of real wood either to build the texture or use as an overlay. Here are the versions of the crates I did using a real wood photo. The steps are the same as this exercise, only you don't spend your time making the wood grain;

**Figure 6.26**
These crate variations were made quickly from the base.

**Figure 6.27**
Sometimes there's nothing like the real thing. Wood-based textures like these crate textures often benefit the most from the use of a reference photo, either to build the texture or to use as an overlay.

you spend your time cleaning and preparing the wood grain (using the techniques from Chapter 4).

## Concrete

Concrete can be as simple as gray noise, but using a few tricks to make the concrete look splotchy and worn is worth the few extra minutes they take. The concrete in our scene is simple, but I will take you a bit further here so you are better able to create concrete for various uses. Subtle stains and weathering can be applied to the base concrete, but stronger details have to be added to a copy of the texture or created with an alpha channel so they can be projected.

### Basic Concrete

1. Start with a new image at **1024×1024**. Name it **Concrete_Base_001**.
2. Create a new layer and name it **base**.
3. Foreground color **RGB: 140,140,140**. Fill the layer.
4. **Filter > noise > Add noise 3%**.
5. **Filter > Blur > Gaussian Blur 0.5 pixels**.
6. **Filter > Brush Strokes > Spatter**: Spray Radius **15**, Smoothness **8**. Now we have a very basic and clean cement. The next step is to add subtle and varied stains.
7. Create a new layer and name it **Grime 1**.
8. **Filter > Render > Clouds**.
9. **Brightness/Contrast**: Brightness **+10**, Contrast **+60**.
10. Change the layer Blending Mode to **Multiply** and take the opacity down to **15%**. Now you should have subtle dark stains on your concrete. Your image should look like Figure 6.28.

### Rougher Concrete

To make the concrete a bit rougher, you can add some small pits, as though the concrete was laid rough or is just worn out.

1. Create a new layer and name it **Pits**.
2. Fill this new layer with **black**.
3. **Filter > noise > Add noise 20%**.
4. **Filter > Artistic > Cutout**: Number of Levels **8**, Edge Simplicity **4**, Edge Fidelity **3**.
5. Take the contrast up **+80** and the little clumps will pop out.
6. Select the **black** portion of the layer with the **Magic Wand** and **delete** it.
7. Change the Blending Mode to **Multiply** and the Fill to **0%**.
8. Add the layer effect **Bevel and Emboss** and change the following settings:
   Depth: 1%
   Direction: Down
   Size: 1 px
   Soften: 2 px
   Highlight Mode Opacity: 36%
   Shadow Mode Opacity: 36%

**Figure 6.28**
A basic concrete with subtle stains.

**Figure 6.29**
A rougher concrete made from the base.

**Figure 6.30**
Concrete with rust stains.

### Stained Concrete

Not all stains are dark. Using orange as a base color, you can make rust stains similar to the way you make grime using black.

1. Create a new layer and name it **Rust Stains.**
2. Make your foreground color orange, **RGB: 167,98,10,** and your background color **white.**
3. **Filter** > **Render** > **Clouds.**
4. You may want to run the **Difference Clouds** filter to get more variation in the pattern, but if you do, run it **twice,** so the colors return to orange and white.
5. Take the opacity down to **10%.** You can play with the brightness and contrast to get stronger or weaker rust stains.

### Grooved Concrete

Another effect you can add is the subtle grooves that concrete retains from when it was smoothed out after it was poured.

1. Create a new layer and name it **grooves.**
2. Render **black and white clouds** on the layer and lower the contrast **−70.**
3. Add some noise: **9%.**
4. **Filter** > **Texture** > **Grain:** Intensity **50,** Contrast **50,** Grain Type **Horizontal.**
5. Lower the opacity of the layer to **10%.**

### Sectioned Concrete

Sometimes concrete floors are poured in sections with a seam or wooden divider between the sections. For seams, you can simply

**Figure 6.31**
Concrete with grooves in it from where it was smoothed after laying.

apply a bevel emboss filter to the base layer of concrete and you will get a neat seam around the concrete square. To make a wooden frame, do the following:

1. Create a new layer and call it **frame**.
2. Fill the layer with a **dark brown**.
3. Use the grid set at **16** units and **1** subdivision and select all of the image except for a **16**-pixel-wide strip on all four sides. **Delete** the selected color in the middle.
4. Add a small amount of **noise** to the frame.
5. Set the background color to **black** and run the **Spatter** filter.
6. Fade the filter by **50%**.
7. Apply the **Outer Glow** layer style and make it **black**. This should be a faint outer glow.
8. Apply the **Bevel and Emboss** layer style and make the depth and size very **small**.
9. Merge everything. **Duplicate** the layer and use the **Free Transform** tool to make the image **8** pixels larger on all sides.
10. **Crop** the image and **flatten** it.
11. When you offset this image, the wooden frame should need little to no work on the seams.

By splitting the wood frame in half, we removed the problem of a double frame being on all sides. If we were to only put the frame on two sides, that would work until the texture hit a wall and the frame ended unnaturally. This way the frame will tile perfectly and we will see half a frame where the texture hits a wall. It just looks neater that way. See Figure 6.32.

For the most part, creating concrete in Photoshop is a process of experimenting with various filters on clouds and noise and then choosing a blending mode. Building a concrete texture involves several very subtle layers, since concrete is generally covered in a variety of subtle stains and discolorations. Concrete is such a subtle

**Figure 6.32**
When putting a frame around the concrete, we split it in half so that we see half a frame where the texture hits a wall. It just looks neater that way.

**Figure 6.33**
With one simple concrete base, you can make many variations.

texture that the best way to create it is to create a consistent base, as we did here, and overlay actual imagery of cracks and concrete textures. Figure 6.33 shows a few variations of concrete made from this base.

## Details Using an Alpha Channel

You can add details such as oil stains (where a vehicle might have been parked), signs, cracks, blast marks, and more, either directly on the texture or by creating an image with an alpha channel to be projected on the texture. The oil stains in this exercise are nothing more than variously sized soft black brushes with the opacity set very low. To create the alpha:

1. Create a new layer named **oil stains** and paint some oil stains on it using variously sized soft, black, round brushes with the opacity set very low.
2. Go to **Select** > **Load Selection** > **Choose** the layer name. In this case it will say Oil Stain Transparency and it will make a perfect selection of the oil stains on the layer.
3. Go to the **Channels** tab and add a new alpha layer. It should appear solid black with the lines of your selection on it.
4. Select the **rectangular marquee, right-click** in your selection, and fill it with **white**.
5. You can copy and paste this alpha channel into a separate image if you need to. Figure 6.34 shows you the texture with oil stains, the oil stains alone, and the alpha created for the stains.

IMAGE

ALPHA

IMAGE OVER TEXTURE

**Figure 6.34**
Detail that would tile if it were part of a texture can be projected in a few places so as to add interest. The detail texture can be masked with an alpha channel so that you can achieve subtle effects like these oil stains.

We focused on concrete used as a floor here, but concrete is also used on walls. Concrete walls can have paint on them, a layer of dirt at the bottom, trim pieces, and even a wood grain. Concrete walls are poured into a wooden form that is removed when the concrete hardens. The concrete often retains the grain of the wood from the form.

## Metal

Metal is similar to concrete with regard to the way it is made in Photoshop, but we are of course going for a different look when we create metal. In this concept sketch, there are three types of metal: lightly rusted on the beams, a dull galvanized sheet metal on the garage doors, and the metal pipes on the wall. Technically we already made metal when we made the frames of the windows, and the techniques are similar.

### Rusted Metal

Creating the rusted metal for the beams:

1. Create a new image **1024×1024** and name it **Metal_Rust_001**.
2. Create a new layer and name it **base**. Fill the layer with a dark brown, **RGB: 81,65,54**.
3. **Filter > noise > Add noise 40%**.

**Figure 6.35**
Concrete wall variations made with one base.

**Figure 6.36**
Our base rusted metal.

4. **Filter** > **Blur** > **Motion Blur**: Angle **45**, Distance **45**.
5. **Filter** > **Distort** > **Ocean Ripple**: Size **10**, Magnitude **10**.

This is a base rust. I used levels to darken it a bit for this scene. I made the image really big so that it can be used in other places. For tiling on the beams, I reduced this image quite a bit. I cropped it so I could make a smaller texture without losing much detail (Figure 6.36).

### Garage Door Metal

The garage door metal is very similar to the wood paneling in that it has the same type of seam running across the texture. The metal itself is a grayish mottled pattern.

1. Create a new image, **512×512**, and name it **Metal_GarageDoor_001**.
2. Create a new layer and name it **base**.
3. Fill this layer with a **medium gray**.
4. Set Add noise to **5%**.
5. Set Gaussian Blur to **2** pixels.
6. **Filter** > **Pixelate** > **Crystallize** > Cell Size **33**.
7. Set Add noise to **1%**.
8. Create a new layer and name it **seams**.
9. Set the Fill to **0%**.
10. Use a hard, small brush and draw a line horizontally across the texture every **64** pixels.
11. Apply the following layer effects:
    **Outer Glow:**
    **Structure:**
    Blending Mode: normal
    Opacity: 51%
    Noise: 13%
    Color: Pure black
    **Elements:**
    Size: 32

**Bevel and Emboss:**
**Structure:**
Style: Outer Bevel
Depth: 111%
Direction: Down
Size: 27
**Shading:**
Highlight Mode: Linear Dodge
Opacity: 46%
Shadow Mode: Multiply
Opacity: 68%

12. Make a new layer and name it **hinge pins**.
13. Select a **dark gray** color and use a **5**-pixel hard brush to draw lines across the image on the inside the bends in the metal. Use **Shift** to get them straight.
14. Apply the following layer effects:
    **Outer Glow:**
    **Structure:**
    Blending Mode: normal
    Opacity: 75%
    Noise: 8%
    Color: Pure black
    **Elements:**
    Size: 10
    **Bevel and Emboss:**
    **Structure:**
    Style: Inner Bevel
    Depth: 100%
    Direction: Up
    Size: 5
    **Shading:**
    Highlight Mode: Screen
    Opacity: 42%
    Shadow Mode: Multiply
    Opacity: 75%
15. **Copy** the layers and **flatten** the image.
16. Offset the image by **256×256**.
17. Check your tiling and clean up the seams (Figure 6.37).

## Pipes

The pipes on the walls are made from one simple texture. In this context, we need to add the highlight, but in other cases, a shader is used.

1. Copy a vertical strip off the base metal of the garage door. Make this strip **128** wide and **512** high.
2. Paste it into a new file. **Ctrl+n** will create a new image the size of the image you copied. Name it **Metal_Pipes_001**.
3. **Lighten** the image a bit using levels.
4. **Blur** > **Motion Blur**: Angle **0**, Distance **22**.
5. Use the **Dodge** tool and a soft **65**-pixel brush to lighten the vertical center of the pipe (Figure 6.38).

If you want dirty pipes, you can go back and grab a copy of your rust texture and slap it on. Play with the opacity and blending modes.

**Figure 6.37**
Garage door metal with hinge pins.

**Figure 6.38**
Pipe metal made from part of the garage door metal and a version with rust on it.

Like virtually every other surface, metal has a wide variety of appearances, depending on the type of metal, the way in which the metal is used, and the environment it is in. Our window frames had a spattering of light dry rust on them, and the beams are evenly covered in a heavier rust. In other contexts, metal may have paint chipping and wearing off it or it may be shiny and new. The list is endless. We will tackle some of those other metal types and conditions in coming chapters.

## Breaking Out the Details

Now that you have built the base materials of the scene, you can start looking for the details you need to create using the base texture or as a new image entirely. Look at the concept sketch again. Let's start to identify the details. The numbers and the stenciled sign are the easiest; the small hanging sign requires a few more steps. The door is fairly complex and involves several steps. We will tackle that last.

### Numbers

You will quickly learn that making signs, banners, and the like is easy with fonts, filters, and some patience. The numbers above the two garage doors are nothing more than a font that is either laid onto a copy of the base brick texture or is an image with alpha channeling. Because the alpha version of this is more challenging, we will take that approach here.

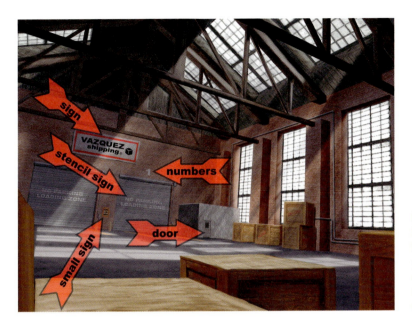

**Figure 6.39**
Now that you have built the base materials of the scene, you can start looking for the details that you will need to create using the base texture or as a new image entirely.

1. Create a new image and name it **Detail_Number1_001**.
2. Fill the background with **black**.
3. Snap one guide at the horizontal center of the background and one at the vertical center.
4. Use the **Text** tool and put a number **1** down; the Arial Black font seems to match the closest.
5. Use the **Free Transform** tool and make the font fill most of the image. Keep it centered and proportional.
6. **Right-click** on the test layer and rasterize it.
7. Make sure your background color is **black** and run **Filter** > **Brush Strokes** > **Spatter**: Spray Radius **16**, Smoothness **–8**.
8. Use the **Magic Wand** tool to select a black splotch on the edge and then **right-click** and choose **Similar**. Press the **Delete** key to remove the black parts of the number. You might want to turn the background layer off so you can see.
9. **Noise** > **Add noise –9%**.
10. Take the opacity of this layer down to **60%**.
11. **Blur** > **Gaussian Blur 0.5 pixels**. If you want to see how the number will look in context, you can drop a copy of the brick texture on a layer behind the number.
12. To create the alpha for this image, you do it just the way we did the oil stains earlier. Go to **Select** > **Load Selection** > **Choose** the layer name. In this case it will say, 1 Transparency.
13. Go to the **Channels** tab and add a new **alpha** layer. It should appear solid black with the lines of your selection on it.
14. Select the rectangular **marquee, right-click** in your selection, and fill it with **white**.
15. You can copy and paste this alpha channel into a separate image if you need to. Figure 6.40 shows you the texture with the number, the number alone, and the alpha created for the number.

*Stencil Sign*

The stenciled sign (Figure 6.41) is done in the exact same way as the numbers—just make the image size larger. In this case I made it 1024×256. I also took the opacity down further, to 40%.

**Figure 6.40**
Painted-on numbers and signs are easy with fonts, filters, and patience. This number is using an alpha channel. Left is the number projected on a wall, middle is the number image, and right is the alpha channel for the number.

**Figure 6.41**
The stencil sign is done the same way as the numbers. Top is the sign projected on the garage door, middle is the image, and the alpha is at the bottom.

## Small Sign

Between the garage doors is a small caution sign. Signs are easy to make and to weather.

1. Start with an image that is **512×512** and name it **Signs_Caution_001**.
2. Create a new layer and name it **base**.
3. Fill this layer with a safety sign yellow, **RGB: 164,145,87**.
4. Add noise **3.5%**.
5. **Blur** > **Gaussian Blur: 2** pixels.
6. The sign is not the same proportions as the square image that we have to work with (power of two), so we need to use the rectangular marquee to trim it down to the general size of the sign. In actual development we would find some other texture to fill in that dead space, because this doesn't need to tile, but for now we will leave it blank.
7. Now drag out a vertical and horizontal line to the center of the sign, not the image.
8. To make the red border, create a new layer and name it **red border**.
9. Set the foreground color to a dark red, **RGB: 160,35,38**.
10. Drag out the rectangular **marquee** on the red border layer until it is about the right size. Use the guidelines to center it vertically and horizontally.
11. Select the rectangular **Marquee** tool and **right-click** in the selection. Choose **Stroke** > **Inside 16 pixels**.
12. Create two text layers. One says **safety** and one says **zone**; the font is **Arial Black** and the color is **black**.
13. The hard hat on the sign in the concept art is the one thing that if you can't draw it, you can replace it using the **Custom Shape** tool or the **Type** tool and the **Wingdings** font. Add a lightning bolt, exclamation point, a hand, and so on.
14. Figure 6.42 shows variations of the sign. Just a filter or two and it takes on a drastically different appearance.

## Big Sign

The big banner over the garage doors is created the same way as the small sign. Start with an image that is 1024×256. Create a base layer. Fill this layer with a very light gray, add a small amount of noise, and Gaussian Blur it slightly. You can use the same settings as you did for the small sign. You make the red border the same way as well as the letters. There is even a Registration in under the Custom Shape tool palette. You may have to load all your shapes to find it. I used the rectangular marquee on a new layer to make the box shape and used the eraser to make the lines on the box. The sign ends up being very bright and clean. I took the contrast, saturation, and brightness down and added a little more noise.

The last thing you can do that would add a lot to this banner would be to draw some folds on it. This is easier than it sounds. Select the **Burn** tool and a large, soft brush. Drag out a few long lines that darken the banner where a fold shadow could be. Just drag from one of the upper corners diagonally to the center. Use the **Dodge** tool

**CUSTOM SHAPE TOOL**

**OUR SIGNS**

**WEBDINGS FONT SET**

**Figure 6.42**
Once you set up a template for a sign, you can crank out a wide assortment of variations quickly.

and do the same, only do this on top of the darker parts (light and shadow). The effect is great looking and easy to do. I did a few more areas and even zoomed in and made some tight folds at the corners of the banner (see Figure 6.43).

## Door

The last detail we have to create is the office door. This is not hard, but it does have many steps.

1. Create a new image **512** wide by **1024** high. Name it **Door_Office_001**.
2. Create a new layer and name it **Material**.
3. Fill this layer with a light blue/gray, **RGB: 155,158,164**.
4. **Filter > noise > Add noise 3%**.
5. **Filter > Blur > Gaussian Blur 0.5 pixels**.
6. Set your grid to **64** with **1** subdivision and turn it on.
7. Duplicate the **Material** layer and name it **Frame**.
8. Use the rectangular **marquee** and select the space where the door will fit into the frame. This should be a **64**-pixel frame on the top, right, and left with the bottom cut out.
9. Make sure the **Material** layer is turned off.
10. Press **Delete** on the **Frame** layer and you will see your doorframe.
11. Layer style for frame: I am having you apply effects you won't see until after the door is more complete. So you won't see much change as you enter the parameters. Apply the following layer styles:
    **Drop Shadow:**
    **Structure:**
    Blending Mode: Multiply
    Opacity: 24%
    Distance: 5 px
    Size: 7
    **Outer Glow:**
    **Structure:**
    Blending Mode: Multiply
    Opacity: 21%

**Figure 6.43**
This banner was as easy to make as the little sign, and the folds in the cloth were just an extra simple step.

Color: Pure black
**Elements:**
Technique: Softer
Size: 10
**Bevel and Emboss:**
**Structure:**
Size: 4
Shadow Mode Opacity: 50%

12. Make sure your background color is **black** and the **Material Layer** is off.
13. On the **Frame** layer: **Filter** > **Brush Strokes** > **Spatter**: Spray Radius **12**, Smoothness **8**.
14. Fade this (**Ctrl+F**) to **25%**.
15. Duplicate this layer and name it **Inner Frame**.
16. Turn on your grid and set the subdivisions to **6**. Keep the grid at **64**.
17. Use the rectangular **marquee** and select a **one-unit** border around the inside of your frame.
18. On the **Frame** layer, press **Delete**.
19. Activate the **Inner Frame** layer, **right-click**, and invert the selection. Press **Delete**.
20. Run the **Spatter** filter on the **Frame** layer again. If it was the last filter you used, you can press (**Ctrl+F**) to run it again with the same settings. I used the **Burn** tool with a **5**-pixel soft brush to put a subtle frame line at the top of the door. Your image should now look like Figure 6.44.
21. Now we will make the door itself. Select the empty space on the inside the Inner Frame.
22. Duplicate the **Material** layer and name it **Door**.

**Figure 6.44**
Your frame and inner frame should look like this.

23. Invert the selection and **delete** the portion of the door behind the frame.
24. **Copy** and **Paste** the layer style from the **Frame** layer. You only need to change the Bevel and Emboss style to **Emboss**.
25. Turn your 64 **grid** on and change the subdivisions to **3**.
26. Look at Figure 6.45 for visual reference. Use the rectangular **marquee** and select the upper window and the three panel spaces in the door. Aside from good proportions, keeping the width of all the frames in the door the same is important. The bottom panel of the door can be a bit larger, like a real door. I made the thickness **two** units all the way around. Make sure that your panel spaces are the same size, too. I made the window **18** units high and each panel **5**. Press **Delete**.
27. Run the **Spatter** filter again and fade it to **25%**.
28. You can use the **Burn** tool with a very small, soft brush to put the seams on the door where the boards meet but were painted over.
29. Select the **Magic Wand** tool and select one of the three empty panel spots in the door, hold **Shift** and select the other two. Duplicate the **Material** layer and name it **Panels**. Paste the layer style and make the following changes:
    **Outer Glow:**
    Turn it off
    **Inner Glow:**
    Opacity: 25%
    Noise: 12%
    Size: 38 px
    **Bevel and Emboss:**
    Technique: Chisel Hard
    Direction: Down
    Size: 6 px
    Highlight Mode: Screen
    Opacity: 47%
    Shadow Mode: Multiply
    Opacity: 18%
30. Run the **Spatter** filter again (**Ctrl+F**) and fade it to **25%** (**Ctrl+Shift+F**).
31. Select the empty place for the window and create a new layer and name it **Window**.
32. Fill the selection with **black**.
33. **Filter** > **noise** > **Add noise 50%**.
34. **Filter** > **Artistic** > **Sponge**: Brush Size **5**, Definition **10**, Smoothness **8**. I took the brightness up **50** and the contrast down **10**.
35. Add the following layer styles:
    **Inner Shadow:**
    Blend: Multiply
    Opacity: 75%
    Distance: 2
    Size: 2
    **Inner Glow:**
    Blend Mode: Screen
    Opacity: 38%
    Noise: 22%
    Color: **RGB: 194,212,235**

**Figure 6.45**
Cutting out the window and panels is easy, but pay attention to the grid and the placement of the elements.

Size: 59 px
**Gradient Overlay:**
Blend Mode: Lighten
Opacity: 18%

Your image should now look like Figure 6.46.

Now we will add the details to the door, such as the knob, the lock, and weather stripping at the bottom.

1. Create a new layer and name it **Knob_Plate_Lock**. Use the rectangular **marquee** and eyeball the knob plate. See Figure 6.47 for where I put it.
2. Fill the selection with a light brown, **RGB: 74,67,62**.
3. To create the lock above this plate, snap a vertical guideline to the center of the selection. Use the **circular marquee** and hold **Shift** to keep the circle perfect. Make the circle approximately the same width as the door plate, then snap it to the guideline and place it above the plate, roughly centered where the three boards of the door meet.
4. Fill the selection with light brown, **RGB: 74,67,62**.
5. **Deselect** all.
6. **Filter** > **noise** > **Add noise 2%**.
7. **Filter** > **Artistic** > **Palette Knife: default** settings.
8. **Copy** and **paste** the layer style from the **Inner Frame** layer and change the size in the Bevel and Emboss style to **3**.

**WHERE THE BOARDS MEET, BUT WERE PAINTED OVER**

**THE DOOR SO FAR**

**PANELS**    **WINDOW**

**Figure 6.46**
Your door with the window in
it should look like this.

9.  Key slot: Use a soft **5**-pixel brush and the **Burn** tool to paint a
    small black line through the lock plate to look like a key slot.
10. **Copy** the layer and **merge** it with an empty layer and use **Motion
    Blur** to blur the layer vertically.
11. Make sure this new blurred layer is under the **Knob_Plate_Lock**.
    Move it down **10** pixels and change the blending mode to
    **Overlay** and the opacity to **50%**.
12. Use the **Smudge** brush to smear the pixels down so it looks like
    rust stains.
13. Create a new layer on top of the **Knob_Plate_Lock** layer and
    name it **Knob**.
14. Use the **Circular Marquee** and the same guideline that you used
    to create the lock to place a selection for the knob. Make the
    selection the same width as the plate—maybe even a pixel or
    two larger.
15. Fill that selection with a brassy color, **RGB: 107,92,57**.
16. Paste the layer style from the **Knob_Plate_Lock** layer and change
    the following settings (see Figure 6.48):
    **Bevel and Emboss:**
    Depth: 101%
    Size: 6 px
    Soften: 3 px
    Highlight Mode: Linear Dodge
    Opacity: 53%

**Figure 6.47**
The placement of the knob plate.

**Figure 6.48**
The stages of the knob and plate.

The weather stripping at the bottom of the door starts with a rectangular piece of the Material layer about 22 pixels high and the width of the door, maybe slightly smaller.

1. Create a new layer and name it **Weather_Stripping**. Make sure that it is under the inner and outer frames but on top of the door layer.
2. Paste the strip of material at the bottom of the door and centered. Nudge it up three or four pixels.

3. Brighten this strip. **Ctrl+U: +20** Brightness.
4. **Filter > noise > Add noise 2%.**
5. Use the **Burn** tool and a **13**-pixel soft brush to darken the bottom half.
6. Use the **Burn** tool and a **9**-pixel soft brush to further darken the very bottom of the strip.
7. Use the **Burn** tool and a **5**-pixel soft brush to make a dark line roughly in the middle, leaving a gap between it and the darkened bottom.
8. Use the **Dodge** tool and a **9**-pixel soft brush to lighten the gap between the darkened bottom and the line you just made. Also, lighten the very few top pixels of the strip.
9. Add a drop shadow with the default settings and a slight outer glow. You will have to change the mode to **Multiply**, the opacity to **35%**, and the size to **8**.
10. Finally, I used the 5-pixel hard brush and a medium/dark gray and placed those five dots that look like nails holding the strip on when the texture is reduced and placed in a game. Even though most weather stripping has guide holes, I purposely eyeballed the placement of the nails and staggered them so it would look like someone hammered that on real quick.

All we have left to do is beat this door up some more. We can make it look weathered, dirty, and chipped.

1. Create a new layer on top of everything else and name it **Weathering**.
2. Fill this layer with **black**.
3. **Filter > Render > Fibers > defaults.**
4. **Filter > Artistic > Colored Pencil > defaults.**
5. Set the layer mode to **Overlay** and play with the opacity; I like **15%**.
6. You can leave it this way or clean off the window, since glass and wood would weather differently. Go to the **Door** layer and select the window hole with the **Magic Wand**, go back to the weathering layer, and **delete** it.
7. Create a new layer and name it **Chips**.
8. Use the **Gradient** tool with black as the foreground. Use the **Foreground to Transparent** preset. Drag the gradient up from the bottom a little over half the way. Hold **Shift**!
9. **Filter > noise >** jack it all the way up!
10. **Filter > Artistic > Paint Daubs**: Brush Size **5**, Sharpness **22**, Brush Type **Dark Rough**.
11. Change the Layer Blending Mode to **Multiply** and the opacity to **27%**.
12. Create a new layer and name it **Dirt**. This will be just a general darkening of the areas people come into contact with the door the most.
13. Change the Layer Blending Mode to **Soft Light** and the opacity to **35%**.
14. Use a big, soft black brush (**100** pixels) and hit the areas around the knob and near the bottom, especially by the inner part of the door where it opens.

**Figure 6.49**
The final door.

Sometimes when I am all done with a texture, after I flatten the file I like to run a filter over the whole thing (usually Dry Brush) and then fade it way down. This can give a texture a more cohesive feeling. Here is the final door (see Figure 6.49).

Congratulations! You made all the textures for the urban environment. Here they all are in the warehouse scene (see Figure 6.50). You may notice things I didn't address in the scene, such as the pipes for the rollup door, the switch, and the yellow stripes and pylons by the door. I left these out because to create them would be redundant. The pipe texture we already made. The yellow stripes and pylons are based on the same techniques you learned in the sci-fi chapter, when we created caution stripes, and the button and switch are created in the same manner as the detail textures from Chapter 5.

## Building It Up Using Overlays

In Figure 6.51, you can see a variation made with some overlays and a lowering of light. The cement looks moldy because I took the rough cement from Figure 6.29 and added a layer above it. I set the Blending Mode to overlay and the opacity to 30%. I then rendered clouds on this layer with black as my background color and a very dark and desaturated green as my foreground color. I used the same technique on the other textures. On the walls I used black and gray

**Figure 6.50**
Here is the final scene. You might notice the shafts of light streaming from the windows and the shadows of the window frames on the ground. The light shafts are super-easy; we will make those in Chapter 9. The frame shadows are simply the alpha channel of the windows projected onto the floor.

for the clouds. The windows use a variation we created earlier in this chapter. I took the glow and light shafts out and replaced them with an illumination map that makes the windows look incredibly dirty and the sunlight barely penetrating.

## Tearing It Down for Shaders

The shaders used in this final scene are simple and addressed elsewhere at great length. This chapter specifically dealt with low polygons, low texture budget, and older technology, and shaders are not a big part of that workflow. If you are interested in the windows, see the illumination map we looked at earlier in this chapter and the light beams we look at in Chapter 9. The bloom or glow shader effect is described in Chapter 3.

## Chapter Exercises

1. Practice breaking the materials and details out of a scene. Take 10 or 20 minutes to do this and compare notes with other people in class. Can you identify the base materials that tile and their details?
2. Create your own bricks. Change the pattern, color, and mortar style. Create a set of tiling textures for your bricks that include the top and bottom of a wall.
3. Create a window texture set that includes either an illumination map or alpha map. Make your own frame design.

**Figure 6.51**
Here is a variation of the final scene using overlays and lowering the light levels. I also took the light shafts out of the scene.

4. Create textures for a set of crates that have a few variations of stenciling and labels—these can be WWII-style, modern-day, or whatever you want. Use images from a Google search for labels and art, and you can get some overlay images as well. Make the wood look stained and worn using images from the Internet.

5. Create a base concrete and a set of overlays for dirt, mold, and fine cracks. Create a set of alpha-channeled details for the floor such as strewn trash, leaves, coins, stains, or whatever you like.

6. Create your own set of signs.

7. Create a door that has variations on color and weathering (stains, dirt, and so on); you can use the overlays that you created for the floor as a base.

8. Advanced: Create a door in the same way we created a door here, only use concrete for the skills. How would you alter the size, shape, and proportions of things to make the door look believable? Use the metal we created for heavy hinges and latches. Try creating a sign that would make this door look even more formidable and ominous.

# Chapter 7

Fantasy Concept, 2005, by Mark Birge-Anderson

# The Fantasy Setting

## Introduction

This is the chapter where we go all-out: We will make our base materials and several highly detailed textures for a high-polygon-count scene. We will also use the Path tool to create the fancy curves you see in some textures of the scene. Finally, we will create the textures needed for a simple shader.

Although we will be creating the art for a typical fantasy setting, this setting can also be a medieval castle. Take away the fantastic elements and you are left with a room in a castle. See Figure 7.1.

## The Concept Sketch

This concept sketch has a great level of detail. Aside from creating all that detail, the challenge with this sketch is that it is in black and white. This is a great exercise, because sometimes you might have to pick the colors of the textures you need to create. We will start with the colors of the familiar materials that we can easily guess, things like wood and stone. But what about the other items? The pitcher, for example—what is that made of, ceramic or silver? Should the color scheme reflect an evil or a good inhabitant? And the door—is that metal or wood? This place looks pretty nicely furnished and well kept, so we can imagine that the colors will be fairly saturated and the materials not as basic as ceramic. Judging by the spellbook and map, this is a magician's room, and the goblet appears to be ornate and have gems embedded in it. The pitcher looks like part of a set,

**Figure 7.1**
This setting can also be medieval.

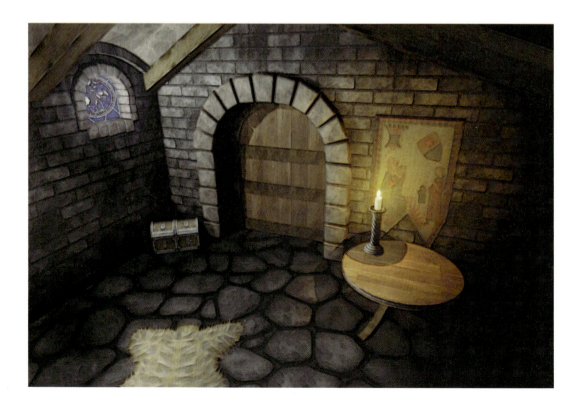

so it is most likely not ceramic but of the same material as the goblet. The chest seems well constructed and locked. I am assuming there are some valuables in there. The windows are made of fine stained glass. There is a thick and plush-looking animal fur on the floor. If I had to guess I would say this was a good magician, based only on the fact that the symbols in the window seem to be of the sun and moon with the earth in front of it. That doesn't look evil to me. The similarity of the symbols on the banner, the book, and the door indicates an order or school of magic. The banner also looks like the type held on a pole when warriors rush into battle, so at the very least this person is well traveled, if not actually an adventurer.

## Breaking Out the Materials in the Scene

The materials common in fantasy settings are rough stone for walls, stone flooring, rough-hewn wood, and coarse metals. The ceiling in this setting seems to be made of a light stucco or plaster. We will add some weathering and wear, because even though this is a very posh-looking room, wear makes things look much more convincing and interesting. The good news is that we are not starting from zero this time. We have already created several textures that we can use as bases for these textures. If you skipped straight to this chapter, don't worry—you can go back to those sections. I will refer to them in the text. The list of base materials we need to create is:

- Stone flooring
- Rough stone wall
- Rough wood beams
- Plaster or light stucco
- Base metals—dark iron, pewter or dull silver, gold

## Breaking Out the Details

Aside from the common base materials, like wood and stone, we need to break out the details—and there are a lot more of them in this scene. I also included my assumptions about each item, because the sketch is in black and white and we need to know, before we create textures, the colors and make-up of the materials as well as other information about the scene.

- Animal-fur rug: Thick and plush bear skin.
- Chest: Wood bound in heavy metal; well worn, too.
- Candlestick: Dark, silver-like pewter. We also must create the flame and the candle itself.
- Spellbook: Metal-bound with a hide cover and inset gems. The symbols on the cover and the spine are embossed.
- Map: Old and worn dark parchment with burnt edges and faded ink.
- Windows: Bright, based on the light shafts, and the glass looks clean and unbroken. The colors are yellow and blue based on the sun and moon.
- Banner: Cloth and the colors are the same as the window, but these colors will be more desaturated based on the material, the location of the banner, and its assumed adventuring history.

- Door: Metal intricately carved with symbols and writing. The symbols and the writing have a magical glow.
- Pitcher and goblet: Gold with red gems.

After I did this exercise, I emailed my assumptions to the artist who drew this scene, who responded by saying that I was on target. He told me that he envisioned this to be the room of a member of an order of magic, only he didn't think of it as good or evil, rather "a more druid-like order." Technically, that's good to me, being in line with nature and all, but he didn't think of it that way as he drew it.

He added that what is most important to him, more than seeing detail, is to feel the room as though he were in it. "Do you smell mold and mildew or strong incense? Is it cold or warm? Do you feel tension or are you at peace in the room? Is the light cold or warm? As I draw, I put myself into the environment. It is how the detail becomes so, well, detailed and 'real.'" These are the same questions that texture artists need to ask themselves as they work. He was successful as a concept artist because his art conveyed all that information to me, and more. I think my assumption about the nature of this inhabitant being good was correct, but it was not conscious on his part. He later e-mailed me and said, "If I had done an evil environment I would have to have been thinking about it. I think I gravitate to light or good naturally without thinking about it." And, he added, "The rug is bearskin."

## Base Materials

We will start, as always, by creating the base materials for our scene. Several of these textures are created using images you already created in this book.

### Stone Flooring

We will start with our floor. We are creating a texture for the floor that is different from the wall (which we will create next) because a floor is exposed to different treatment than a wall. A floor has been laid down for a different purpose—walking on—and therefore needs to be smoother than a wall. It will have different light and shadow than a wall. And last but not least, having the same stone on the floors and walls would look bad. There would be no division, no distinction, between the wall and the floor.

The way we will be creating the stone floor is very versatile. You can adjust the space between the stones, the size of the stones, and the color and texture of the stones and mortar all by changing a few variables.

1. Create a new 1024×1024 image and name it **fantasy_stone_floor**.
2. Fill the background with a dark gray: **RGB: 68,68,68**.
3. **Filter** > **noise** > **Add noise 10%**.
4. **Filter** > **Artistic** > **Cutout**: Number of Levels **8**, Edge Simplicity **2**, Edge Fidelity **2**.

5. **Filter** > **Brush Strokes** > **Accent Edges**: Edge Width **4**, Edge Brightness **23**, Smoothness **3**.
6. Create a new layer and name it **stones**.
7. Fill this layer with **white**.
8. Make sure that your foreground color is **black**.
9. **Filter** > **Texture** > **Stained Glass**: Cell Size **45**, Border Thickness **10**, Light intensity **0**.
10. **Filter** > **Other** > **Offset 512×512**.

I found these settings to be best for this application, but these are some of the variables that you can change to make a different type of stone. Smaller cells mean more and smaller stones. Border thickness helps determine the space between stones. You will notice a hard line running in both directions down the center of the image. Use a hard brush and the **X** key to toggle between black and white to fix the tiling problems now. It is much easier than trying to tile the stones later. See Figure 7.2. I also used this opportunity to make the cells/stones a bit less uniform. As you are doing this, zoom in to work and zoom out to look at your stones. You will have to do more than just smooth the lines. Even after the lines are smoothed, you will probably notice that the spaces between the stones still run too straight and will need to be tweaked.

11. **Filter** > **Blur** > **Gaussian Blur 10 pixels**.
12. **Filter** > **Artistic** > **Cutout**: Number of Levels **8**, Edge Simplicity **4**, Edge Fidelity **1**.
13. Run this filter at least three more times using **Ctrl+F**.
14. Use the **Magic Wand** to select the center of a stone. **Right-click** and select **Similar**.
15. Look at your selection. If you find that the stones are too far apart, you can use **Select** > **Modify** > **Expand: # pixels** to close the gap. Contracting the selection will widen the gap between stones.
16. **Right-click**. Fill with the selection with **white** (the stones should be white).
17. Select **inverse**. Fill the spaces with **black**.
18. Offset this image again and clean it up. Sometimes there are gaps or artifacts to fix, and they are so much easier to deal with now. Remember to use black and white, not the eraser. This is also an opportunity to remove any edges that may be too pointy or straight. You can even run the Ripple Filter on this, but don't make the lines too wavy.

**Tip 1:** I find it easier not to try to paint the black lines perfectly but rather to use one large brush (about 45 to 65 pixels) and cover the general area with black, overlapping the stones on either side of the lines. Press the X key and paint the white stone back in. I find this is not only easier but it also looks better because the larger brush makes for a smoother stone edge.

**Tip 2:** Offset the image again to check your tiling, only this time don't enter exactly 512 for a 1024 image; try 256. The reason for this is

**BASE MATERIAL PROGRESSION**
1.    2.    3.    4.

**STONES**

STAINED GLASS

OFFSET

CLEAN UP

BLUR

CUT OUT

STONES

**CLEAN UP DETAIL**

AFTER OFFSET

ERASE HARD LINES

REPAINT

**Figure 7.2**
The progression of the base material and the steps to creating our stones.

that an exact offset often covers a mistake in tiling that you won't notice until you are finished with the texture and have it tiling across a floor. The few minutes it takes to recheck things like this make your work go much faster in the long run.

19. Use the **Magic Wand** to select the space between the stones and delete it. If you have wide spaces between your stones and

want to work on the mortar between the stones by itself, you can create a new layer and fill the selection in.

20. Create a new layer on the top of the stack and name it **stone material**.
21. Set your foreground color to **black** and the background color to **white (D)**.
22. **Filter** > **Render** > **Clouds**.
23. **Image** > **Adjustments** > **Brightness/Contrast** > **–50 (legacy)**.
24. **Filter** > **Render** > **Lighting Effects**.
    Light Type: Spotlight
    Intensity: 10
    Focus: 69
    Gloss: 42
    Material: 56
    Exposure: 0
    Ambience: 10
    Texture Channel: Blue
    Height: 87

    See Figure 7.3 for the Lighting Effects dialog box and how to adjust the spotlight. In the window to the left you can see the small version of your texture and the circle that represents the spotlight. There are four squares along the edge of this circle. Drag the right-hand square out until the spotlight circle is completely outside the image.

25. You can run the Lighting Effects filter once more if you want a rougher stone. I did not in this case.
26. You can also run the **Filter** > **Brush Strokes** > **Accent Edges**: **Edges** to get a richer stone. I did.
27. Save a copy of this base stone as a separate image in your asset library for later use.
28. Duplicate the layer. We are doing this so the stones will look like they are made from random stones and not one sheet of stone.
29. Flip the layer vertically and horizontally (use **Ctrl+T** and **right-click** on the selection).
30. Offset this layer by **512** in both directions. Clone out the hard seams.
31. Turn both new layers off: stone material and stone material copy.
32. Select the **stone** layer.
33. Select about half of the stones with the **Magic Wand** in a random pattern. I find that occasionally turning the layer off so you can see the selection by itself makes it easier to see the distribution of selected stones.
34. **Invert** the selection.
35. Select the stone material layer and press **Delete**.
36. Deselect the layer and use Levels (**Ctrl+L**) and darken the stones slightly.
37. Merge this layer with the **stones** layer.
38. Select one of the remaining white stones on the **stone** layer and select **Similar. Invert** this selection.
39. Go to the **stone** material copy layer and press **Delete**.
40. Merge these layers. You should have two layers remaining: the stones and the background.

**Figure 7.3**
The major steps in creating the stones.

41. Add layer effects to the stones and change the following settings:
    **Drop Shadow:** Use the default settings
    **Outer Glow:**
    **Blending Mode:** normal
    Opacity: 54%
    Noise: 20%
    Color: Black
    Size: 27 px
    **Inner Glow:**
    **Blending Mode:** Hard Light
    Opacity: 60%

Color: Black
Noise: 20%
Size: 40 px
**Bevel and Embos:**
**Technique:** Chisel Soft
Soften: 10 px
Highlight Mode Opacity: 60%

42. Copy the stone and background layers into a set and merge the copies.
43. Set your background color to **black.**
44. **Filter > Brush Strokes > Accent Edges 2, 20, 4.**
45. **Filter > noise > Add noise 4%.**
46. **Filter > Brush Strokes > Accent Edges 2, 20, 4** (yes, again).
47. Clean up: The stones already tile, but you need to do two things to clean them up. First, use the **Crop** tool to remove the excess pixels from outside the canvas area. When you merge a layer with an effect on it like Outer Glow with another layer, the effects cease to be a dynamic effect and become actual pixels outside the canvas area. If you can't visualize this, tile the image before you crop it and you will see what I mean.
48. Offset this image. You also need to use the **Clone** brush to remove the line across the image where the effects were frozen.

If you want, you can create two versions of the stone layers as you did in the previous exercise, both offset exactly 50% from the other. They would be identical, but after they were merged the line that runs through the texture would be in different places on the textures. Just offset one of them and they will line up perfectly; then you simply erase the hard line from the top image to expose the good part of the one below. I chose not to do this, because although my goal is speed on one hand, I also want things to look good, and this was an opportunity for me to mix up the light and dark stones. The rendered lighting effects tend to lighten the middle stones. Your image should look like Figure 7.4. Also note that by working in layers, I could create the displacement map for this texture in seconds (literally) and the result is pretty impressive. The map is black and white with some gradient and no detail from the stones themselves.

## Rough Stone Wall

To create our stone wall, we will use the pattern of the brick texture that we created in the warehouse in the urban chapter and the stone material we created for the floor.

1. Start by opening a copy of the brick pattern you created in the chapter on urban textures (**brick_pattern**), or go back and create it now. Save this file as **fantasy_stone_wall.**
2. Set the grid at 32 with **1** subdivision.
3. **Free Transform** the **Brick Shape** layer and drag the bottom handle down until the bottom two rows of bricks are off the canvas.
4. Crop the image at its current size to remove the outer portions of the layer. Simply drag the **Crop** tool across the canvas. Make sure that you do not change the canvas size of the image.

**Figure 7.4**
Two variations of the final stone floor texture. The stones displaced using a displacement map created in seconds.

5. The bricks are now vertically thicker and still tile perfectly. You might want to run the Offset Filter to make sure the image tiles perfectly.
6. We want to wear down the edges with a hard eraser as we did for the urban bricks. Turn off the grid and use a **13**-pixel eraser

and zoom into the image so you can work accurately. Be patient and subtle. Don't take too much off; we just want the bricks to look older and hand-carved from stone. You will notice that you have more leeway to remove stone vertically, because stretching the bricks made the mortar spaces wider horizontally but not vertically. Your image should look like Figure 7.5 at this point.

7. Select the background layer and change the color to a dark gray, **RGB: 73,73,73**.
8. **Filter > noise > Add noise 5%**.
9. **Filter > Brush Strokes > Accent Edges**: Edge Width **2**, Edge Brightness **13**, Smoothness **4**.
10. Copy and paste a copy of the **stone_material** on the top of the stack from the stone floor image.
11. **Duplicate** the layer.
12. Flip the layer vertically and horizontally (use **Ctrl+T** and **right-click** on the selection).
13. Offset this layer by **512** in both directions.
14. Turn both these new layers off.
15. Activate the **Brick Stone** layer.
16. Select about half the wall stones with the **Magic Wand** in a random pattern and invert the selection.
17. Activate the **stone_material** layer and press **Delete**.
18. Deselect the layer, use Levels (**Ctrl+L**), and darken the wall stones slightly. Merge this layer with the **Brick Stone** layer.
19. Add layer effects to the bricks and change the following settings:
    **Drop Shadow:** Use the default settings.
    **Outer Glow:**
    **Blending Mode:** normal
    Opacity: 54%
    Color: Black
    Size: 18 px
    **Bevel and Emboss:**
    **Technique:** Chisel Soft
    Size: 5 px
    Soften: 4
    **Highlight Mode:** normal
    Opacity: 38%
    Shadow Mode Opacity: 40%

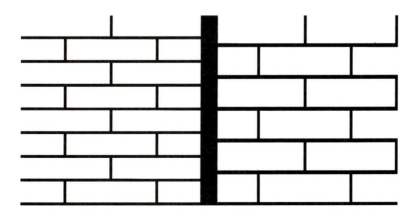

**Figure 7.5**
The bricks from the Urban Scene on the left and on the right after we stretch them down.

**Figure 7.6**
This is what the stone wall looks like so far.

20. Add a new layer on top of the stack and name it **dirt**.
21. **Filter** > **Render** > **Clouds**.
22. **Filter** > **Blur** > **Gaussian Blur: 5 pixels**.
23. **Image** > **Adjustments** > **Brightness/Contrast**: Brightness **+25**, Contrast **−50**.
24. Change the Blending Mode to **Multiply** and the Opacity to **45%**.

    Depending on how and where you are using this texture, you might need to play with the Levels and the Brightness/Contrast. Your image should look like Figure 7.6.

25. Create a layer set and put the three layers into it we just created. You will have to duplicate the background layer to include it in the layer set.
26. **Duplicate** the layer set. **Hide** the original set. Flatten the new layer set (**Ctrl+E**).
27. **Filter** > **Artistic** > **Sponge**: Brush Size **2**, Definition **2**, Smoothness **11**.
28. Fade this filter **50%** (**Ctrl+Shift+F**).
29. **Filter** > **Artistic** > **Poster Edges**: Edge Thickness **4**, Edge intensity **5**, Posterization **2**.
30. Fade this filter **25%** and set the Blending Mode to **Multiply**.
31. **Filter** > **noise** > **Add noise 5%**.
32. Crop the image to remove the excess image that is outside the canvas and offset the image to check your tiling.

Your image should look like Figure 7.7.

## Rough Wood Beams

We will base this texture on the wood fill from the warehouse. This will be used as a horizontally tiling beam, so we will make it longer and narrower and add some detail.

1. Open a copy of the image named **Wood_Fill_001**.
2. Change the image size to **256**, with constrained proportions.
3. Duplicate the **wood** layer and make the canvas size **1024** in height. Keep the same width.
4. **Tile** this wood four times to fill the layer, and merge the four layers.
5. **Liquify** this layer and create three or four knot holes. Pinch the grain together in some spots along the beam.
6. Use the **Burn** and **Dodge** tools to create an uneven, hewn look to the beams' edges. Go easy; don't create any hotspots that will show up later when you tile the beam.
7. Check your tiling both ways. Even though this is designed as a vertically tiling beam, smoothing out the lines where the horizontal edges meet will make this texture easier to use and more versatile.
8. Use **Levels** to darken the wood slightly if you like. See Figure 7.8 for the steps I described here.

**Figure 7.7**
Here is the final stonewall texture and a few simple variations.

### Plaster or Light Stucco

The plaster ceiling is based on the concrete texture we created in the warehouse. We will do a few things to make this concrete look like old stucco.

1. Open the image you created for the concrete with pits in it in the urban chapter, or go back to that chapter and create the image.
2. Colorize the image (**Ctrl+U**): Hue **38**, Saturation **6**, Lightness **–39**.
3. Create another layer on top of the stack and name it **cracks**.
4. **Filter > Render > Clouds**.
5. **Filter > Artistic > Cutout**: Number of Levels **8**, Edge Simplicity **1**, Edge Fidelity **2**.
6. You can select and delete various parts of the resulting pattern.

   Depending on what you select and what you delete, you will get various crack patterns. The variations are endless. You can apply a variety of layer effects, such as a very light Bevel and Emboss and Inner Glow, to give the stucco depth. Use the shape to mask off another image to get the effect that plaster is falling away from the wall and exposing the material behind it. Figure 7.9

**Figure 7.8**
The stages of the rough-hewn wooden beam.

**Figure 7.9**
Variations of the stucco using the same technique but with altered variables.

shows the various effects I achieved using this method. I also used this cracked stucco as an overlay on the stone wall for the medieval version of this room at the end of the chapter.

7. Create a new layer on top and name it **dirt**.
8. **Filter** > **Render** > **Clouds**.
9. **Filter** > **Render** > **Difference Clouds** two times.
10. Change the Layer Blending mode to **Multiply** and the opacity to **39%**.

You can also create one strong crack in your stucco.

11. Use the **Gradient** tool with a black-to-white gradient on a new layer named **crack**.
12. **Filter** > **Render** > **Difference Clouds**.

**Figure 7.10**
A harder, more defined crack using a different method.

13. Adjust your Layer (**Ctrl+L**) by dragging the center arrow of the input to the left.
14. Zoom in and use the **Magic Wand** to select the darkest center of the crack and select **Similar**.
15. **Invert** the selection. Press **Delete**.
16. Now you can apply a **Bevel and Emboss** to the crack to add depth. See Figure 7.10.

There are several variables you can play with. The width and tightness of the gradient determine the chaos of the line. See Figure 7.11 for an illustration of this idea. You can also expand or contract the selection before you delete the pixels outside the crack.

### Base Metals: Dark Iron, Pewter or Dull Silver, Gold

Dark iron, pewter, or even a dull silver can simply be the base metal we created for the sci-fi hall.

1. Open a copy of **sci_fi_metal_base** and save it as **fantasy_metal_base**.
2. **Image** > **Adjustments** > **Brightness/Contrast**: Contrast **–50%**.

That's all you need to do. We will be using this base in various ways, and it works perfectly as a hand-crafted, beaten-up metal. As we use it, we will do specific things to the metal, depending on where it is and what it is used on. When we make the gold, it will be a very basic texture with a special shader applied to it.

## Detail Textures

These detail textures will have a lot more detail in them than the previous textures and will require many steps to complete. We will start with the easiest and work up to the more complex textures.

**Figure 7.11**
The width and tightness of the gradient determines the chaos of the crack line.

### Table Trim

In the concept art, you can see the trim on the side of the table. This is simple and based on the wood we created for the heavy beams.

1. Open a copy of the **wood beam** texture and name it **fantasy_table_trim**.
2. **Image > Rotate Canvas > 90 degrees**.
3. Crop the image so it is **1024** wide and **128** high.
4. Create a new layer and name it **trim**.
5. Fill the layer with a color; it doesn't matter what color.
6. Using the **grid** and the **circular selection** tool, cut the arches out of the wood by clicking **Clear** and moving the selection. If you set the grid to **32**, you can make the arches 7 units (224 pixels) with one unit between them all.

7. Use a hard, medium brush to make the circles (around **20** pixels).
   Apply **Layer Effects** and change the following settings:
   Fill: 0
   **Drop Shadow:**
   Size: 25 px
   **Outer Glow:**
   Blend Mode: normal
   Opacity: 33%
   Color: Black
   Size: 38 px
   **Bevel and Emboss**
   Highlight Mode Opacity: 50%
   Shadow Mode Opacity: 60%
8. You can copy these layers and merge the copies so that you
   can offset them to clean up the seams. See Figure 7.12 for a
   progression of the table trim.

## Fur Rug

The animal fur on the ground is a thick, plush bearskin rug. This
requires a little hand painting, but it's easy and looks great. You do
need to be patient and methodical, but you don't need very much
artistic talent.

1. Open a new **512** wide×**1024** high image and name it **fantasy_
   bearskin**. Make sure your background is **black**.
2. Create a new layer and name it **bearskin**.
3. Fill this layer with a light brown, **RGB: 144,109,30**.
4. Use the **Lasso** tool and outline the general shape of half the
   bearskin. We are doing half for one of two reasons: This texture
   can be mirrored on the 3D model that it will be applied to, which
   saves texture memory, or you can complete half and then copy
   and mirror it. This saves a lot of work. If you need to, you can
   spend a few extra minutes on the entire rug to make it look less
   "mirrored." See Figure 7.13.
5. **Invert** the selection and **delete**.
6. **Filter** > **noise** > **Add noise 10%**.
7. **Filter** > **Blur** > **Motion Blur**: Angle **0**, Pixels **32**.

**Figure 7.12**
Progression of the table trim
texture.

**Figure 7.13**
The workflow of the bearskin and the hair brush.

8. **Filter** > **Brush Strokes** > **Angled Strokes**: Direction Balance **6**, Stroke Length **13**, Sharpness **5**.
9. Use the **Smudge** tool and the hair brush (see the note) and start by smearing out the edges of the bearskin. You will have to adjust the size of the brush (use the **[** and **]** keys to do this quickly) and the amount of smear. I find that around **50%** works best.

**Note:** To make your own hair brush, open the image on the CD in the Projects folder for this chapter. Select the entire canvas and go to **Edit** > **Define Brush Preset** and name your new brush. This brush is perfect for painting hair. It has five dots, so no matter what direction you drag, you are getting a good, even hair shape. Change the brush settings so that there is no spacing and so the Shape Dynamics are set to **Fade**. Adjust the number to the right of this to the amount you want the brush to fade. This number depends on the size of the image you are working on, among other factors such as the length of the hair and your own preferences. This number determines the number of brush increments, not pixels, that the brush takes to fade away. Therefore, a larger brush with the same value entered will take a longer distance to fade away.

10. This is the fun part—actually, it's the tiresome part that is really fun when you are done because it looks so cool. We start by gradually outlining the general flow of the fur and will spend time building the fur up in layers. It's not hard, just a bit tedious.

**Figure 7.14**
Create your own hair brush and start the bear skin. These are the stages of the bearskin rug. The fur looks great when it is done, but it starts with a simple layout that builds on itself.

Because fur actually grows in layers and tends to clump, you don't have to draw individual hairs, and it looks great when you are done. Use the **Burn** tool—**Midtones**, exposure **38%**—and a soft brush (**13** pixels) and start by making basic lines and triangles defining the general pattern of how the fur grows from the pelt.

11. Dodge with a larger soft brush (**27** pixels) and give each triangle a quick dash of highlight. You don't have to be too exact—just a general swoop down the middle.

**Figure 7.15**
The complete bearskin rug.

12. Burn with the hair brush hairs across the rug. This is where you need to be a bit more patient. Zoom in a bit and hit the ] and [ keys a few times to make the brush larger and smaller as you work. Start on the edges and work your way inward.
13. Dodge highlights by doing the last step again, but use the **Dodge** brush.
14. Burn some depth into the rug using a large, soft brush (**100** pixels) by darkening the edges and a few major clumps of fur.
15. **Dodge** a highlight on the clumps you created.
16. **Burn** over the fur again with your hair brush to make it pop a little more. You don't need to do quite as much; use this opportunity to hit areas that might be a little too light.
17. **Dodge** the highlights too and focus on the too-dark areas.
18. **Filter** > **Artistic** > **Dry Brush**: Brush Size **2**, Brush Detail **10**, Texture **1**.
19. Fade this to **30%** (**Ctrl+Shift+F**).
20. You are going to want to tweak a little with the **Burn** and **Dodge** tools, and use the **Smudge** tool again on the edges. The painted hairs might look like they are dead-ending into the edge of the fur, and smudging them will blend the painted hairs into the edge. See Figure 7.15 for the final bearskin rug.

### Chest

This chest is made of wood bound in heavy metal. We will use the base metal that we created from the sci-fi metal. The beam we created in this chapter is actually a little too rough to use for the chest, so we will use the wood planks that we created in Chapter 6.

In this exercise I will provide you with a UV template (Figure 7.16). This is an image that has all the parts of a 3D model that needs a texture laid out flat and efficiently. The art of laying out a UV map efficiently and creating the texture for a UV-mapped model could fill another book altogether. But I do want you to get a feel for what it is like to work with a UV map. Once you do this, you will see the relationship between model and texture more clearly.

UV mapping a model before the texture is created is pretty common. It is also common for one artist to create both the texture and the model. The benefit is that the artist is able to switch among the texture, the UV editor, and the model, changing all three, and is not held to painting on one template. Although that seems easier, UV'ing a model in advance and using the template is far easier and nets better results. Also, a lot of your work has been done for you if you are the texture artist getting the UV map; you don't need to examine the model and do the tedious work of laying the UVs out and placing them in the square texture space in the most efficient way. This template may not be as efficiently laid out as possible (that wasn't my focus when I did it), but it will give you a taste of creating textures within boundaries. There are some quick, but major, efficient practices I did exercise. Notice that in this texture layout, parts of the image are used in repeated places on the model. The panels are repeated and the inner part of the panel is used as the top of the lid. The metal trim of the panel is used on all the small edges of the chest. This might

**Figure 7.16**
A typical template for a UV-mapped model—in this case, our chest.

not be a valid layout for some projects that are using specific material systems or shaders, and other projects could demand a more efficient use of textures and may have even more overlap.

I always heard that guys like big chests in the fantasy genre, so let's give 'em what they want and make a big chest. The chest texture is composed of the following elements:

- The side panels
- The arched side panels on the top of the chest
- The lock
- The braided decorative band wrapped around the chest

These elements can all fit with room to spare on one texture, and we can make them all the same relative size. Relative sizing is important because if we made the side panels really big and then had to squeeze the lid panel in, making it smaller to fit, you would see the resolution difference on the final model.

Open the image from the CD/DVD **fantasy_chest_UV_MAP** and save it as **fantasy_chest**.

1. I pasted **Wood_Planks_001** into the image and tiled four copies of it on the layer wood. The image **sci_fi_metal_base** is on the metal layer.

2. Turn off the **wood** and **metal** layers.
3. Open the layer set **UV Map**. This layer set has the UV map in it as well as a layer with text labels identifying the parts. There is also a layer with dashed lines that indicate where the parts of the chest are that we don't need to create art for, since they use parts of the existing texture. Select the layer with the UV map on it. You can turn the other layers off as you work.
4. Use the **Magic Wand** tool and select the darker blue **inner section** of the chest lid and panel. These will be the wooden parts of the trunk.
5. Go to the **wood** layer, **invert** your selection, and press **Delete**.
6. Duplicate the metal layer and name it **panel frames**. Make sure that this layer is on the top of the stack.
7. Go back to the UV map and select the lighter blue **outer portion** of the panel and lid (the metal frame around the wood panels we just created) and the decorative plate in the center of the panel. **Invert** this selection.
8. On the **panel frames** layer, press **Delete**. If the metal layer is still visible, you won't see anything happen, so turn it off.
9. Apply **Layer Styles** with the following settings:
   **Outer Glow:**
   **Blend Mode:** Linear Burn
   Opacity: 15%
   Noise: 13%
   Color: Black
   Size: 62 px
   **Inner Glow:**
   **Blending Mode:** Vivid Light
   Opacity: 45%
   Noise: 17%
   Color: White
   Size: 35 px
   **Gradient Overlay:**
   **Blend Mode:** Vivid Light
   Opacity: 29%
   **Bevel and Emboss:**
   **Technique:** Chisel Soft
   Contour: Default Texture
   Scale: 412%

   Your image should look like Figure 7.17.

10. Create a new layer and name it **bolts**. Copy the layer styles from the **panel frames** layer and change the following settings:
    **Drop Shadow:** Default Settings
    **Outer Glow:**
    Opacity: 24%
    Size: 29 px
11. Use a hard brush with a medium gray and place the large bolts on the corners of the chest frame and lid frame. I eyeballed this, but if you like you can use four guidelines to get them placed perfectly.
12. Duplicate the **metal** layer and name it **lock**.
13. **Copy** the layer style from the **bolts** layer and **paste** it on the **lock** layer.

**Figure 7.17**
The beginnings of the chest with the major metal and wood parts in place.

14. Go to the **UV Map** layer, **select** the parts of the lock, and **invert** the selection.
15. On the **lock** layer, press **Delete**.
16. Duplicate the **bolts** layer and name it **lock bolts**. Clear this layer of pixels (**Ctrl+A** and **Ctrl+X**).
17. Use a small, hard brush and a medium gray and place the small bolts on the lock.
18. Change the following settings in the layer style:
    **Drop Shadow:**
    Distance: 4
    Size: 6
    **Outer Glow:**
    Opacity: 35%
    Size: 8 px
    **Inner Glow:** Turn it off
19. Duplicate the metal layer and name it **band**.
20. Select the band on the **UV Map** layer and **invert** the selection.
21. On the **band** layer, press **Delete**.
22. Duplicate the **band** layer and name it **band top**. Press **Delete** on this layer, too. You should have two identical layers at this point: band and band top.
23. Copy the layer style from the **lock bolts** layer, paste it into the **band** layer, and change the following settings:
    **Bevel and Emboss:**
    Size: 9
    Soften: 7

24. Copy the layer style from the **band** layer and paste it into the **band top** layer.

25. We need to cut the diagonal spaces into the band top. Use the grid and the **Polygonal Selection** tool to create a diagonal selection, move it along the grid, and press **Delete**. You can see the chest in the final render, but Figure 7.18 shows the texture with a close-up of the chest. Notice that the top of the lid is the side panel texture, and the trim parts inside the metal frame are the trim from the metal bands on the lid.

## Candlestick

The candlestick is actually three separate images:

- Candlestick: metal, pewter with etched leaves
- Candle flame: small, separate illumination-mapped texture
- Candle wax: illumination-mapped, but differently than the flame

## Metal Candlestick

1. Open a copy of the **base metal** we made for the sci-fi setting. Change the image size to **512×512**. Save this image as **fantasy_candlestick**.

2. **Filter** > **Brush Strokes** > **Crosshatch**: Stroke Length **10**, Sharpness **6**, Strength **1**. This helps the metal look more worn and smoother than the rough base metal.

3. Duplicate this layer and name it **pewter**.

4. Duplicate it again and name it **ridges**. Make sure that this layer is on top.

5. Using the **grid** and a hard-brushed eraser (**9** pixels), erase four evenly spaced horizontal lines. Don't forget that the top and bottom must have a half-line erased from each, or offset the image vertically and erase the line. We are doing this horizontally because not only is it much easier to work horizontally and rotate the texture on the model, but we can also more easily use this texture in other places with a horizontal orientation.

**Figure 7.18**
The final chest texture with a close-up of the chest from the fantasy scene.

6. For this step, you can apply layer styles, including Bevel and Emboss, or use the Burn and Dodge tools to create the highlights and shadow on the metal. I opted to use Burn/Dodge because in the end it looked better and was easier to tile. Here are the settings you need to change from the layer styles:
**Outer Glow:**
Color: Black
Size: 6 px
**Inner Glow:**
Opacity: 51%
Noise: 13%
Color: White
Size: 29 px
**Bevel and Emboss:**
Depth: 61%
Size: 64

7. Link the **pewter** and **ridges** layers, create **new set from linked**, and duplicate the layer set.

8. Hide one of the layer sets and merge the other.

9. Crop to remove the excess pixels outside the canvas area of the merged layer set.

10. Duplicate the layer and offset it 256 pixels in both directions. Use a large, soft brush to remove the seams.

11. Link these layers and merge them. The last thing we have to do is create the leaf pattern.

12. Create a new layer and name it **leaf**.

13. Use the **Custom Shape** tool, select the **Leaf 3** shape, and make one big leaf on the new layer. Use the **Free Transform** tool to size and rotate the leaf until it fits on about one fourth of the top band. Apply **Layer Effects** and change the following settings:
Fill: 0
**Outer Glow:**
Blend Mode: Color Burn
Opacity: 45%
Noise: 11%
Color: Black
Size: 13 px
**Bevel and Emboss:**
Style: Pillow Emboss
Depth: 60 px
Size: 12
**Gradient Overlay:**
Blend Mode: Color Dodge
Opacity: 58%

14. Duplicate the **leaf** layer and flip the leaf. Vertically adjust the two layers back and forth until the leaves look right, taking up about half the band (eventually you'll want to fit four of them across). See Figure 7.19. Change the following settings in the layer effects:
**Color Overlay:**
Blend Mode: Overlay
Opacity: 70%

15. Now that these two leaves look good, duplicate them and place them on the other half of the band. Keep duplicating leaves until

**Figure 7.19**
The candlestick metal with the first leaves in place.

you fill the texture. You can leave all these layers unflattened and output the texture as you need it. Even if I flatten a texture before I output it, I always copy layers that I might want to change later.

That's it. Here is the final texture with the model applied (Figure 7.20). The candle itself doesn't look good, because we haven't made the wax and flame yet.

*Candle Flame*

16. Create a new **256** wide by **512** high image with a black background and name it **candle_flame**.
17. Snap a vertical guideline to the center of the image.
18. Create a new layer and name it **orange**.
19. Use a large, soft brush (**200** pixels) and put a big, fuzzy orange circle at the bottom of the layer in the center: **RGB 255,127,0**.
20. Use the **Free Transform** tool and stretch this ball up by using the middle top handle. You will have to zoom way out to do this, and it will put a lot of nearly invisible pixels outside the canvas area, so you will want to crop the image to remove them. You should also clean the edges with a small, hard eraser and a larger soft one if you see a hard line in the orange.
21. Create a new layer and name it **white**. Set your foreground color to **white**.

**Figure 7.20**
The final candlestick texture
with the model.

22. Use a smaller soft brush (**65** pixels), open the **Brushes** palette,
    and set the Shape Dynamics to **Fade** and the Fade Size to **55**.
    Start very near the bottom and hold **Shift** to keep the flame
    straight and draw upward. I also smudged the tip of the flame to
    get a better-looking flame tip.
23. I put a small black line in the center for the wick and brushed
    some white over the tip to blend it into the flame. See Figure
    7.21 for the candle flame and its stages.
24. To create the alpha channel, simply duplicate the layer or the
    entire image, depending on how you need to handle the alpha
    channel, and desaturate it (**Ctrl+Shift+U**). Use the Hue/
    Saturation (**Ctrl+U**) to make the flame darker (Lightness **–43**) so
    that it is more transparent. Use a white brush and make the wick
    solid **white** so that it is not transparent at all.
25. To create an illumination map, copy the alpha image and use
    **Hue/Saturation** to make it much brighter. The illumination map
    makes areas of the object mapped with white fully bright and
    not affected by light while black areas have no illumination
    and usually light normally, depending on the game engine or
    technology you are using. The lightness and darkness of the
    grayscale determine the amount of illumination.

## Candle Wax

1. Create a new image **256** wide and **512** high. Name it **candle_wax**.
2. Create a new layer and name it **wax**.
3. Fill this layer with a desaturated light yellow: **RGB: 198,184,135**.

**Figure 7.21**
The stages of creating the candle flame.

4. **Filter** > **noise** > **Add noise 20%**.
5. **Filter** > **Blur** > **Gaussian Blur 5 pixels**.
6. **Filter** > **Brush Strokes** > **Spatter**: Spray Radius **6**, Smoothness **6**.
7. **Filter** > **Render** > **Clouds**.
8. Fade (**Ctrl+F**) Blending Mode: Overlay, Opacity **65%**.
9. Use the **Burn** tool and a large, soft brush (**100** pixels) to slightly darken the horizontal edges of the candle.
10. Use the **Dodge** tool and a smaller, soft brush (**45** pixels) and do a faint line or two of highlight up and down the horizontal center of the candle. If you want the candle to look more like shiny wax, also add another stronger, more narrow line to the highlights.
11. To get the dripping-wax effect, create a new layer and name it **dripping wax**. Apply layer effects and change the following settings:
    Fill: 0
    **Drop Shadow:**
    Opacity: 38%
    Distance: 3 px
    Size: 13 px
    **Outer Glow:**
    Blend Mode: Color Burn
    Opacity: 38%
    Color: Black
    Size: 35 px
    **Bevel and Emboss:**
    Size: 16 px
    Soften: 3 px
    Highlight Mode Opacity: 60%
    Shadow Mode Opacity: 31%
    **Texture:**
    Pattern: Molecular
    Scale: 474%
    Depth: +102%
    Check the invert box
12. To make the drips, use a soft **27**-pixel brush, paint along the top, and draw a drip or two coming down the candle. Copy the layers and merge them so you can offset them and clean the tiling edge.
13. To make an illumination map, do it the same way as the candle flame: Copy the image, desaturate it, and adjust the darkness and

**Figure 7.22**
The candle flame with and
without the illumination
map. Makes a big difference,
doesn't it?

lightness of the image to get the illumination effect you desire.
In this case, I used a black-to-white gradient (black starting at
the bottom of the candle) and faded it to 70% and changed the
blending mode to Linear Burn. I also tweaked the brightness
at the top and the darkness at the bottom of the candle. This
illumination map will make the candle appear to glow with the
light of the flame. Figure 7.23 shows the candle with and without
the illumination map in both a lit and nonlit scene.

## Spellbook

Now we will create the spellbook, which is a bit more complex. This
book has a metal cover binding a dragonscale hide and is inset with
gems. There are embossed writing and symbols on the cover and spine.
For the writing, we will use one of my favorite techniques: fonts. I got
permission from the font's creator to use it in the book and it is on the
CD, too. You will need to install this font before you start this exercise.
We will also create the unique shapes on the cover using paths. These
shapes are also used on the door, banner, and map. Creating them
using paths is flexible and you can drop the shapes into the other
textures that use them. If you hand-paint the shapes on the texture,
you will be repainting them every time you need them. Finally, we will
create the decoration on the spin, the page edges, and the gems.

The spellbook is similar to the chest in that we will be using a UV
map template. The main parts of the spellbook on the UV map in
Figure 7.24 are:

- Metal binding, trim, and spine
- Dragon scale hide cover inset

**Figure 7.23**
Candles 1 and 2 are in a very low-light scene; you can see the difference between the one with the illumination map and the one without. Candles 3 and 4 are in a brighter scene, but the illumination map still helps the candle look more authentic because the glow brings the perception of translucence to the candle. The bottom-left image is the candle texture and the bottom right is the illumination map.

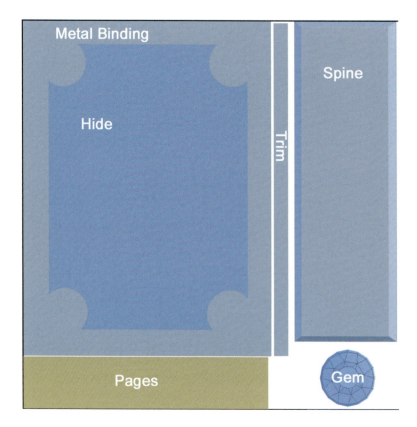

**Figure 7.24**
UV map template for the spellbook.

- Page edges
- Gem

## Metal Binding, Trim, and Spine

1. Open the image from the CD/DVD **fantasy_spellbook_UV_MAP** and save it as **fantasy_spellbook**.
2. The metal layer has the sci_fi_metal_base already there for you.
3. Turn off the metal layer.
4. Open the layer set **UV Map**. This layer set has the UV map in it as well as a layer with text labels identifying the parts. Select the layer with the **UV map** on it. You can turn the other layers off as you work.
5. Use the **Magic Wand** tool and select the lighter blue sections of the book. These will be the metal bindings of the book. Make sure you get the book frame, trim piece, and all the parts of the spine.
6. Go to the **metal** layer, invert your selection, and press **Delete**.
7. Apply layer styles with the following settings changed:
   **Outer Glow:**
   **Blend Mode:** Linear Burn
   Opacity: 15%
   Noise: 13%
   Color: Black
   Size: 62 px
   **Inner Glow:**

**Figure 7.25**
The metal binding of the book.

**Blending Mode:** Vivid Light
Opacity: 45%
Noise: 17%
Color: White
Size: 35 px
**Gradient Overlay:**
**Blend Mode:** Vivid Light
Opacity: 29%
**Bevel and Emboss:**
**Technique:** Chisel Soft
Contour: Default Texture
Scale: 412%

8. **Filter** > **Brush Strokes** > **Crosshatch**: Stroke Length **16**, Sharpness **6**, Strength **2**.
9. Set your background color to gray, **RGB: 120,120,120**.
10. **Filter** > **Artistic** > **Smudge Stick**: Stroke Length **4**, Highlight Area **12**, Intensity **4**.
11. You can create a place for the gems to be set in by duplicating the metal layer. Save it as **gem settings** and clear the layer contents. Set the Fill to **0** and use the **circular selection** tool to place a setting and stroke it on the inside of the selection.

## Runes

The runes are very easy. First, make sure the Tengwar-Gandalf font from the DVD is installed.

1. Create a new layer set named **runes** and a new text layer named **runes**. Set the font to **Tengwar-Gandalf**. Make it about **42** pts.
2. Set the Tracking to **–10** (tracking is the space between the letters).
3. Type whatever you want until the line of text fills the space between the gems.
4. Apply layer effects with the following settings changed:
**Inner Glow:**
**Blending Mode:** Vivid Light
Opacity: 62%
Noise: 4%
Color: White
Size: 10 px
**Bevel and Emboss:**
Style: Outer Bevel
Technique: Chisel Soft
Depth: 101%
Size: 2 px
Contour: default
**Color Overlay:**
Blend Mode: normal
Opacity: 100%
Color: **RGB: 67,90,106**
5. You can duplicate this layer and use the **Free Transform** tool to rotate it to line up on the four sides of the book binding. You might have to delete or add letters to make a nice fit. You can also type different words if you want to make sure that the runes look different on every side.

6. We also need to do the runes on the book spine, too. For this I pressed **Return** after each letter and made the font a little larger (about **60** pt) and adjusted the leading (the vertical space between the letters) to **35** pt. I linked all the runes so I could collapse them, but you can keep them separate if you think you will want to edit them later. Your image should look like Figure 7.26.

## Spine Decoration

The decoration on the spine is broken down into three steps: top, middle, and bottom.

1. Create a new layer set named **spine decoration**. Create a new layer named **top**.
2. Use the **Shape** tool, select the shape **Leaf 3,** and start by making the center leaf; make it big to start with. The color doesn't matter.
3. Copy the **leaf** layer three times and use the **Free Transform** tool (**Ctrl+T**) to flip and rotate the leaves into position. Use **Liquify** and a very large brush to move the leaves around until they look good. Merge the layers together.
4. Duplicate this half you just created, flip it, line up the two halves, and merge them. Copy and paste the layer effects from the **runes** layer. Your image should look like Figure 7.27.

**Figure 7.26**
Runes on the cover and spine of the book.

5. The middle of the spine decoration is a twist pattern. Select the **Type** tool and set the font to **Eras Demi iTC**. Create a new text layer, type a capital **S**, and make it pretty big.

6. Rasterize the layer and erase the ends of the S. **Free Transform** the curve down to a size small enough that you can stack them into the twist shape.

7. Snap a guide to the center of the resulting curve and copy the curve vertically using the guide to keep the curves centered. You can use the **Free Transform** tool to manipulate the complete twist to fit it into the spine the way you like it.

8. Copy the layer style from the top layer and paste it to this layer. See Figure 7.28 for the progression of the creation of the twist.

9. Create a new layer named **bottom** and copy the layer style from the top or twist layer and paste it to this layer.

10. Use the **Shape** tool and select the **Fleur-De-Lis** and drag one out on this layer. You will need to use the **Free Transform** tool to flip it vertically and resize it to fit on the spine below the twist and between the runes. Figure 7.29 shows the finished book spine with runes and decoration.

**Figure 7.27**
The progression of the creation of the top of the spine decoration.

**Figure 7.28**
The progression of the creation of the curve for the spine decoration.

## Dragon Scales

Here I introduce the Pen tool. The Pen tool creates *paths*, which allow for the easy creation of smooth and complex curves. The great thing about paths is that they are editable. You can lay them down quickly without being too exact, and then you can add and subtract points, move them, and adjust the handles to get any curve you can imagine. You can also save paths, fill them, stroke them, and more.

1. Create a new layer set and name it **scales**.
2. Create a new layer and name it **scale**.
3. Select the **Pen** tool. I turned on the **grid** for this part of the project. See Figure 7.30 for the general placement of the anchors and points, the final path, and the final scale shape.
   a. Click somewhere in the upper-left side of the image.
   b. Click and drag a little in the lower left of the image to create an anchor point.
   c. Click and drag between the center line and the last anchor point.
   d. Click once on the center line.
   e. Hold **Shift** and move the line straight up and click once at the top center, at the same horizontal height as the starting point.
   f. Click once on the starting point to close the path off.
4. After you have created the path and adjusted it to your liking, go to the **Paths** palette and save the path and name it "scale" so it is still there after you close the file and reopen it later.
5. Fill the path with a medium green, **RGB: 77,145,66**. **Right-click** and choose **Fill Path**.
6. Turn off the path. Go to the **Paths** palette and click outside the **path** layer.
7. Go back to the **Layers** palette and copy and paste the scale half. Flip it horizontally and line it up with the other half and merge the two layers. At this point you might not like the shape you

**Figure 7.29**
The finished book spine with runes and decoration.

**Figure 7.30**
Initial path point placement, the final half-scale path, and the final full-scale shape. Note that you click and drag where the arrows appear. This creates curved lines instead of straight ones.

created. You can either use **Free Transform** or go back and adjust your path.

8. **Filter > noise > Add noise 10%**.

9. **Filter > Blur > Gaussian Blur 1.5 pixels**.

10. Now you will use your **Dodge** and **Burn** tools, just as we did on the banner in the warehouse and on the fur recently. Start by dodging a light line down the center of the scale using a soft, **45**-pixel brush. Look at Figure 7.31 for a progression of the painted scale.

11. Dodge the edge of the scale. You can use short, choppy strokes if you don't have a graphics tablet or the ability to draw a continuous fluid line. Actually, the lumpiness of a choppy line helps the scale look more organic than a smooth line. I dodged those two extra ridges in the sides of the scale to make it more interesting.

12. Burn the outer edge of the scale and in between the highlights to build up the depth of the scale. Go slow and use this opportunity to burn in between the bright spots to get a lumpy appearance, unless you want a smooth scale.

13. Set your background color to **black**.

14. **Filter > Brush Strokes > Accent Edges**: Edge Width **10**, Edge Brightness **22**, Smoothness **3**.

15. **Filter > Brush Strokes > Spatter**: Spray Radius **8**, Smoothness **8**.

16. **Filter > Artistic > Plastic Wrap**: Highlight Strength **11**, Detail **8**, Smoothness **2**.

17. I went back and strengthened some of the highlights and shadows with Dodge and Burn again.

18. For this next step, I turned off all other layers.

19. Create a copy of this layer and hide it. You want to keep one large copy of the scale in case you need it later.

20. Use the **Free Transform** tool and size the scale down until you like the size. I made it about **200** pixels high.

21. Apply the **Drop Shadow** layer effect to the scale and change the following settings:
    Uncheck the Use Global Light option
    Opacity: 25%
    Distance: 12 px
    Size: 10 px

**Figure 7.31**
The progression of the painted scale.

22. I found it easier at this point to copy this layer and merge it with an empty layer to freeze the layer effects. You can also go to the Layers menu and Create Layers and merge the two as well. I am just in the habit of creating an empty layer and linking and merging faster than I can click through a menu.

23. **Select All** and use **Ctrl+Alt** to copy the scale on the layer. You don't want the first row of scales to touch or overlap. Lay them out on the grid with roughly half a scale space between them like in Figure 7.32. Start at the bottom and when you have a row, duplicate the layer and move it up half a scale, and center it between the scales below.

24. Merge all the scale layers together and name the layer **finished scales**. I thought my scales were too bright so I used **Ctrl+U** to lower the saturation and the lightness a bit.

25. **Filter** > **Brush Strokes** > **Spatter – Spray Radius 8, Smoothness 8.**

26. **Filter** > **Artistic** > **Plastic Wrap – Highlight Strength 9, Detail 7, Smoothness 2.**

27. **Filter** > **Brush Strokes** > **Accent Edges – Edge Width 7, Edge Brightness 22, Smoothness 2.**

28. Turn all the layers back on (except for the UV layer set and the saved scale). Mostly you want to see the metal layer and how the scales look under the metal frame of the book. **Free Transform** the scales until you like the size.

29. Go to the **metal** layer, select the empty inside of the cover with the **Magic Wand,** and invert the selection.

30. Go to the **scales** layer and press **Delete.** Your cover should look like Figure 7.33.

**Figure 7.32**
Scales laid out on the grid to create the cover. The top row of scales (1) is the first row you create. This goes at the bottom of your image. The second row (2) shows the duplicated layer placed above the first. The third row (3) shows the scales filling up the layer. You work from the bottom up, overlapping scales like a roofer laying tiles.

## Cover Symbols

We will use paths again to create the symbols on the cover. These symbols will be used again on the map, banner, and door. When you create these shapes, don't try to make them to fit the book cover; make them large so they can easily be reused.

1. Create a new layer set and name it **symbols.**
2. Create a new layer and name it **symbol.**
3. Select the **Pen** tool. I turned the grid off for this part of the project.
   a. Click somewhere in the lower-left side of the image.
   b. Click and drag in the upper-right-middle of the image to create an anchor point.
   c. Click to the right and a little lower of the last anchor point.
   d. Click down and a little to the left.
   e. Click and drag a little higher and to the left of the last point.
   f. Click once on the starting point to close the path off.
4. After you have created the first shape and adjusted it to your liking, go to the **Paths** palette and save the path as **symbol path** so it is still there after you close the file and reopen it later.
5. Fill the path with any color. **Right-click** and choose **Fill Path.**
6. Turn off the path: Go to the **Paths** palette and click outside the **path** layer.
7. Go back to the **symbol** layer and use the **Magic Wand** tool and select the shape.

**Figure 7.33**
The cover with the finished scales.

8. **Select** > **Modify** > **Contract**: Select a number of pixels to contract the selection that looks good to you. Press **Delete**.

9. To create the circular shapes on the cover, create a new layer named **circle**. Create a circular selection and fill it.

10. Snap a guideline line to the vertical and horizontal center of the circle.

11. Drag out a circular selection centered on the circle using the guides and press **Delete**.

12. To make the half-moon shape, create a new layer named **half-moon** and drag out an oval selection. Make sure that this selection is a little thicker vertically. Snap this selection to the center of the guidelines. Fill this selection.

13. Drag a circular selection out from the center of the guidelines that is a bit larger than the circle on the circle layer.

14. Press **Delete** to remove the middle of the oval and erase the remaining left portion of the shape.

15. Now you have all the shapes you need to create the symbols on the cover. Duplicate the symbols layer set and name it **cover symbols**. Now all the original large versions of the shapes are there for you to create the other textures in the scene.

16. In the cover symbols layer, copy and manipulate the shapes until they look like the symbols on the cover and merge all the layers. See Figure 7.34 for the general placement of the anchors and points, the circular shapes, and the final shape.

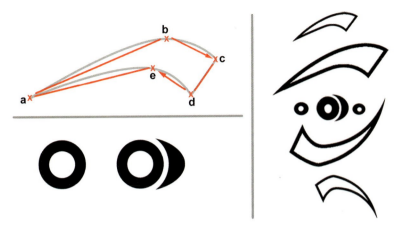

**Figure 7.34**
Initial path point placement, the circular shapes, and the final shape.

17. Apply layer effects with the following settings changed:
    Fill: 0%
    **Outer Glow:**
    **Blending Mode:** Multiply
    Opacity: 100%
    Color: Black
    Spread: 9%
    Size: 18 px
    **Bevel and Emboss Style:**
    **Inner Bevel Technique:** Chisel Soft
    Depth: 131%
    Size: 5 px
    Contour: default
    Color Overlay Color: White
    Opacity: 50%
    Gradient Overlay: default

See Figure 7.35 for the book cover with the symbols in place.

## Page Edges

The book has old, well-worn page edges. These are easily created.

1. Create a new layer set named **pages**.
2. Create a new layer named **pages**.
3. Go to the **UV Map** layer set and the **UV Map** layer and select the pages area with the **Magic Wand** tool.
4. Go to the **pages** layer and move the selection up to the middle of the canvas. Use the **Select** > **Transform Selection** command to rotate the selection **90** degrees.
5. Reset your colors (**D** key) to **black and white.**
6. Fill the selection with **black.**
7. **Filter** > **Render** > **Fibers:** Variance **10**, Strength **15**.
8. Colorize this (**Ctrl+U**): Hue **45**, Saturation **27**, Lightness **–57**.
9. Reset your colors (**D** key) to black and white and swap them (**X** key).
10. **Filter** > **Distort** > **Glass:** Distortion **4**, Smoothness **7**, Scaling **62%**.
11. Rotate the pages back horizontally and position them over the UV area for the pages.

**Figure 7.35**
The cover with the symbols in place.

12. You can use the **Burn** tool to darken the top, bottom, and side edges of the pages. See Figure 7.36 for the progression of the pages.

*Gem*

Finally, we need to make the gem for our spellbook—another easy task.

1. Create a new layer set and name it **gem**.
2. Create a new layer and name it **gem**.
3. Go to the **UV Map** layer set and select the **gem** area of the UV map.
4. Go back to the **gem** layer and fill the selection with it with any color you want. You want to use a color that's not too close to black or white. A pretty well-saturated color works best.
5. Keep the selection active or lock the layer transparency.
6. Apply layer effects with the following settings changed:
   **Inner Shadow:**
   **Blending Mode:** Multiply
   Color: Black
   Opacity: 49%
   Distance: 30 px
   Choke: 7 %
   Size: 38 px
7. Use the **Dodge** tool and lighten the lower edge of the gem.
8. Create a new layer and name it **highlights**.

**Figure 7.36**
The progression of the pages.

9.  Use a soft brush of various sizes and paint on some white highlights. Having the highlights on a separate layer allows you to edit them. Sometimes you might want to repaint them. If the highlights are too strong, you can apply a Gaussian Blur or take down the opacity. See Figure 7.37 for the stages of the gem.

A final step that makes the gem look great—that is, in other contexts, but not in this case, because the gem will be mapped to geometry— is to apply a large outer glow and a strong inner glow. Try these settings:

**Outer Glow:**
**Blending Mode:** normal
Opacity: 75%
Color: The color you chose for the gem
Spread: 10%
Size: 250 px
**Inner Glow:**
**Blending Mode:** normal
Opacity: 83%
Color: White
Choke: 3%
Size: 116 px

You are finished all the details of the spellbook. Figure 7.38 shows the final spellbook texture.

### Old Map

Now we will create the old map on the table. This map is old dark parchment with burned edges and faded ink. You can see the complex torn edges of the map and the holes in it as well. For this effect we will use an alpha channel.

1. Open a new **1024×1024** image and name it **map**. The background color should be **black**.
2. Create a new layer and name it **paper**. Fill this layer with the color **RGB: 193,166,101**.

**Figure 7.37**
The progression of the creation of the gem. The last one on the right is the gem with added effects that look great in other contexts, but not here. It's a neat trick, though.

**Figure 7.38**
The final spellbook texture.

3. **Filter** > **noise** > **Add noise 15%.**
4. **Filter** > **Blur** > **Gaussian Blur: 5 pixels.**
5. Reset your colors to black and white (**D** key).
6. **Filter** > **Render** > **Clouds.**
7. Fade the clouds (**Ctrl+F**). Opacity **20%**, Blending Mode: **Multiply**. See Figure 7.39.
8. Now we need to tear up the edges of the map. I started by making a square selection that had a 32-pixel border all the way around (I used the grid for this). Invert the selection and press **Delete**.
9. Use the eraser with a large, hard brush (**40** pixels) and erase the general outline of the torn paper (Figure 7.40).
10. Use the **9**-pixel Drippy Watercolor brush. You might have to load the **Wet Media** brushes to make the brush a little larger and start eating away the edges of the paper. I experimented with a few brushes at various sizes to get different torn edge effects. One was the Brush Heavy Flow Scatter.
11. Apply layer effects with the following settings changed:
    **Inner Glow:**
    Blending Mode: Overlay
    Opacity: 52%
    Noise: 5%
    Color: Black
    Choke: 9%
    Size: 90 px

    See Figure 7.41.

12. Create a new layer named **terrain** and set the opacity to **49%** and the blending mode to **Overlay**. Use a small black brush (**3–5** pixels) to draw some details on the map. Don't worry; they can be pretty simple. We will add more detail shortly. And don't

**Figure 7.39**
The parchment base.

**Figure 7.40**
The parchment with the beginning of a worn edge.

**Figure 7.41**
The parchment with torn and burned edges.

worry if the lines don't look like the old ink you want it to; we will process that later. You can look at Figure 7.42 to see what I drew before it was processed.

13. Now go back to the **spellbook** and copy the **symbol** layer into the map. Turn off all the layer effects and add a new one:
    Stroke Size: 1 px
    Position: inside
    Blending Mode: Overlay
    Opacity: 49%
    Color: Black

14. Now you can copy and resize a few of these symbols around the map. You can erase portions of the symbols, flip them around, do whatever you think will look good.

15. Select the **Text** tool, then select the **Tengwar-Gandalf** font and make it **82** points. Type whatever you want on the map. Make a few short lines of text, as though notes were written on the map. You might need to adjust the spacing between the letters and the lines of letters. Set the layer Fill to **0** and add the following layer effects:
    **Color Overlay:**
    Blending Mode: Color Burn
    Color: **RGB: 92,45,45**
    Opacity: 50%

16. Use the **Free Transform** tool to rotate the text up on the right side so that it looks more handwritten.

17. Create a new layer and name it **dirt**.

18. Use the **Color Picker** to set your foreground color to a color close to the map's color. Just select anywhere on the map.

19. **Filter > Render > Render Clouds**.

20. **Filter > Render > Render Difference Clouds 2X**.

21. **Filter > Blur > Gaussian Blur: 25 pixels**.

**Figure 7.42**
The terrain lines; they don't have to be too good at this point.

22. Set the layer blending mode to **Overlay** and the opacity between **40%** and **55%**, depending on how dirty you want your map. See Figure 7.43.
23. Link all the layers except for the background and create **Layer Set From Linked**.
24. Duplicate this layer set and unlink the text layer. Merge all the linked layers and make sure that the text layer is on top.
25. Select the paper layer in the original, unflattened layer set.
26. **Selection** > **Load Selection** > **Press Okay.** The proper filename and layer should be the default when the correct layer is selected.
27. Hide the unflattened layer set.
28. Invert the selection.
29. Highlight the new flattened layer with the map on it and press **Delete.**
30. **Filter** > **Brush Strokes** > **Spatter:** Spray Radius **8**, Smoothness **8**.
31. **Filter** > **Distort** > **Ocean Ripple:** Ripple Size **12**, Ripple Magnitude **4**.
32. **Filter** > **Brush Strokes** > **Accent Edges:** Edge Width **4**, Edge Brightness **24**, Smoothness **4**.
33. Turn the **text** layer back on. See Figure 7.44.
34. Create a new layer, name it **alpha,** and fill it with **black**.
35. Select the paper layer in the original, unflattened layer set.
36. **Selection** > **Load Selection**, press **OK**.
37. Turn off every layer but the new alpha layer.
38. Select the **alpha** layer and fill the selection with **white** (right mouse, Fill).

## Windows

The windows are bright, based on the light shafts, and the glass looks clean and unbroken. The colors are yellow and blue based on

**Figure 7.43**
The map getting dirty.

**Figure 7.44**
The final old and worn map.

the sun and moon symbols. The seams are the bulgy lead seams typical of stained glass. We will create an illumination map, which is simply a grayscale image based on the complete texture to be used in a shader.

1. Open the **512×512** image **fantasy_window_UV.psd** on the DVD. See Figure 7.46.

**Figure 7.45**
The alpha channel for the map.

**Figure 7.46**
UV Map template for the window.

2. This image is a UV template like the chest, only not nearly as complex. This image is rather simple to create and really simple to map onto a piece of geometry. You will notice some space to the right of the window shape—that is semi-wasted space. In a real-world scenario, we could use this for the candle flames or find another use for this space. Here the focus is creating the art itself and not laying out UV coordinates as efficiently as possible. I wanted you to be aware of this fact so that in actual practice you could address this issue.

3. Use the **Magic Wand** to select the shape.
4. Create a new layer and name it **lead**.
5. Look at Figure 7.47. You can see the pattern of the lead seams very clearly. Correcting for the angle of the drawing and given the fact that we are working from a template, we should be able to recreate this fairly easily. Also, there is no reason for this one-of-a-kind texture to be tileable, on the grid, or exact in any way. That makes recreating it a lot easier.
6. The easiest thing to create first is the frame that surrounds the glass. If your selection is no longer active, use the **Magic Wand** again to select the shape and activate the newly created lead layer.
7. Stroke the inside of the selection with a **5**-pixel black line.
8. Snap a guideline to the vertical center of the window frame and one to the horizontal center. Look at the concept art. The next easiest thing to do would be to draw the line that runs up the center of the window. Refer to Figure 7.48 for a progression of the lead seams as they are drawn.
9. Select a hard, **5**-pixel brush and draw the line up the center and go a little beyond where the guidelines meet.
10. Use the **Circular Marquee** and hold down the **Alt** and **Shift** keys to make the marquee symmetrical and to make the start point the center of the selection. Make the circular selection about **160** pixels and vertically centered on top of the straight line we just drew, like a lollipop (see Figure 7.48-A).
11. Make another circular selection as we just did, only make it about **130** pixels and move it to the left and press delete before stroking it **5** pixels (see Figure 7.48-B).
12. Select a **5**-pixel hard brush and draw a line dividing this new circle in half.
13. Make a new circular selection of about **43** pixels in the center of this line, press **Delete**, and stroke it **5** pixels (see Figure 7.48-C).

**Figure 7.47**
The stained-glass windows from the concept sketch and the finished frame we created in Photoshop.

**Figure 7.48**
A progression of the lead seams being drawn for the stained-glass window (A–D).

14. There is a cool moon/crescent moon below the large moon we made first. Make a circular selection that is **70** pixels, centered on the vertical line and just a tad under the horizontal line (see Figure 7.48-D).
15. Press **Delete** to remove the line, stroke this **5** pixels/inside, and then move the selection over to the right until the left edge snaps to the center guideline.
16. Stroke the **5** pixels on the outside of the selection.
17. Deselect and use a hard eraser to erase the unwanted outer ring of the moon. Be careful erasing where the two rings overlap.
18. All that's left to do is create those ray-like lines coming from the main moon/sun. Choose a hard, **5**-pixel brush and click a dot where you want the line to start, hold **Shift**, and click where you want it to end and you will have a straight line between the two points.

    We will apply the layer effects to the lead seams after the glass panes are in place. Logically, we need to see what's below the lead seams before we are able to tweak and adjust their layer effects.

19. The glass is easy to make now that the frame is made. Activate the **lead** layer and use the **Magic Wand** to select the areas in the frame where the darker, blue glass will be. Look at the concept art as a guide.
20. Create a new layer and name it **panes**. Fill the selection with blue: **RGB:74,90,171**.
21. Go to the lead layer and select the remaining areas inside the frame except for the small moon inside the larger moon at the top of the window and the large crescent to the right. Activate the **panes** layer and fill these spaces with yellow: **RGB: 175,172,89**.
22. Go back to the **lead** layer and select the small moon inside the larger moon and the large crescent. Activate the **panes** layer and fill these two spaces with **white** (Figure 7.49).
23. Deselect the selection.
24. Reset your colors to **black and white** (**D** key) and switch them (**X** key) so black is your background color.
25. **Filter** > **noise** > **Add noise 10%**.
26. **Filter** > **Distort** > **Glass**: Distortion **8**, Smoothness **4**, Texture Frosted, Scaling **100**.
27. **Fade Filter 50%**.
28. **Filter** > **Artistic** > **Sponge**: Brush Size **2**, Definition **2**, Smoothness **1**.
29. **Filter** > **Distort** > **Glass**: Distortion **2**, Smoothness **7**.

**Figure 7.49**
The window glass, colored.

30. **Filter** > **Artistic** > **Plastic Wrap:** Highlight Strength **13**, Detail **5**, Smoothness **2**.
31. **Fade Filter 50%, Blending Mode Vivid Light.**
32. **Filter** > **Blur** > **Gaussian Blur: 1.5 pixels**.
33. **Filter** > **Distort** > **Glass:** Distortion **3**, Smoothness **3**, Scale **58%**.
34. Add the following layer effects and change these settings:
    **Inner Shadow:**
    Distance: 6 px
    Size: 10 px
    **Inner Glow:**
    Blending Mode: Multiply
    Opacity: 59%
    Noise: 5%
    Color: Black
    Size: 24 px
    **Gradient Overlay:**
    Blend Mode: Vivid Light
    Opacity: 29%

    At this point I was happy with the blue and yellow glass, but the parts that we left white still looked too plain to me, so I selected their spaces on the lead layer and ran the ink Outlines filter on the panes layer: Stroke Length 12, Dark intensity 6, Light intensity 9.

    Meanwhile, back at the lead seams:

35. Turn on the **lead** layer and apply the following layer effects.
    **Drop Shadow:** Default settings
    **Outer Glow:**
    Blending Mode: Multiply
    Opacity: 47%

**Figure 7.50**
The final window texture.

Noise: 2%
Color: Black
Size: 32 px
**Bevel and Emboss:**
Technique: Smooth
Depth: 111%
Size: 1
**Contour:**
Cone: inverted
**Texture:**
Scale: 127%
Depth: 371%
**Gradient Overlay:**
Blend Mode: normal
Opacity: 50%
Style: Radial
Scale: 65%

See Figure 7.50 for the final window texture.

The illumination map is nothing more than a grayscale image. Black is dark and white is fully illuminated.

36. Duplicate the window image and name it **fantasy_window_illumination**.
37. On the lead layer, turn off the **Bevel and Emboss** layer effects and apply a solid black **Color Overlay** layer effect.
38. Go to the **panes** layer and desaturate it (**Ctrl+Shift+U**).
39. **Image** > **Adjustments** > **Brightness/Contrast**: **+22** brightness, **+48** contrast.

40. You will still need to use large, soft brushes of various sizes to airbrush the centers of the panes white and leave only a small amount of darkness at the edges. Figure 7.51 shows the illumination map with the texture in a dark room with and without the illumination map.

### Banner

The banner is cloth and the colors are the same as the window, but these colors will be more desaturated based on the material, the location of the banner, and its assumed adventuring history. In this exercise we will use the shapes we created for the spellbook cover, as we did on the map. We will also create new paths to define the outline of the banner. Finally, we will create the alpha channel for this banner and put a fake shadow in it. The great thing is that if you don't want the shadow, you can turn it off.

1. Open a new **1024×1024** image and name it **fantasy_banner**.
2. Create a new layer and name it **banner outline**.
3. Look at the shape of the banner in the concept sketch. We will create half of the banner using paths and then flip it. See Figure 7.52 for the shape breakdown of the banner.
4. Drag a vertical guide out to the 400-pixel mark on the canvas. Hold down **Shift** and the guide will snap every 10 pixels. We don't want to build the shape in the exact center, because we want to leave some space for the alpha-channeled objects.
5. Select the **Path** tool and drag out the shape of the banner. I detailed the creation of a shape using the Path tool a few times.

   If you don't know how to use the Path tool, go back to the relevant earlier sections of this chapter and practice on those shapes. See Figure 7.53 for the banner path click and drag points.

**Figure 7.51**
The illumination map for the window and the texture in a dark room with and without the illumination map.

**Figure 7.52**
The breakdown of the banner shape. From left to right: the banner cropped from the concept sketch, the straightened version, the half-banner path line, and the final shape.

6. Once you have half the banner outlined, you can save the path if you like. Make sure you are on the banner outline layer and still have the **Direct Select** tool selected, then **right-click** to fill the banner with blue, **RGB: 62,98,163**.

7. Turn off the path. Duplicate this layer and flip it horizontally.

8. Line up the two halves, link them, and merge them. Make sure the resulting shape is solid and that there is no seam between the two pieces. Also make sure there is enough space at the bottom between the end of the banner and the edge of the banner if you plan to put a drop shadow in.

9. **Filter** > **noise** > **Add noise 5%**.

10. **Filter** > **Brush Strokes** > **Crosshatch**: Stroke Length **31**, Sharpness **10**, Strength **1**.

11. **Filter** > **Artistic** > **Poster Edges**: Edge Thickness **1**, Edge intensity **1**, Posterization **3**.

12. **Filter** > **Blur** > **Gaussian Blur: 1.5 pixels**.

13. **Filter** > **Artistic** > **Paint Daubs**: Brush Size **6**, Sharpness **0**, Brush Type **Dark Rough**.

14. Open the **spellbook** file and find the symbols layer that has the original, large version of the shapes you created for the cover of the spellbook. Copy this layer into the banner image. If you didn't copy the entire layer set, create a new layer set so all the shapes and symbols are easily collapsed and organized later.

15. Refer to the concept art and start the process of laying out the banner shapes with the symbol shapes you already have. I was able to create all the shapes by copying the original shapes and using Free Transform. The only shape I needed to create by hand were the cross bars in the lower symbol. I took some time and filled in the circles and erased them, making them look a little more organic or handmade. See Figure 7.54 for the progression from basic shapes to the final banner decoration.

16. Collapse all the symbols onto one layer and apply layer effects with the following settings:
Fill: 0%
**Outer Glow:**
Blending Mode: Multiply
Opacity: 71%
Color: Black
Noise: 8%
Spread: 5%

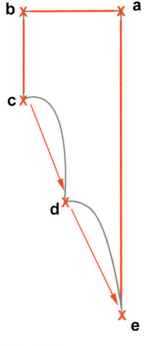

**Figure 7.53**
The click and drag points of the banner path.

**Figure 7.54**
The progression from basic shapes to the final banner decoration. Using shapes previously created saved us a lot of time presently.

Size: 29 px
**Bevel and Emboss:**
Style: Inner Bevel
Technique: Chisel Hard
Depth: 81%
Size: 5 px
Contour: default
Texture: default
**Color Overlay:**
Color: yellowish, **RGB: 178,166,38**

17. The next thing we need to make is the fringe that borders the banner. Create a new layer and name it **fringe**.
18. Go to the banner outline layer and use the **Magic Wand** to select the area outside the banner and invert the selection.
19. Go back to the **fringe** layer and stroke the selection: inner Stroke and 16 pixels.
20. Remove the very top line of the stroked outline using a hard eraser or the Selection tool (pressing the **Delete** key).
21. Copy the layer effects from the symbols layer and paste them into the layer.
22. Duplicate the fringe layer. Now we can erase the gaps in the top layer to make the border fringe look wound. You can eyeball this with a small, hard eraser or use the grid with a selection, moving the selection and pressing Delete, if you want the gaps perfectly spaced.
23. Duplicate one of the fringe layers, make sure it is on the top of the other two, and clear the contents from this layer (**Ctrl+A** and **Ctrl+X**). Change the following settings in the layer style of this layer. **Bevel and Emboss:**
Technique: Smooth
Size: 21
24. Use a 40-pixel hard brush and put the balls on the ends of the banner points. Your image should look like Figure 7.55.
25. Link all the layers except for the background and choose **Create Layer Set From Linked**.
26. Duplicate this layer set and name it **banner flat** and flatten it. Hide the original unflattened layer set.
27. **Filter** > **noise** > **Add noise 5%.** I also took the saturation and contrast down just a little on the banner.
28. **Filter** > **Artistic** > **Dry Brush:** Brush Size **3**, Brush Detail **5**, Texture **1**.
29. **Filter** > **Brush Strokes** > **Accented Edges:** Edge Width **4**, Edge Brightness **26**, Smoothness **2**.
30. To create the alpha channel and to make the drop shadow part of the texture, you need to go to the original unflattened banner layer set and duplicate it. Name it **alpha**.
31. Turn off all the **Outer Glow** layer effects in the layer set but leave the rest of the layer effects on. Flatten the alpha layer set.
32. **Select** > **Load Selection** > choose **OK**, and go back to the banner layer. Invert the selection and press **Delete**. The outer glow should disappear. Make sure that this is the only active layer if you don't see this happen.
33. We also need to create the end cap. Create a new layer and name it **end cap**.

**Figure 7.55**
The banner with the fringe on it.

34. Use the **Shape** tool with the **Fill Pixel** option chosen and set your foreground color to a **medium gray.**
35. Choose the **Fleur-De-Lis** shape and drag out a shape that fills in part of the empty space. This doesn't have to be too big and doesn't need to be constrained using the Shift key. I made mine a little longer than wide.
36. Erase the bottom three smaller tips of the shape and apply the following layer style and settings:
    **Bevel and Emboss:**
    Style: Inner Bevel
    Technique: Chisel Soft
    Depth: 111%
    Size: 27 px
    Soften: 3 px
    Contour: default
    **Texture:**
    Pattern: Satin
    Scale: 341%
    Depth: +34
    **Color Overlay:**
    Color: yellowish, **RGB: 178,166,38**
37. Duplicate the end cap layer and link it to the alpha layer and merge them.
38. Put a **solid black** color overlay on the alpha layer and a **drop shadow** to your liking. I changed only the distance (**17** px) and the Size (**21** px). If your background layer is black, you won't see any of this, so make it a light gray.
39. Create a new layer and link it to the alpha layer and merge them so that the effects are baked in and become pixels rather than an effect.
40. **Select** > **Load Selection** > **OK.**

41. Go to the **Channels** tab and create a new alpha channel. Fill the selection with white. You should only have to right-click to do this here.
42. Now the alpha channel contains the fake drop shadow. Figure 7.56 shows the banner, the alpha channel, and the banner with the alpha enacted with the faked drop shadow. And Figure 7.57 shows a couple of variations on the banner using the same technique (I used an overlay of an image for the one on the right).

### Magic Door

The door is metal and intricately carved with symbols and writing. The symbols and writing have a magical glow. The door was easier to do than I originally anticipated. By the time you get to this point in the fantasy setting you have all the shapes, symbols, and magical writing you need for the door. Plus the curves you see in the door are not made by you with paths; they are part of the model and hence part of the UV map.

1. Open the image from the CD/DVD named **fantasy_door_UV_Map.psd**. See Figure 7.58.
2. You'll see the familiar setup, the UV map, and the labels for the parts.

**Figure 7.56**
Left to right: the banner, the alpha channel, and the banner with the alpha enacted showing the fake drop shadow.

**Figure 7.57**
A couple of variations on the banner using the same technique (I used an overlay of an image for the one on the right).

3. Paste the base metal in you made for the fantasy setting on the top of the stack of layers and name it **metal**.
4. Duplicate the metal layer and name it **door frame**.
5. Turn both layers off and go to the UV map and select the frame, select similar, and invert the selection.
6. Select the **door frame** layer to turn it on and press **Delete**.
7. Apply layer styles with the following settings changed:
   **Drop Shadow:**
   Blend Mode: Multiply
   Opacity: 53%
   Distance: 6 px
   Size: 18 px
   **Outer Glow:**
   Blend Mode: Linear Burn
   Opacity: 19%
   Noise: 17%
   Color: Black
   Size: 65 px
   **Bevel and Emboss:**
   Technique: Smooth
   Depth: 151%
   Size: 9
   Highlight Mode Opacity: 57%
   Shadow Mode Opacity: 57%
   **Texture:**
   Pattern=Molecular, Scale=537%, Depth= +95
8. Now we will create the magical writing all over the door. Create a new layer set and name it **writing**.
9. Select the **Text** tool and the **Tengwar-Gandalf** font. Make it **35** pt.
10. Type whatever you want and then use the **Warp Text** tool to fit the text into the spaces in the door. This is a trial-and-error process. You have to experiment with more or fewer letters and

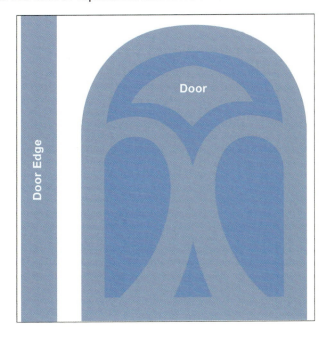

**Figure 7.58**
UV map template for the magic door.

different warp settings. I also used the Character Palette and adjusted the tracking (horizontal spaces between letters) and moved the letters closer to each other. See Figure 7.59 for the layout of the text on the door.

11. When you have placed all the text, select one layer and apply layer styles with the following settings changed:
**Outer Glow:**
Blend Mode: Color Burn
Opacity: 24%
Color: Black
Technique: Precise
Size: 9 px
**Bevel and Emboss:**
Style: Outer Bevel
Technique: Chisel Soft
Depth: 127%
Direction: Down
Size: 2
Highlight Mode Opacity: 69%
Shadow Mode Opacity: 74% Color Overlay

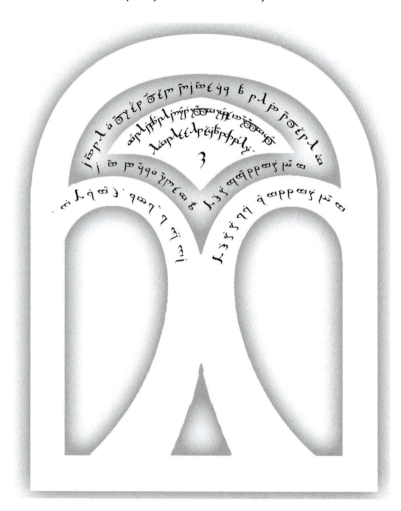

**Figure 7.59**
Placing the text on the door is a trial and error process, but well worth the effort.

Blend Mode: normal
Color: **RGB: 167,255,239**

12. Link all the text layers, copy the layer style from the initial text layer, and select **Paste Layer Style to Linked**.
13. The shapes on the door are the last thing to do. You can open the shapes you saved elsewhere and paste them into a layer set named **shapes** and manipulate them with the **Freeform Tool** and **Liquify**, or you can easily create these shapes using paths, or even the circular selection tool. For the little shapes toward the bottom, I used a few brushes so there would be variety and interest there. See Figure 7.60 for the layout of the door shapes.
14. Once one side of the door is complete, you can duplicate the layer, flip it horizontally, position it, and alter it a little so that it looks more interesting and not like a perfect mirror of the other side.
15. Copy the layer style from the text layers, paste it onto this layer, and change the following settings:
    **Color Overlay:**
    Blend Mode: Vivid Light
    Opacity: 47%

**Figure 7.60**
The layout of the shapes on the door.

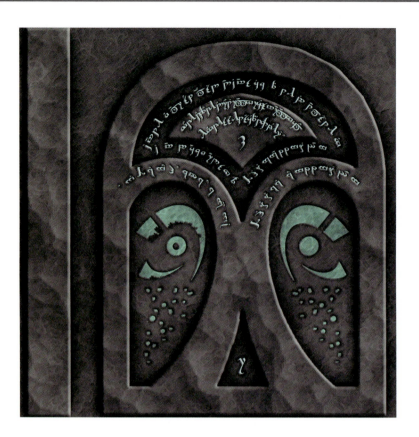

**Figure 7.61**
The final magical door
texture.

16. See Figure 7.61 for the final door. You may notice that there is
the door edge to the left; that is a simple layer shape based on
the UV map with the layer Fill set to 0 and a Bevel and Emboss
applied.

## Tearing It Down for Shaders

### *Pitcher and Goblet Set*

The pitcher and goblet are made of fine metal with inset gems.
Although highly polished, these vessels have seen their share of
use and bear many dents and scratches. To get a reflective gold
metal that has bumps and scratches in the surface—ones that look
real—we need to use a shader. Shaders are becoming very common.
In fact I don't think there is a game today on any console or desktop
computer that doesn't use some form of shader. Even games on
mobile devices that look like traditional 2D games often use the 3D
capabilities of the hardware and software for the game. I discussed
shaders way back in the beginning of the book, defining the term and
looking at some visual examples. I noted that as artists, we are most
often concerned with the input and the output of the shader and not
the code itself. One of the primary tasks you will perform as an artist
will be to create several images that the shader will use to process
various real-time effects. You will often redo these images and adjust
them until you get the visual results you want.

We will use this part of the fantasy scene to take the creation of a basic shader step by step. If you are not familiar with shaders, you might be surprised at how simple some of them can be. Not to oversimplify a potentially very complex topic, but most of the common shaders are fairly easy to work with. In this case we will use a common shader that uses the following map types:

- Diffuse (or color) map: Contains almost exclusively color information
- Bump mapping: Grayscale image that simulates bumps and scratches
- Environment (or cube) map: A series of images used to fake a reflection
- Environment mask: Grayscale image that alters the reflective value of the cube map

I will not step you through the creation of these maps. Based on their simplicity and what you have already learned in this book, making them should be easy for you. Let's look at the pitcher before any visual information is applied. In Figure 7.62 you can see that this is a relatively simple mesh.

## Diffuse Map

The diffuse map is what most people are talking about when they use the word *texture*. Previously, the diffuse map contained virtually all the visual information that would be applied to the 3D geometry of a game. The diffuse map is still referred to as a texture, but more commonly it is again being referred to as the diffuse map or color map, since it now contains virtually nothing but color information. See Figure 7.63 for the diffuse map and the map applied to the pitcher. Notice how plain it is.

In this book we created textures that contained all of the visual information pertaining to an object or surface: color, highlight, shadow. Having all this visual information painted into the image, and therefore static or nonreactive to the environment, is often referred to as *baking*, as in, "The shadows are baked into this texture." The techniques in this book don't bake the visual information into the source image; therefore, you can easily go back and split out the visual information before flattening the PSD file to make maps for a shader. Learning to paint a texture is the best way to get the strong basis you will need to create effective shaders. You can't rely on technology; shaders are a tool and not a replacement for artists.

## Bump Map

Bump mapping makes the surface of the texture appear to be … bumpy. White on the bump map represents the highest parts of the surface and black the lowest. You can use bump maps to simulate etched letters with solid black and hard edges, or dents with lighter gray and soft edges. The bump map adds detail that makes the geometry look far more detailed than it really is. See Figure 7.64

**Figure 7.62**
The pitcher mesh before we apply any visual information.

**Figure 7.63**
The diffuse map and the diffuse map applied to the pitcher. Notice how plain it is. Now that shaders process many visual details in real time; we don't need to add this detail to the texture.

**Figure 7.64**
The bump map for the pitcher and the pitcher with the bump map applied. White represents the highest parts of the surface and black the lowest. To the far right is the pitcher with the diffuse and bump map applied.

for the bump map of the pitcher and the pitcher with the bump map applied. Notice that the letters are solid black with hard edges and the dents are softer and lighter in color, so they are not as harsh and deep as the letters. You can also see in Figure 7.65 the effect of using high- and low-resolution images for the bump map.

**Figure 7.65**
The resolution of the bump map image affects the outcome. A low-resolution image was used for the bump map on the left and a high-resolution image for the one on the right.

### Environment or Reflection Map (Cube Mapping)

We will create a reflective surface on our pitcher using an environment or reflection map. The environment map uses a series of images called a *cube map* to fake the reflection on the surface of an object. Cube maps, as mentioned earlier, are so named because the reflections you see are actually six images arranged in a cube. These images are rendered from the spot the reflective object is located, so the cube map reflects the object's surroundings accurately. These six images cover all directions: up, down, front, back, left, and right. Ideally they will all line up, meaning that the images meet at the edges so the reflection is seamless. The images of the cube map are most commonly static, or always the same. If you are looking into a reflection created by a static cube map, you won't see yourself (or your in-game character).

This is the most efficient way to handle cube mapping, but there are also other techniques for generating real-time reflections. One of those techniques is called *dynamic cube mapping*. This method redraws the six images in the cube map every frame. If the object mapped with the environment map moves or something in the environment around it moves, the cube maps are updated to render an accurate reflection in real time. See Figure 7.66 for an illustration of the (static) cube map as it was created for this scene and Figure 7.67 for the cube maps arranged as if the cube were folded open like a box. If you don't have access to a 3D package, you can also use an image of clouds, or a blurry nondescript image, for a cube map.

**Figure 7.66**
The six images that form the cube map were rendered from the location of the pitcher so the metal looks as though it is reflecting its surroundings.

**Figure 7.67**
The six images that form the cube map arranged as if the cube were folded open like a box.

Figure 7.68 shows the pitcher with only the cube map applied in its initial state. The cube map is clear and reflecting at 100%.

Because this metal pitcher has seen a good deal of use, the metal shouldn't reflect like a mirror, so there are several things we can do to make this reflection look much more realistic. First I blurred the cube maps so the reflection appears less crisp and mirror-like. I also desaturated the images a little. Figure 7.69 shows the pitcher with a blurred and desaturated cube map.

**Figure 7.68**
The pitcher with only the cube map applied in its initial state. The cube map is clear and reflecting at 100%.

**Figure 7.69**
The pitcher with the blurred and desaturated cube map.

**Figure 7.70**
The pitcher with the color map, bump map, and reflection active.

At this point, if you turn on your color map and bump map, you will see the pitcher taking shape.

The final step that adds a final level of realism and finishes this surface off nicely is a mask for the reflection. This mask determines how strong various parts of the reflection are based on grayscale values. White is fully reflective and black is matte, or nonreflective. I used some light-gray areas so that the pitcher looks well worn. Figure 7.71 shows the progression of the pitcher from simple mesh to finished product. You will notice the gems in the concept art and the final scene. These were smaller, red diffuse maps, but used the same environment map as the pitcher.

## The Complete Scene/Variation

That's the end of the fantasy setting. Here is the complete scene using all the textures you created (Figure 7.73). And as I mentioned in the beginning of the chapter, the medieval setting is simply the fantasy setting stripped down (Figure 7.74).

## Chapter Exercises

1. Create a set of textures that make this setting look as if an evil person lives here. Consider color, shape, and other visual clues that might tell an observer what type of person lives here.

**Figure 7.71**
The pitcher with the final detail, masking the reflection.

**Figure 7.72**
The pitcher in all of its stages.

2. Create a stone floor with smaller stones.
3. Create three variations of a wall based on the information in the section "Plaster or Light Stucco." Can you create a stucco that's falling away from boards?
4. Paint a fur rug that is from a shorter-haired creature with a pattern like a tiger or zebra. What about a yeti fur? This would affect the shape of the skin.
5. Create a chest texture that is all metal—and looks good.
6. Create a spellbook texture that has some or all of the following differences: different shapes for the metal parts, differently colored and shaped dragonscales, color the metal like gold

**Figure 7.73**
Here is the complete scene using all the textures you created.

**Figure 7.74**
As I mentioned in the beginning of the chapter, the medieval setting is simply the fantasy setting stripped down

or brass. Try wood and various other surfaces instead of dragonscales.

7. Create a map that has different burn patterns and tears, a different mapped location, and for one extra Schrute buck, paint folds into the map and make it look like it is hanging on a wall. Go back to Chapter 6 if you need to review how to do this.

8. Windows: Create your own window pattern. Create an illumination map for the window texture.

9. The door: Try creating this out of various materials and try different runes or symbols on the door. Can you make it look like an evil door, a good door, or a total mystery?

# Chapter 8

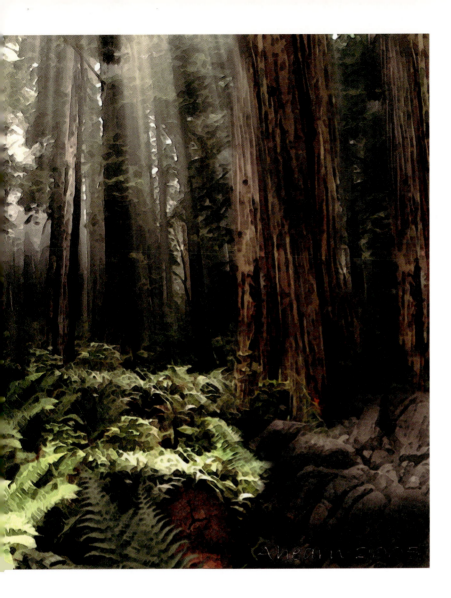

Forest Concept, 2005, by Luke Ahearn

# The Outdoor Setting

## Introduction

In this chapter, we will create a set of textures for a forest that can be altered to look spooky, friendly, or fanciful. Using the basic approach presented here, you can also create a similar simple set of textures for any outdoor environment: jungle, desert, and so on. I will also introduce the use of photo sources in texture creation. I mentioned in the very beginning of the book that the use of a photo source to create textures is not only common but also preferred. It makes your job faster and easier and gives your textures an extra layer of richness that can take a lot of time to achieve otherwise. I find that using overlays when creating assets for the outdoor environment is particularly useful. The surface of a rock, the bark on a tree, and the veins in a leaf are all challenging to create for most, whether by hand or in Photoshop—or are time-consuming at the very least. Using an overlay of a real leaf over a solid leaf shape will create a better texture quicker than either hand-creating the leaf or trying to manipulate a digital image into a workable asset.

With overlays, you still use the same workflow as in all the previous chapters. Although working with overlays may take the most time and tweaking, they are generally added later in the creation process, after a good foundation is laid. Using digital imagery will greatly enhance and speed up your work, but you don't want it to be a crutch that you must always lean on. You should look on using photo sources as primarily the icing on the cake, not the whole meal.

Texturing a large, foliated outdoor environment can be challenging, but once you break the task down to its basic elements, a game environment can be fairly easy to create. The distinction here is that we are building a game environment, not a real environment. A real outdoor environment has many species of trees and plants, all with specific details. All we have to do is make the game space look good and look believable. To do this, we need to understand what should be in a certain environment, and for the game artist the focus is mainly on color and shape. We do need to have some degree of accuracy, which we can obtain from pictures, but ultimately the environment we will create will not stand up to the scrutiny of a botanist.

## The Concept Sketch

Creating assets for the outdoor setting can be fun because it can actually be simpler than creating assets for most other types of game settings and net more impressive results. We are now experiencing truly impressive outdoor environments in games, due to technological advancement. Remember when 3D games were set in confined spaces such as hallways? As computers become more powerful, things will keep opening up and we will continue to see more of the outdoors. Already we are seeing impressive outdoor spaces being built for games, with expansive terrain and high-poly-count models, and things are only getting better.

These large, impressive, and elaborate environments can be challenging to create in many ways, but they are also actually easier to create compared to just a few years ago. Partly this is due to the fact that most outdoor environments consist of similar elements (grass, dirt, leaves, bark, and stone), and a good set of assets can go a long way if they are used correctly with newer technology. A relatively small set of textures can be mapped to an equally small set of meshes and then the models placed, rotated, scaled, and arranged to produce an enormous amount of variety. This technology alone gives us the ability to create a more convincing forest or jungle. But the major reason that creating outdoor environments is now easier is that the tools are more powerful, more refined, and more user-friendly. Some game engines allow for the combining of multiple layers of textures on terrain in a manner similar to how Photoshop handles layers. This approach allows the terrain textures to be composed predominantly of one material and therefore makes them easier to tile. Add to this the fact that we are also able to use much larger textures and you can get some really great-looking outdoor environments.

It used to be that the terrain mesh was tiled with one (smaller) texture and if you wanted something like a road or dirt patch, you had to create various versions of that one texture to place on specific polygons on the terrain where you wanted the road to run or the dirt patch to appear. This was limiting, to say the least; roads ran in straight lines and right angles and you had to create a separate texture for any unique terrain detail. Now we can create a few large textures of a specific terrain material (packed dirt, grassy dirt, dried dirt, grass, dead grass) and paint them onto the terrain. You can lay down a base layer of grass on your terrain and paint on darker grass patches, add an organic winding dirt road—you can create any type of terrain you can imagine. Painting and erasing layers on terrain is easy and the results are superior to any previous technique.

The front plate shows a pretty typical forest with towering trees and ferns. In addition to the obvious tree bark and ferns, we also need to create assets for the rocks, branches, ground, and the end of the log in the lower-right corner. You can even see the sky, so we will need to create that, too, and that involves a bit more planning and a different technique than typical texture mapping.

I did a few quick color studies of this environment. The goal with the initial concept was to create a neutral location—just a plain forest. These variations are intended to explore the potential of the environment using various color schemes. I would use one of these color studies as a guide when texturing and lighting a scene to recreate the feel of the study. In addition to spooky/dark/desaturated and happy/bright/colorful, I created a bleak, dreary place that is more emotionally disturbing than scary. Altering the concept art was easier than altering all the textures and loading them into a game editor or 3D application to see the results (see Figure 8.1).

**Figure 8.1**
A few quick color studies. Upper image: a bleak, dreary place that is more emotionally disturbing than scary. Middle image: happy/bright/colorful; and bottom: spooky/dark/desaturated.

## Breaking Out the Materials in the Scene

This set will contain the following:

- Forest floor
- Tree bark
- Tree branches
- End of log
- Rock
- Ferns

### *Forest Floor*

This concept art is a visual guide for the look and feel the environment should have, but it isn't a game-specific piece of art.

Sometimes, as a specific location of a world is being designed, you will start creating assets for it and will have information based only on a piece of art that is a representation of the look and feel of the game. We need to anticipate and create the assets most likely needed for a game world based on a look-and-feel piece. So, although you can't see it, the ground needs to be created, because it is pretty likely that in a game the player will see the ground.

In a dense forest like this, the ground tends to be covered with a dark, moist, matted blanket of rotting vegetation. For this texture, I started with an image of the ground after rain. I added an image of some dead grass on top of this. Even though the grass looks dead and dry in the original image, it worked great because of the contrast. When overlaid, it looks as though the grass occasionally grew but died and matted down with the rest of the forest floor. In addition, I created a texture that I could use as a path through the trees. A path will be worn, packed dirt, but also needs to blend into the scene in terms of color, contrast, and so on. I created a new image and used a third image of some packed dirt with small rocks in it on top of a copy of the forest floor texture. I blurred the forest floor to get the overall color and general feel of the ground (the subtle pattern of the forest floor remains; see Figure 8.2). I made this image a bit lighter because it is dirt in the open and would be drier. You also need a little contrast so that the path stands out. See Figure 8.3.

## Tree Bark

Tree bark is actually a bit hard to photograph digitally. It is usually found in less than ideal lighting conditions, and it is wrapped around a cylindrical shape. This means that even though you can see about half of the trunk facing you, only a small portion of the bark is actually positioned facing you straight on. I used the Fiber filter, stretched the image vertically, used Liquify to make some fine adjustments (as we did with the wood crate in Chapter 6), and colorized the image. See Figures 8.4 and 8.5 for the progression of the tree bark.

## Tree Branches

For the tree branch, I used a digital photo of a branch with no leaves on it that I was able to capture with only the contrasting blue sky behind it. I used the Extraction tool (under the Filter menu) and took the background out. I did have to do a little clean-up with the eraser, but not too much, and I colorized the branch. I took another digital image of a close-up of the redwood needles and did the same. I copied and pasted this only a few times. I made an alpha channel by selecting the transparency of the merged branch elements the way we have done previously. See Figures 8.6 and 8.7 for the progression of the branch and the evolving scene.

At this point I started to adjust my color and lighting a bit to more closely match the concept art. I tend to work on the dark side. As you build textures you may find that you have certain pitfalls that you gravitate toward, so be sure to refer to the concept art often to make sure you are on track (see Figure 8.8). I also added the tree line backdrop. I used a

**Figure 8.2**
The progression of the forest
floor and path texture.

photo and the same steps as I used to create the branch (Figure 8.9). In
order to work, a tree line backdrop must be where the player can never
get to it and usually needs to be desaturated and darkened to emulate
the color and luminance that we lose with distance.

### End of Log

To create the end of the log, I used a digital image of—that's right—
the end of a log. I enhanced the image with the sketch filter (circles);
see Figure 8.10.

### Rock

The rock texture was simply a colorized image of some rock.
I lowered the contrast and saturation, and I made it tile. Actually,

**Figure 8.3**
The beginning of the scene with only the terrain in place.

**Figure 8.4**
The progression of the tree bark.

**Figure 8.5**
The next stage: trees. They are usually added after the branches are on them, but I wanted you to see the stages of the texturing.

**Figure 8.6**
The progression of the tree branches. Left: the original image; second: the extracted branch; third: the cleaned-up and rotated branch; far right: the final branch texture.

**Figure 8.7**
The evolving scene with the branches added to the trees.

**Figure 8.8**
The scene with the tree line backdrop added and some color corrections to more closely match the concept art.

I made it seamless. It technically doesn't tile, because I left the bottom of the texture darker to simulate shadow and moisture, as though the boulders were sitting in the ground a long time. If this texture were tiled across a large surface, you would see the repeating pattern. This texture was made specifically to be wrapped around the boulders (Figure 8.11).

**Figure 8.9**
The tree line backdrop: a photo, the Extract tool, and a little bit of work with the eraser.

## *Ferns and the Complete Scene*

The ferns were all made from one fern leaf, just like the tree branch (Figure 8.12). I went outside, digitally photographed a fern leaf, extracted it in Photoshop, and created an alpha channel. Figure 8.13 shows the final scene with the ferns in place.

## Additional Information: the Sky

A good sky adds a lot to the feeling of depth and atmosphere in a virtual world, even if only glimpsed through trees in a scene like this one, but it's almost not worth having one at all if it is poorly implemented. If there are mistakes in the sky (the player can see

**Figure 8.10**
The scene with the fallen tree added and the end of log progression inset.

**Figure 8.11**
The stone texture progression and the scene with boulders in place.

seams, for example), the illusion is shattered. Typically, in a game, the sky is handled a few ways:

- Single image
- Sky dome
- Skybox

The single-image technique is used in only a few games (generally older ones) that have a limited view of the world. Most older 3D

**Figure 8.12**
The fern texture progression. Upper left: the original image; upper right: the extracted fern; lower left: the cleaned-up fern frond; lower right: the final fern texture.

**Figure 8.13**
Here is the final scene with the ferns in place.

games and many driving games kept players on a certain path. You were in some form of a 3D world, but your view was restricted to a 2D plane; you could look only left and right, not up and down (you could often walk up and down stairs but could not tilt the camera to look up at the sky). These games used an equally limited technique for the sky: A single image moved only left to right and up and down as the player moved about the world. I won't step you through this technique, simply because it is rarely used, if at all, in any game of quality. With mobile gaming exploding in popularity, it may well become prevalent again; nevertheless, if you can create one panel of a skybox, you have the required asset for this technique.

The sky dome technique is simply a fixed model that is part of the game map and is large enough to encase the entire world. This approach is referred to as a sky "dome" because typically a dome shape looks best using this approach, but you can also use a simple cube (if it works) and save a lot of polygons. Mapping a texture to a dome is easier, whereas a cube requires more tweaking to get things to look right. See Figure 8.14 for an illustration of the sky dome and Figure 8.15 for an example of a skybox with a seam showing. Personally, I don't like this method, for several reasons; it's harder to work in the map with the sky in the way, and if I hide the sky dome, the level doesn't look like it will in the game and it's harder to accurately judge the work that I am producing. In the game the dome is also a physical limit, and the player has to be kept away from it. This isn't at all conducive to the larger worlds that we are able/required to create today, especially those worlds on the scale of a present-day/near-future massively multiplayer online (MMO).

The skybox technique is actually a separate area in a map (like a little room) with only the sky elements in it. There is a camera centered in the area that doesn't move but swivels in the same direction the player looks. What this camera sees in the sky box is composited with what the player sees, and the result is impressive. I like this method because it is easier to work with, you get better results, and the player can walk forever and never reach it or can view it from an angle where it doesn't look its best. Because the sky moves with the

**Figure 8.14**
The sky dome is a fixed model that is part of the game map and is large enough to encase the entire world. This approach is called a sky "dome" because typically a dome shape looks best with this approach, but you can also use a simple cube (if it works) and save a lot of polygons.

**Figure 8.15**
The sky dome, using a cube. The seam can often show.

player, you can control precisely how it looks to them. It is easier to get a skybox looking perfect from one angle than every conceivable angle. See Figure 8.16 for an illustration of how the skybox works.

## Additional Information: Terrain

Although it's not texture creation, I wanted to go over a few aspects of outdoor creation that often fall to the artist and do have some overlap or similarities to texture creation. Basic terrain creation and editing are common to most game tools, and there are three general ways to create terrain for games: manually using a 3D application, using tools in a game editor, and using a terrain generator. You usually end up relying on one way and using the others in the course of your work. Because in-game terrain tools are usually tailored to that game/game engine and combine basic

**Figure 8.16**
Number **1**: The camera is in its own location and swivels to look where the player looks, but it doesn't move. Number **2**: The view of what the skybox camera sees. Number **3**: The players' view with no sky. Number **4**: The sky and players' view composited together.

terrain-editing features with proprietary features, we will first look at the basics of terrain creation, followed by a brief discussion of terrain-creation software. After you understand the basics of terrain editing, you should be able to quickly pick up almost any terrain in-game editor.

## Manual Terrain Creation

Creating terrain manually can be tedious; it's great if you are on a budget or simply don't need an overly large or elaborate piece of terrain. Manual creation involves a few basic operations that can be used alone or in conjunction with each other: forming the terrain mesh using a displacement map, sculpting the mesh by hand, and using application specific tools to manipulate the mesh. You can also hand-paint the displacement map, but that takes a great deal of time and skill. I believe that you are better off working on the mesh directly. Importing a rough displacement map is useful if you need to build terrain that fits a certain map (Figure 8.17) and work from there.

First, let's look at using a displacement map to distort a mesh. This is a pretty simple concept. Basically, a grayscale map is used to determine the height of any given point on a mesh. This is best understood in illustration—Figure 8.18 shows samples of displacement maps and the effect they would have on a mesh. You can see that the finer the transition is from black to white, the smoother the physical transition on the mesh. What makes hand-painting terrain so challenging is that each shift in grayscale is a change in elevation. You can see how the slightest shade difference can cause an ugly artifact in your mesh (Figure 8.19). In this case, the artifacts were caused by extreme image compression.

When you need to hand-manipulate terrain in a traditional 3D application such as Max or Maya, there are many tools to help you and each program has different tool sets. Maya has a set of mesh-sculpting tools, and Max has features such as soft selection and paint deformation. So, you can import a height map (Figure 8.20), manipulate it by hand (Figure 8.21), and apply various modifiers to it as well (Figure 8.22). Modifiers can include noise, ripples, waves, meting, relaxing, and much more. Modifiers tend to affect an entire mesh, but in Max you can use soft selection to apply the modifier to a portion of the mesh and have the effects fade out with the soft selection (Figure 8.23).

## Terrain Editing Basics

Like any mesh, terrain is composed of polygons and pixels and has resolution (Figure 8.24). The big difference in this mesh is the way the game engine handles it due to its size and intended use. And, because it is mesh, you can manipulate the vertices and polygons in much the same way. Note that there is a difference between

**Figure 8.17**
Importing a rough height map.

the resolution of the mesh and the resolution of the height map: Both affect the end result of the terrain (Figure 8.25). The mesh is composed of polygons, and the more polygons, the smoother the mesh. The height map is composed of pixels, and the more pixels, the finer the control it has over the mesh. Thus, if one of these is low quality, that will be reflected in the other.

The basic tool for terrain editing is a brush much like the brush in Photoshop. You can determine the overall size of the brush and the hardness of the brush. The softer the brush, the more gradual the slope of the terrain. In Figure 8.26, you can see the effect of various brush settings. This is an important concept to understand, because so much of terrain manipulation and painting is based it.

## Freeform Terrain Painting

With the brush, you can physically manipulate the terrain to achieve various effects. Most simply, you can raise or lower your terrain, as in the brush example. But there is a lot more that you can do. Keep

**Figure 8.18**
Height map.

in mind that we are not talking about textures or any other aspect besides the physical shape of the terrain mesh.

### Push/Pull Lower/Raise

You can set the size and softness of the brush as well as strength. This allows for the subtle manipulation of the surface or a radical change in the surface (Figure 8.27).

### Smoothing/Erosion

Another useful effect is smoothing or erosion. This differs from a simple lowering of the brush in that it smoothes the angles between polygons instead of just lowering them from the center of the brush (Figure 8.28). A good terrain editor will mimic actual erosion, which will look better than a simple smoothing of polygons. The distinction is that the smooth effect occurs mathematically, opening up the angles on the affected polygons, whereas actual erosion pulls material down and piles it up below the brush (Figure 8.29).

**Figure 8.19**
Mesh artifact.

**Figure 8.20**
Importing a height map.

## Noise/Turbulence

Another simple but useful ability is adding random noise or
turbulence to your terrain (Figure 8.30). After shaping and
smoothing, your terrain may look too smooth and need some random
movement along the surface. Of course, there are settings that will
determine the area and strength of the effect, and often there is even
a choice of which mathematical algorithm to use when calculating
the turbulence.

**Figure 8.21**
Hand manipulation.

**Figure 8.22**
Modifiers applied to mesh.

**Figure 8.23**
Modifiers fading out using
soft selection.

**Figure 8.24**
Same height map with terrain of varied resolution.

**Figure 8.25**
Same terrain mesh with height maps of varied resolution.

**Figure 8.26**
The Terrain Brush and various settings. Notice how the brush works: everything inside the inner circle is affected 100%, and everything outside the larger outer circle is not affected at all. The area between the two is where the terrain-editing effect transitions between 0 and 100 percent.

**Figure 8.27**
The same brush with different strength settings.

**Figure 8.28**
Most terrain editors allow for a smoothing or eroding function to help you shape your terrain.

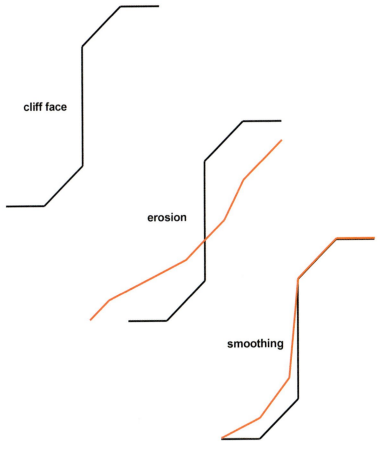

cliff face

erosion

smoothing

**Figure 8.29**
Smoothing versus erosion.

SIMPLE PULL RAISES TERRAIN

NOISE ADDED

**Figure 8.30**
Adding random movement
along the surface.

## Flatten/Set to Height

Sometimes you might want to establish a part of your terrain as a
flat, inorganic space where a building may be located, for example.
Terrain editors allow for the flattening of polygons, and you can

usually choose to flatten the terrain to a certain height that you enter numerically or to the height of the first polygon that you select before you start flattening the terrain (Figure 8.31). For the jungle river in the illustration, I flattened the terrain along the river path so that the water table would be clearly visible to me and then eroded the banks of the riverbed.

### Other Features

Good terrain editors also allow for the creation of terrain features such as cliffs and steppes. Most are starting to support tools that aid in the creation of roads (Figure 8.32).

### Terrain Texturing

At its most basic, terrain texturing is done using several tiling textures of the surfaces most common to the environment you are creating. The textures are stacked like layers in Photoshop and either alpha-channeled or combined to make a single large texture. Many large terrains in a game are using several maps just for the base level of texture: one large low-resolution color map; a smaller set of higher-detailed color maps that are chopped into tiles and loaded and displayed only when the player is on the section of the terrain that needs it; and a smaller, highly detailed map that is often a bump or normal map for the area immediately around the player where such fine detail would be appreciated (Figure 8.33).

The terrain texture can be painted by hand in the terrain editor or generated by the terrain editor. Hand-painting terrain is much like working with Photoshop layers.

**Figure 8.31**
Flattening terrain.

**Figure 8.32**
Road created in a terrain
editing program.

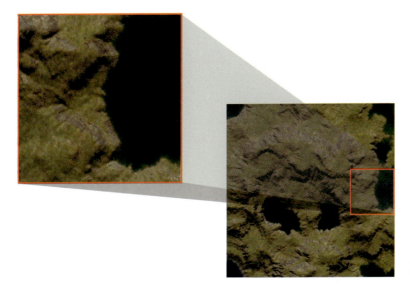

**Figure 8.33**
Terrain texture map tiles.

## Terrain Generation Software

There are many programs that can generate terrain for you, and
they range in price from very costly to free and differ according to
intended use. Some, like Bryce 3D and Vue, are designed for high-
detail renders and not real-time gaming; they use some very complex
code that simulates various real-life behaviors. Still others are
barely more than mesh manipulators that allow for layered painting
on terrain. The reason that game developers are ill served by both
of these tools is that the high-end tools do not produce assets
easily used in games and the others generate vast terrains that
programmatically and generally lack the degree of close-up control
the game developer needs. The simplified terrain-editors require
that every inch of the terrain be hand-crafted or that information
from other sources be imported to aid the developer and save them
from creating the entire terrain by hand. So, on one hand there is not
enough fine detail control, and on the other we have all the control
and lack tools that can speed up and enhance our work.

### L3DT (Large 3D Terrains)

L3DT is a Windows application for generating artificial terrain maps and textures developed by Aaron Torpy, the proprietor of Bundysoft. There is a free standard version and a very reasonably priced professional version. The standard version can do a lot, and it is free to use commercially. L3DT was developed primarily for game developers making large worlds typical of massively multiplayer online (MMO) games, but the artist can use this as well to generate terrain for other uses.

I have found that L3DT serves the game developer best. This application can generate a terrain and all associated maps (height, normal, light map) and output the mesh and textures in various formats. It also allows for the up-close editing and control needed by the developer. Even the auto-generation can be controlled to a great degree by the developer, as you will see. The most impressive aspect of this terrain generator is the wizard that walks you through all the steps of terrain generation.

The best thing about L3DT is that it supports several modes of operation. You can set a few general parameters and let the program do all the work, and you can also manually edit your map and use a design map after the fact. The design map is the middle ground between vast uncontrolled terrain generation and tediously pushing every vertex where you want it and painting every pixel. The design map lets you paint the attributes of your terrain in broad strokes. You can determine the shape of the terrain as well as specify where things like mountains, plateaus, and volcanoes go. You can add or subtract height, place cliffs, increase or decrease erosion, and more. When L3DT generates the terrain, it looks at your design map and generates the fine details from there. There is even a terrain wizard that walks you through the steps of creating your terrain from the design map to the finished texture and everything in between. Quick steps to create a small simple map by simply clicking a few buttons are shown in Figure 8.34.

**Figure 8.34**
Basic L3DT steps.

Figure 8.35 shows a map created using the same parameters as in Figure 8.34, but the design map has been changed to include one place where the terrain is higher and more jagged. A larger, more radically altered map is shown in Figure 8.36. Using the design map, I painted in a lower valley with the temperate climate in the middle of this arctic wasteland.

L3DT also supports the common editing tools discussed previously. You can shape and sculpt your terrain, and use tools like the road builder and erode brush. Figure 8.37 illustrates the tools in action. And when you are finished, you can recalculate the associated maps, including the light, normal, and texture maps. In Figure 8.38 you can see how altering the terrain in various fashions produces a different texture. A flat surface is grassy, a smooth hill is slightly eroded, and at a steeper angle you get exposed rock. Note that I lowered the terrain below the water table; the area is filled with water and the textures reflect it. The shores are sandy and the terrain under the water is darkened and tinted based on the depth of the water.

The ability to control the climate is extensive. You can auto-generate the climate, alter it on the design map, and even create your own climates and save them as presets (like you can most other aspects of the terrain). The climate modeler distributes textures in a realistic fashion; this includes fresh and salt water effects. In Figure 8.39, you can see that the same terrain has had its climate changed and rerendered. The water can be automatically and manually designed using the water-flooding aspects of the program or tweaking it all

**Figure 8.35**
One design map parameter changed.

**Figure 8.36**
More radically altered map using the design map.

**Figure 8.37**
Road builder, erode, and other common functions in L3DT. Note that the erosion looks like real-world erosion—the material has slid down to fill the area below. This is not just a smoothing algorithm.

by hand. And this is not a simple water plane that fills the entire world at one level. It is possible to have an island on the sea with a mountain lake on a higher elevation (Figure 8.40).

L3DT was designed to generate vary large maps. The free standard version has a cap on the map size, but the professional version allows for maps up to 131,072 × 131,072 pixels in size for the height map and 2M × 2M for the texture. You don't need gigs of RAM for

**Figure 8.38**
Texture calculated by angle, depth, climate, and other factors. This is all done automatically by L3DT.

**Figure 8.39**
Same terrain in different parts of the world: temperate, desert, and arctic.

these maps—L3DT includes an automatic paging system that swaps map "tiles" from RAM to the hard disk drive as required. It's called a mosaic map, and it usually caps RAM usage in the 100–200 MB range (even for gigabyte- or terabyte-sized maps).

**Figure 8.40**
Water at multiple elevations.

**Figure 8.41**
Gradient fade.

## Tutorial: Clouds

It has always bothered me that I couldn't render clouds or a lens flare on a transparent layer. In Photoshop, when you create clouds or a lens flare, you must have a background color. In other words, clouds must be rendered with two colors and can't fade into transparency like a gradient can (Figure 8.41).

For most Photoshop users, the Blending Mode function is the answer for a realistic cloud or lens flare overlay. You can render clouds on a

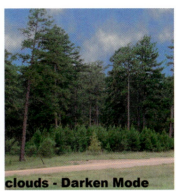

source image   clouds - Normal Mode   clouds - Darken Mode

**Figure 8.42**
Blending clouds into a still image.

**Figure 8.43**
Foreground and background color in black and white.

layer above your image and play with Blending Mode until the clouds look the way you want them to (Figure 8.42).

In game development and interactivity, the images created often need to be used in applications that don't have the sophistication and power of Photoshop. We don't have access to blending modes, and the image must come into the application with transparency already in place. As a result, I have developed a quick way of creating a lens flare or clouds on a transparent layer. I will step you through the process using clouds, but this can be applied to lens flares as well.

Open Photoshop and create a canvas of any size. Keep in mind that because of the way that the Clouds Filter works, the larger the canvas the finer the clouds will be. I used a 512 × 512 image size. For standard clouds, select white as the foreground color and black as the background (Figure 8.43).

You might think that sky blue would be the better choice for a background color, but that will leave a bluish cast in the image. You can see in Figure 8.44 that on the left I used an image created using this tutorial using blue as the background color and on the right I used black. The blue tint is not desirable, as it limits the flexibility of the image and makes accurate color work harder.

Create a new layer by clicking on the **Create a new Layer** icon and name this new layer **Clouds** (Figure 8.45). **Filter** > **Render** > **Clouds** on this new layer.

**Note:** You can hold down the Alt key while running this filter to make your clouds pop more. The default clouds are on the left and the clouds with more contrast are on the right. These images were originally 512 × 512. For this exercise I used the softer clouds on the left (Figure 8.46).

**Figure 8.44**
Don't use blue as your
background color for clouds.

**Figure 8.45**
Create a new layer.

To create the alpha, or transparency, image for the clouds, simply duplicate the **Clouds** layer by dragging it onto the **Create new Layer** icon and rename it **Alpha**. Using a separate image to dictate transparency is the way many applications function (Figure 8.47).

Apply Auto Levels to the image: **Image** > **Adjustments** > **Auto Levels,** which alters the pixels in the image so that they function better as an alpha map for games. You can also skip this step. The results are still good, just different (Figure 8.48).

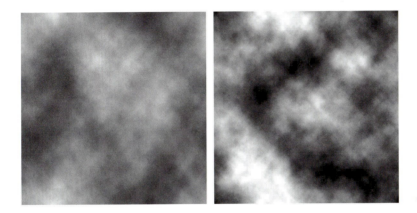

**Figure 8.46**
Clouds with contrast.

**Figure 8.47**
Creating the cloud alpha.

You can see how an alpha map works in Figure 8.49. The source image is to the left and the alpha mask is in the middle. The resulting image has a delicate transparency that makes the clouds look real and soft. The second example uses a figure with a more distinct outline. This makes it easier to see how the alpha mask works.

To actually remove the pixels from the layer in Photoshop—creating a layer with transparency and not just a separate alpha image—follow these steps.

1. Select the entire Alpha layer and copy it; **Ctrl+A** selects all and **Ctrl+C** copies it. Go to your Channels tab and create a new alpha channel (Figure 8.50).
2. Paste the copied **Alpha** layer (**Ctrl+V**) into the new **alpha** channel (Figure 8.51).
3. From the menu, **Select** > **Load Selection** and check the **Invert** box. Make sure that you have the **Alpha Channel** selected (Figure 8.52).
4. Go back to your original **Clouds** layer and press **Delete**. You can play with brightness a little if you like, but it shouldn't need much. Here I changed my background color to a sky blue so that you can see the clouds (Figure 8.53).

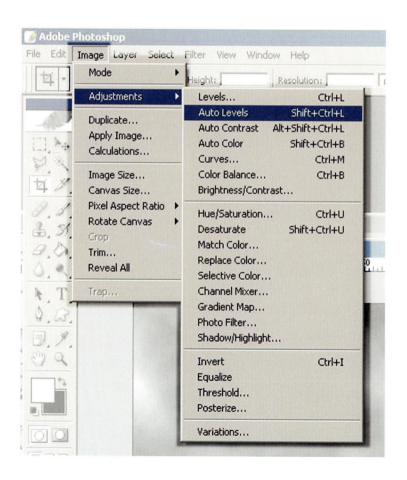

**Figure 8.48**
Adjusting levels.

5. To thin out your clouds, press **Delete** a couple more times before deselecting (Figure 8.54).

Figure 8.55 shows the cloud image in a 3D application using the alpha mask that we created. Note that the clouds tile automatically using this method. Also note that I used two layers of clouds (using the same image), making one layer display the clouds larger and move slower to add more depth.

## Single Clouds

If you want a single cloud rather than a tiling sky full of clouds, use the Lasso Tool with a very large feather. I used a 512 × 512 image and a 45-pixel feather. Simply draw an organic curvy shape and render clouds. You can use a large, very soft eraser to gently sculpt the clouds a bit if you need to (Figure 8.56). Figure 8.57 shows a giant single cloud I created for this 3D scene.

**Figure 8.49**
How alpha mask works.

**Figure 8.50**
Create a new alpha channel.

**Figure 8.51**
Step two in creating an alpha channel.

**Figure 8.52**
Selecting the transparency.

**Figure 8.53**
Deleting the pixels.

**Figure 8.54**
Thinner clouds.

**Figure 8.55**
Same cloud, multiple layers.

**Figure 8.56**
Creating a single cloud.

**Figure 8.57**
Single cloud in scene.

## Water

In games, water can be made using a simple flat water plane or shaders that deform the geometry, followed by adding any number of effects with maps such as normal maps, specular maps, and alpha maps, among others. Particle systems even play a part in some water effects for things such as mist. Usually a good-looking water source in a game uses several of these combined. A water plane is a large, flat polygon with a water texture. Sometimes an alpha channel is on this texture. If it is supported, the texture can be multilayered and animated (Figure 8.58). The plane can consist of a large number of polygons and be animated so that the waves have physical depth, like the real ocean. Add to this the use of shaders to control the reflection, light effects, and normal mapping for smaller waves, and the water starts to look really good. Top it all off with a mist of spray using particle effects and you get some really convincing water (Figure 8.59).

### Caustics Generator

One effect that water causes is called caustics. An extremely simple definition of caustics is the pattern you see when the sun shines through water into a shallow pool or clear ocean (Figure 8.60). If you find yourself without access to a high-end 3D program, you can download this free Caustics Generator at www.lysator.liu.se/~kand/caustics/.

The subject of caustics is quite complex and involves the process of light converging with light. Caustics are caused by light that is reflected or refracted several times before actually hitting a surface, such as through waves. The more light that is refracted to the same area on a surface, the brighter the area will be lit; hence, the bright

**Figure 8.58**
Water can be a simple plane or use many complex shaders. Top, flat plane; second, opaque; third, two layers animated; and bottom, bump mapping and specular highlights added.

**Figure 8.59**
Water in games can now look this good, thanks to pixel and vertex shaders.

pattern we see. To calculate the effect of light refracting through water requires complex math, but thankfully, because of the Caustics Generator (Figure 8.61), all we have to do is push buttons and look at pictures. The Caustics Generator produces rendered frames that are tileable. You can also generate multiframed animations. There is no alpha channel support, but that is a simple thing to create. The Caustics Generator is available in two versions: freeware for everyone and a commercial version intended for professional users.

**Figure 8.60**
Caustics are the pattern you see when the sun shines through water into a shallow pool or clear ocean.

**Figure 8.61**
Interface of the Caustics Generator.

**Chapter 9**

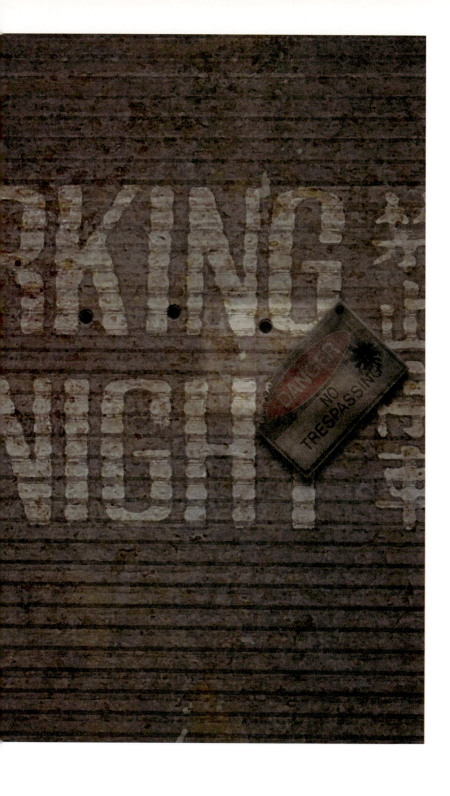

# Game Effects

## Introduction

Games are full of visual effects—probably even more than you realize. These effects are important not just as eye candy but also for giving the player clues and information about what is happening in the game world. These effects also add a great deal to the level of immersion that a player will experience in a game. For example, in some games you can shoot at a wall and nothing will happen—so you wonder, did a bullet come out of your gun? In another you can shoot a wall and a few pixels may fly from the point of impact; how satisfying is that? Shoot a gun at a wall in a recent game of any quality and you will see a hole or abrasion on the wall, a small shower of debris fly from the point of impact, and a puff of dust dissipate into the air. Typically, if you shoot at any surface in a game—wood, metal, concrete, and their variations—you will see and hear a different effect for each surface. Effects also include the glow around a candle, light shafts from a window, even raindrops—and a whole lot more. The assets for these effects are fairly easy to create. Actually, asset creation is the easy part of creating effects in a relative sense. It does take work to create the art and it must look good, but the systems that run the effects can still be complex and challenging to work with. There are generally three types of effects for which you will create assets:

- Static
- Animated
- Particle

## Static Effects

Most effects are based on a fairly simple texture and mesh set, and the texture and mesh of the static effect don't move. Effects such as the light beams streaming from the windows in a warehouse and fantasy settings and the glow around candles in fantasy settings are static effects. Some of the most common static effects are the marks left on a wall after the impact of a bullet, like those in the opening image of this chapter. We'll create all the various impact marks on each of the different surfaces in this chapter. See Figure 9.1 for an illustration of the bullet-hole image (with alpha) mapped to a two-triangle polygon to create the decal and how it looks when placed in the world. Effects like the bullet holes are called *decals* because they are displayed like a decal on a surface in the game world.

A bullet hole is easy to make; it's the programmers who have the difficult job of getting the decal to appear at the right time, display correctly on the surface, fade away after a certain amount of time, and control of numerous other variables. Some game engines rotate the image, cycle through different images for each bullet hole, and even animate the images on the decal. Though usually simple, these effects add a lot to the game world they appear in.

## Animated Effects

Animated effects are based on the texture/mesh arrangement except that the texture is animated and plays like a mini-movie on the face

**Figure 9.1**
An illustration of a bullet-hole decal—a simple texture with an alpha channel applied to a two-triangle polygon. Below: A row of bullet decals placed on a wall.

of the mesh. There can be anywhere from a few to many frames in an animated progression, and the frames can exist as one large image or as separate images. As one large image, the separate frame images are displayed one after the other, and as separate images, the frames are all on one image and the game engine displays the various areas of the image in order. The program flips through these frames and plays the images like a movie.

Animated sequences were usually used as fire in previous games, blinking lights on a console, oozing blood, and many other effects. Fire was created by using a flat plane that always faced the camera and the animated sequence was mapped to it. Animated effects can also be applied to nonmoving models, like the lights of a computer console (Figure 9.2). I put the entire console image in the figure so that you can see the animation in context, but for a game the lights would be a separate image with an alpha channel to save memory. Some current games, and probably all future games, are increasingly using nonanimated particles because the particle systems and the hardware have evolved enough that a much higher degree of control can be achieved, more particles and emitters can be used, and effects exist that process in real time that make the particle systems look much better than a static, or prerendered, asset.

Animated effects are still used to animate some decals, such as a weapons blast. Imagine the burst of energy from a blaster hitting a metal wall beside you in a space station. The blast mark is bright from the heat of the blast and the glow fades and shrinks as it quickly cools; see Figure 9.3. This animated sequence was made quickly in Photoshop. Animated images are a little more challenging to work with, and the job of creating a 2D animation for an effect often falls to the artist, who might not be used to traditional animation nor have access and the knowledge to use a 3D package. Animated effects are commonly used in the muzzle blast from a gun and are often used

**Figure 9.2**
Animated effects are based on the texture/mesh arrangement except that the texture plays like a mini-movie. There are several frames in the animated progression, and the frames can exist as one large image or as separate images. The computer console is an example of an animated sequence in context.

**Figure 9.3**
The creation of an animated particle or decal doesn't always have to be difficult. This laser blast was made quickly in Photoshop.

for explosions and smoke, so you will most likely see them around a little while longer. You can use ImageReady to create and test animated effects.

## Particle Effects

A particle system is a system that can display an assigned asset in great numbers (the asset is usually a small polygon—two triangles—with an applied texture that has alpha transparency on it). The system tracks the particles in 3D space using a set of parameters that the artist can change. These parameters typically alter the rate, size, speed, position, and life span of the particle as well as telling the particle to shrink, fade, or always face the camera (which it usually does). Particles can even physically interact with the game world, colliding and bouncing off surfaces. Figure 9.4 shows the same scene with the same particle system in use with a different texture used in each scene. Actually, the particle used for all the effects (except the sparks in the upper-left corner) is mapped with the same texture; however, in each case the texture has been colorized with a different hue and saturation. The texture itself is simple to create:

1. Create a **512×512** image, **black** background.
2. Create a new empty layer.

**Figure 9.4**
Particles are used in these scenes to create various effects such as sparks (upper left), gaseous flames (upper right), volcanic smoke or ash (middle), poisonous gas (lower left), and steam (lower right). These scenes use the same particle system, with a different texture used in each scene. Actually, the particle used for all of the effects (except the sparks) is mapped with the same texture. In each case, the texture has been colorized with a different hue and saturation.

3. Drag out a circular selection with a **22**-pixel feather centered in the image.
4. Render clouds.
5. **Select** > **Load Selection** > **Load** the transparency of the layer.
6. **Dodge, Burn, Airbrush,** and/or **Colorize** this image to get the effect you want.

A particle system can be used to simulate a wide variety of effects, from smoke to a flock of birds. Traditionally, the use of particle systems with large numbers of particles coming from them was too big a drain on a computer, so game developers were able to achieve only limited effects. But as software gets more complex and game hardware more powerful, smoke and fire and other impressive effects are being very effectively generated using a much larger number of particles.

Dealing with particle systems can be the most difficult part of effects work. Understanding and effectively using the systems that drive the particles, especially a good system with lots of options, can take a lot of time and patience. But even a complex particle system usually uses the same simple texture and geometry setup for the visual particles. See Figure 9.5 for the progression of a static magical sparkle. Figure 9.6 shows a simple particle system. In the upper set of images, the particles are represented by crosses (so that you can see what the particle system is actually doing), and the lower images are the same as the upper but with the sparkle asset attached to each particle.

The point at which the particles are spawned, or appear, is called an *emitter*. An emitter can be of any size. A small emitter with lots of particles coming out in a spray might be what you would use for a garden hose, whereas a very large emitter high in the sky of your game world with a few particles falling from it might be used for rain or snow. See Figure 9.7 for the effect of using different emitter sizes. Often, special particle systems are written for specific uses. Specific particle systems that handle weather effects, for example, are commonly created because weather systems have a more limited function but cover a larger area than a typical full-featured particle system usually does. These special versions of particle systems allow the developers to make them run more efficiently, which is achieved in part by dropping many of the features of a typical particle system that are not needed for a more specific-use particle system. Emitters are typically represented by some sort of icon in the game editor

**Figure 9.5**
A magical spell starts with a small static sparkle.

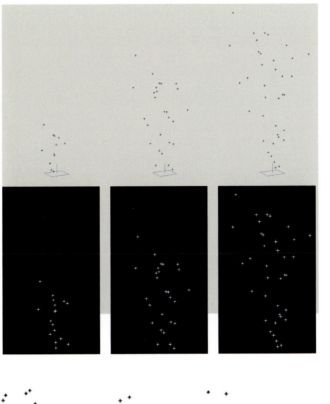

**Figure 9.6**
This is an illustration of a simple particle system, a magical spell. The upper set of images shows the particles represented by crosses, so you can see what the particle system is actually doing, and the lower images are the same as the upper but with the sparkle image attached to each particle.

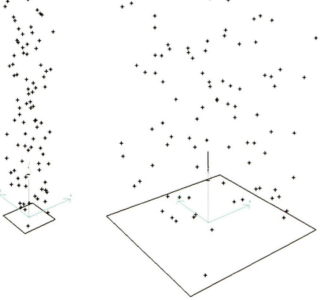

**Figure 9.7**
Emitters are where the particles come from and can be of various sizes. The same number of particles is coming out of both emitters in the figure, but the wider emitter has spread the particles out over a larger area.

but are invisible in the game—you see only the assets spawning at the emitter point being controlled by the particle entity to which they are attached. Usually the game artist, when placing an emitter, makes sure that it looks as though the particles are coming out of something—not just from thin air.

Although a simple particle system may contain only an emitter, a polygon, and a texture, more complex particle systems can contain multiple emitters and multiple textures and use 3D meshes as particles. An explosion is usually composed of a quick ball of fire and a spray of debris, then smoke that drifts from the blasted area and dissipates into the air. This effect is typically created using a blast decal and several systems, one for each effect: flash, debris, and smoke. Additionally, particle systems are usually associated with sound events. Sound adds a lot to the effect that a particle system has. What would rain be without the rumble of thunder? How effective would a silent explosion be? When a fire crackles as you get near it, it adds another level of realism and immersion to a game.

We will start with some simple weather effects and then tackle some of the more common effects for a game, such as lighting and weapons effects.

## Weather

As complex as nature can be, the particles for the most common weather effects are easy to create. Rain and snow are both tiny simple images. You can see the effect that a few hundred of these tiny particles can have on a scene; see Figure 9.8. Notice that the images are blurred a little. The rain is blurred toward the back of the drop to simulate the blurring of a real raindrop as it falls to the ground.

**Figure 9.8**
The particles for the most common weather effects are easy to create. Rain and snow are both tiny simple images. You can see the effect that a few hundred of these tiny particles can have on a scene.

## Lighting

If you understand the math and science of light, then more power to you. But most of us mortals can understand this stuff only on a basic level—it can get really complex. Of course, it helps to understand how light works, but it is absolutely no guarantee that you can create the art that makes a light look good in a game. In fact, an artist is probably better served by observing a variety of light sources in various situations and studying them at a purely visual level than trying to wrap his or her mind around a subject that may have inspired an interest in art in the first place. Fortunately, we are artists and we have to make things look good, not write the code that controls the particle. Several of the more common lighting effects are easy to understand and recreate in a game setting. These effects are accomplished with a simple mesh and texture set. You have already seen a few of these effects in the previous chapters.

## Light Shafts

Do you remember the shafts of light that streamed in from the windows in the warehouse and the windows in the fantasy setting? In the real world, light shafts are created when light passes through the atmosphere and reflects off tiny floating particles. Light shafts are prevalent in games because they look cool, but they can also be important visual clues. These days light shafts are created using the simple mesh/texture set. In the future they will probably be rendered in real time, but for now, see Figure 9.9 for the components of the light shafts as I created them for the scenes in this book.

To produce that texture, I created an image that was 256 pixels wide and 1024 high. I turned on the Fade option in the Shape Dynamics for the brush and drew a few white lines with a soft brush from top to bottom. Then I Motion Blurred it down a few times and Gaussian Blurred it a little, too.

If you are able to use these textures in a 3D application, keep the following points in mind:

- Exclude the geometry from being affected by the light sources in the world so that it doesn't cast a shadow.
- Turn the full-bright (or illumination) on the texture all the way up. When you do this, the texture displays at full brightness and seems to glow. Because light shafts are located near a source of light that is brighter than the surrounding (relative) darkness, they look great and will never be in a situation where they are bright for no reason (well, I guess you can make a door close and the light shafts will remain, but you shouldn't do that).
- Turn collision off so that your light shafts don't block anything (like real light); the collision process is a processor hit, so it's always a good idea to turn collision off anything that doesn't need it.

I have seen this effect augmented in some creative ways: with animated textures that make the shafts seem to waver or shift,

**Figure 9.9**
The components of the light shaft are a simple mesh and texture.

with particle systems that simulate dust drifting through the light shaft, and a projected shadow like the one I used on the floor of the warehouse so it appears that the light is actually casting a shadow.

### Candle Glow/Corona

At night, light sources often seem to have a glow or halo around them. This effect in the real world is caused by the light, the atmosphere between the light source and the viewer. As the light hits water droplets in the air, it is broken up into various colors based on the many variables that can exist in the light source (distance, color, brightness), the atmosphere (amount of moisture in the air, pollutants), and even the viewers' eyes. Although a game might have one corona for many light sources, occasionally creating a few special-case coronas for drastically different-colored light sources, in reality each corona you see is unique because of the many variables involved. Fortunately, a game is usually designed around a theme or setting, which allows for the use of a smaller, more focused, set of assets—coronas being one of them.

In the fantasy setting, we had a glow around the candle flame, which is also a corona, but has a different texture made to look like a candle glow rather than an electric light source (see Figure 9.10). The light shafts are static, but a corona needs to move. To simulate a glow

**Figure 9.10**
The fantasy setting uses a glow around the candle flame, which is also a corona entity with a texture made to look like a candle glow rather than an electric light.

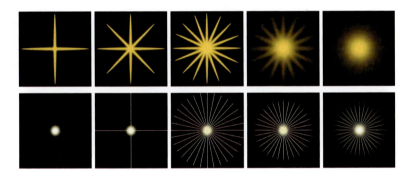

**Figure 9.11**
The progression of the candle glows.

around a light source effectively, many games rely on a technique that uses a moving polygon with a simple corona or glow image mapped to it. The corona entity allows the artist to control several parameters that make the corona image shrink, grow, and fade in and out as the player moves toward and away from it.

I actually created two glows for the candles in the fantasy scene: one that was more diffuse and faint for the background candle and a brighter, more fanciful glow for the candle on the table in the foreground, to give the impression that it is magical. See Figure 9.11 for the progression of both glows. The steps are as described here.

### Candle Glow, Faint and Diffuse

1. Create a new image, **1024×1024**. I work this large so that I can get finer gradation in the glows. You do lose some of that when you resize, but I find that it makes the corona smoother.
2. Make a layer named **center** filled with **black** and snap two guides to the horizontal and vertical center of the image.
3. Create a new layer named **lines**.

4. Use a small, soft brush with the Fade option set to about **75** pixels.
5. Draw yellow-orange lines from the center to all four points of the compass. Copy, paste, and rotate this four times.
6. **Filter** > **Blur** > **Gaussian Blur 20 pixels**.
7. **Filter** > **Blur** > **Radial Blur**: Amount **100**, Quality **Best**.
8. Create the **alpha** channel in the same manner as you did for the candle flame in the fantasy chapter.

### Candle Glow, Brighter and More Fanciful

9. Create a new image, **1024×1024**.
10. Make a layer named **center** filled with **black** and snap two guides to the horizontal and vertical center of the image.
11. Create a new layer named **lines**.
12. Use a smaller, soft brush and set the foreground color to a very desaturated yellow, **RGB: 255,248,218**.
13. Set the foreground color to **white**, reduce the brush size a few steps, and put a white center in the yellow circle.
14. Create a new layer named **lines**.
15. Invert your colors and use the desaturated yellow and a small, hard brush, **5** pixels. Draw lines across the canvas until you have a complete circle of tight thin lines. You can draw two lines using the guides and then copy, paste, and rotate them. Merge all the line layers together when you are done.
16. Use an inverted circular selection with a **42**-pixel feather to remove the ends of the lines.
17. Gaussian Blur this **4** pixels.
18. Radial Blur this, too: Amount **100**, Blur Method **Zoom**.

### Traditional Corona

The traditional corona is a little more involved than a candle glow. You can use the **Render** > **Lens Flare** filter to get a variety of effects that are great references when creating a corona, but you can't use the resulting lens flare as a corona texture, because you can't render the effect on an empty layer. This makes the creation of a decent alpha channel a challenge. Also, the lens flare is meant to simulate the flare from a camera lens, not the glow from a light source, so there is a good deal of extra visual information in the effect that would be next to impossible to remove. The steps to create a corona start as the candle glow:

1. Create a new image, **1024×1024**.
2. Make a layer filled with **black**, and snap two guides to the horizontal and vertical center of the image.
3. Create a new layer named **center**.
4. Use a large, soft brush and set the foreground color to **white**. Put the center white glow in.
5. Coronas can have many colors in them, but they should be subtle. We will start by creating a faint circle in the background. Create a layer named **brownish circle** behind the glow on the center layer. Use a circular marquee with a **22**-pixel feather and fill it with a brown, **RGB: 80,71,59**.

6. Create a new layer named **ring1** under the center layer.
7. Set your foreground color to **RGB: 40,47,40**.
8. Use the circular marquee with the **22**-pixel feather still on it and stroke an **8**-pixel line outside of the brownish circle.
9. You have the option of adding a circle or two more if you like. Ultimately, the corona's color and intensity will be based on the setting it is in.
10. Either paint or smudge the white lines out from the center. Note that the lines are fewer than the fanciful candle glow and are of varying lengths.
11. Finally, Gaussian Blur this about **4** pixels. See Figure 9.12.

## Weapons

Now we are going to tackle weapons effects. These can be the most involved and complex effects to set up, given the number of weapons in a typical game, the number of effects each weapon has associated with it, and the effect that the weapon's projectile might produce when impacting any given surface of the game world. Though these effects are usually complex and involved to set up, the assets they use are fairly easy to create.

### Muzzle Blasts

The plume of fire that discharges from the barrel of a weapon is called a *muzzle blast*. In reality, every type of weapon has a distinct muzzle blast, but most people can't distinguish between the muzzle blasts from similar firearms to any great degree. A muzzle blast from a rifle will do the job for most rifles in a game, but using a muzzle blast from a rifle on a handgun might be noticeable. Although the muzzle blast from various weapons will have various patterns and sizes, currently they are all made in the same basic fashion: they are a combination of geometry and texture. First, let's look at the elements of the typical muzzle blast in Figure 9.13 and the complete muzzle blast in front of a backdrop (Figure 9.14).

Here are the steps to create the muzzle blast. See Figure 9.15 for a visual progression of the steps. To create the circular part of the muzzle blast:

1. Open a new **512×512** document in Photoshop with a **black** background.
2. Create a new layer named **orange**.
3. Set your foreground color to orange, **RGB: 255,150,0**.
4. Use a very large soft brush (**300** pixels) and put a large **orange circle** in the middle of the image using a horizontal and vertical guide.

**Figure 9.12**
The progression of the traditional corona.

**Figure 9.13**
The plume of fire that discharges from the barrel of a weapon—a muzzle blast— is created with a combination of geometry and texture. Upper right: the muzzle blast texture. Middle: the model of a gun with the geometry for the muzzle blast in place. Bottom: the muzzle blast with the texture and geometry together.

**Figure 9.14**
Here is the completed muzzle blast in front of a colored backdrop.

**Figure 9.15**
The progression of the steps to create the muzzle blast.

5. Use a smaller, soft brush (**200** pixels) and put a **white circle** in the middle of the orange circle.
6. Use the **Smudge** tool (**27** pixels, **74%**) and smudge out the color from the center of the image.
7. **Filter** > **Distort** > **Ripple**: Amount **75%**, Size **Large**.
8. **Filter** > **Blur** > **Radial Blur**: Amount **10**, Blur Method **Spin**, Quality **Good**.
9. **Filter** > **Blur** > **Radial Blur**: Amount **25**, Blur Method **Zoom**, Quality **Good**.

To create the elongated part of the muzzle blast:

1. Open a new **512×512** document in Photoshop with a **black** background.
2. Create a new layer named **orange**.
3. Set your foreground color to orange, **RGB: 255,150,0**.
4. Use a large, soft brush (**100** pixels) and set the Shape Dynamics to **Fade** (**25** pixels). Drag a long orange line from the bottom to the top.
5. Use a smaller brush (**50** pixels) and set the Shape Dynamics to **Fade** (**55** pixels). Drag a white line from the bottom to the top of the image.
6. Use the **Smudge** tool (**27** pixels, **74%**) and smudge out from the center of the image and upward.
7. **Filter** > **Distort** > **Ripple**: Amount **75%**, Size **Large**.
8. **Filter** > **Blur** > **Motion Blur**: Angle **90**, Distance **25 pixels**.
9. **Filter** > **Blur** > **Radial Blur**: Amount **25**, Blur Method **Zoom**, Quality **Good**.
10. I did a little more smudging to strengthen the flames.

### Impact Effects: Bullet Holes and Debris

When you fire a gun in a game, the muzzle blast may be notable, but it's the effect the bullet or projectile has on the surface it strikes that is really satisfying. If little to nothing happened when you fired a weapon, you wouldn't feel as immersed or excited by the game. The effect is not only cool, it also is an important interaction with the game world. In fact, a player is usually made aware of the effect of his interaction on the game world (other players being part of the game world) through visual effects. Impact effects give players important visual clues as to how close they are to hitting the target they are aiming at. It is a particularly tense event in a game to hear the sound of a bullet impact near you and see the hole and debris and realize that you are the target. In a stealth shooter, where you are both hunter and prey, this is an important part of game play. Of course, auditory and even tactile effects (such as a vibrating controller) play an important role, too, but you can more easily play a game without speakers than without a monitor.

This section is entitled "Impact Effects" with the additional phrase "Bullet Holes and Debris" because almost any interaction with a game world is an impact that spawns an effect: weapons effects are just a subset of impact effects. But weapons effects are usually the most commonly needed and complex effects created for a game.

I limit the examples of impact effects in this chapter to basic weapons effects because the same principles apply to the creation of virtually all other effects. The bloody hole and red spray from a gunshot wound, the tracks left behind and dust kicked up by a vehicle's tires in the desert, a swarm of insects, and most other effects are all created in the same manner as the effects created in this chapter.

Some effects are relatively simple—you fire a gun and blow dirt from the ground or leave a hole in a metal panel—but some can be pretty dramatic. In some games, you can shoot a window and blow the glass pane into a thousand shards. If you are in the position of creating effects such as these for a game, you will quickly realize that you need a spreadsheet to track the weapon types, ammunition or projectile, world surfaces, and the description and needed assets for each impact effect. This spreadsheet can also include the associated sound files and even special-case events such as malfunctions and misfires. Here I will walk you through the basics of creating impact effects for an average bullet on the most common surfaces.

First, we list the most common surfaces in an average game world:

- Cloth
- Concrete (plaster)/brick
- Dirt
- Glass
- Grass
- Metal
- Water
- Wood

For each of these surfaces, we must create a texture that the game engine can display over the surface (like a decal) and look as though a bullet left a mark at the point of impact. We also need to create a particle/debris image for each surface and variations for some of the surfaces. For example, a bullet hitting the thin metal of a tin garden shed might simply put a neat hole right through the metal with little to no debris coming from the point of impact, but the same bullet slamming into the heavy metal of a blast door might dent the metal only slightly but send a shower of debris, or even red-hot sparks, flying from the point of impact.

Although you can come up with a neat list of the materials in your world, these might all look vastly different in variations of each material. For example, heavy metal can be rusted or freshly painted, and wood can be old (desaturated and brownish) or new (brightly painted furniture or highly polished panels). The challenge here is to create a bullet-hole decal for a certain material (wood, for example) that will work equally well in many situations (old wood, painted wood, and so on). I find that a grayscale image with good light, shadow, and alpha treatment works best because it tends to blend with the material that it is displayed on top of. This method also allows you to focus your efforts on the way a given material will react to a bullet impact, regardless of the color or condition of the material. For example, wood generally splinters, glass shatters, metal is dented or punctured, and so on. By leaving the color information out, you can create an effect that will adopt the color of the surface it is displayed on and spew the appropriate particles for the material type. The key to creating a good impact and debris set is to consider the physical properties of the material first; how hard, brittle, or squishy is the material, and how will it react to the impact of the specific projectile that will be hitting it? Then focus on the highlight and shadow of the hole and debris. Experiment with the effects in Photoshop and in the game and adjust the alpha channeling to obtain the best results. A deeper hole may be small, with an almost solid black center; a shallow dent may be wider and almost transparent, with only a hint of light and shadow.

Here are the basic surfaces I usually work with in a game. They are listed alphabetically, not by importance.

### Cloth

If you kick in the door of the average crack house and start blazing away with your nine, chances are you will hit a sofa, a stained mattress, or some dope shag carpeting. When you are taking down that stained mattress, you want to know it's really dead, so the game artist better give you some good visual feedback.

Cloth tends to rip and tear and leave strings or fibers when it is destroyed. To create the impact and particles for cloth, I started with a simple stringy pattern and applied the Bevel and Emboss layer style, finally adding some additional strings and darkening the hole to give it depth. See Figure 9.16 for the progression of the cloth bullet hole and Figure 9.17 for the bullet hole, debris, and the effects in context.

**Figure 9.16**
The progression of the steps to create the bullet hole for cloth.

**Figure 9.17**
The cloth bullet hole, debris, and the effects in context.

### Concrete (Plaster)/Brick

These three materials are very common in game worlds and similar in their effects. The holes and debris are almost interchangeable, but you might want to differentiate between light concrete, heavy reinforced concrete, and/or bricks and heavy ceramics because of the frequency and wide variety of these types of materials.

Light concrete or plaster will leave a cleaner hole and produce a more wispy puff of debris. See Figure 9.18 for the light concrete/plaster effects set. This effects set was created like most of the other effects, using various brushes and the Bevel and Emboss Layer Style as a beginning.

For the heavier, reinforced concrete, I made the holes shallower and rougher and the debris essentially the same as the lighter concrete. I also added a puff of dust to the context image we created earlier in the chapter in the section on particle effects, so you could see a more complete example of an effect (Figure 9.19).

**Figure 9.18**
The light concrete/plaster effects set and the effects in context.

**Figure 9.19**
The heavier concrete effects set and the effects in context, with a puff of dust that drifts away after the initial impact. We created the puff earlier in this chapter in the section on particle effects.

For the bricks, I went with a simple circular hole as though the brittle brick were blown out in a large shallow circle. I think the shallow, carved-out look works for most brittle brick and tile surfaces. I made the debris contain some small chunks, since it seemed like the brick would be blasted outward, whereas the concrete would powder under the impact (Figure 9.20).

### Dirt

Dirt tends to crater when impacted, so I created a wider, shallower, crater-like hole and a longer, wider, spray of dirt grains (see Figure 9.21).

### Glass

In general, one of three things can happen when glass is impacted in a game world. In one case the glass remains intact and a decal of a bullet hole is laid on the surface, followed by a small amount of

**Figure 9.20**
The brick effects set and the effects in context.

**Figure 9.21**
The dirt effects set and the effects in context.

debris shooting out from the hole. In the second, the glass shatters into pieces and falls out of the frame. The third option is a hybrid of the two: You shoot the glass several times, putting holes in it as you weaken it, then it shatters out of the frame after several shots.

When glass breaks out of a frame and falls to the floor in pieces, this usually involves the model of the glass pane being removed from the scene on the impact of the projectile and a particle system of falling glass shards spawned at the place the glass pane used to be. This involves less asset creation because you are making a few tiny shards and more technical setup because you are coordinating events in a chain reaction:

projectile impact >
    remove pane mesh >
        play breaking glass sound effect >
            spawn falling glass shard particle system >
                play tinkling glass sound effect ...

For the first option, the hole-decal and debris, the effect is technically simpler to set up but involves more asset creation, and this is the effect we will create since this is an asset creation book. As I said, this effect mimics the effect of thick, reinforced, or bulletproof glass being impacted by a projectile but not breaking. When impacted, the glass pane remains and a hole appears with spidery cracks emanating from it. A small shower of glass shards is thrown back from the hole. For this effect the hole is simply a black circle with a faint inner glow for some depth and thin white lines emanating out from the center (use the Fade option for this). The glass debris consists of some simple shapes that I dodged and burned. See Figure 9.22.

**Grass**

I created the grass effects set based on the techniques we used for the cloth and dirt set. The hole created when grass is shot wouldn't be a clear hole but rather a dark patch where the grass was

**Figure 9.22**
The glass hole and debris effects set and the effects in context.

displaced, with a few blades overhanging. The debris would be dirt and grass blades. I colored the debris greenish so that it would look like grass blades, but I could have left it desaturated if I needed it to be more versatile. See Figure 9.23.

## Metal

Metal is another potentially big category. I created three basic scenarios: the light metal with a clean hole, the heavier metal that will get dented inward and punctured when shot, and a dense metal that will only dent when impacted. Each hole is a variation on a Bevel and Emboss with some dodging and burning. See Figure 9.24 for the light metal, Figure 9.25 for the heavier metal, and Figure 9.26 for the dense metal.

### Water

When water is shot, it sprays upward and outward. Here I show you the simple decal/debris version that we have been working with.

**Figure 9.23**
The grass effects set and the effects in context.

**Figure 9.24**
The light metal effects set and the effects in context.

**Figure 9.25**
The heavier metal effects set and the effects in context.

**Figure 9.26**
The dense metal effects set and the effects in context.

Some games make the water splash more complex, resembling the muzzle blast of the gun that we looked at earlier. See Figure 9.27 for the water impact and splash.

**Wood**

Wood will splinter when shot, so I created a simple hole similar to the grass impact. There is a depression with splinters that overhang the hole. The debris is obviously splinters or chips of wood. See Figure 9.28.

That's a basic rundown of in-game effects. The asset creation is the easy part; it's working with the various systems to get the desired effect that is the real challenge. This chapter has provided you with a basis for creating the assets for any effect that you may be required to create for a game.

**Figure 9.27**
The water effects set and the effects in context.

**Figure 9.28**
The wood effects set and the effects in context.

# Chapter 10

ILLUMINATION

SPECULAR

# Normal Maps and
# Multipass Shaders

## Introduction

This chapter focuses on normal mapping—specifically on creating normal maps in Photoshop, with a look at creating them using a 3D program and creating the supporting maps for a typical environment. I will explain how 3D applications are used to do this, but we won't be doing that in this book.

To understand what a normal map is, first we will look at how lighting in games generally works. In short, a normal map creates an illusion of depth by recalculating the highlights and shadows on a low-polygon surface using the information from a high-polygon model—and does it all in real time. Earlier in the book we looked briefly at bump and normal map shaders; these add 3D depth to an otherwise flat surface. Although bump maps are grayscale and display the most limited 3D effect, the normal map adds more depth using a color map with lighting information stored in it. A painting can be created that looks like a real scene, but it will look good only from one fixed angle. When you change your viewing angle, you suddenly see that the painting is a flat 2D image. Imagine if you could create a painting that repainted itself every time you moved and did it so fast that it seemed as though you were seeing a real 3D scene. That is essentially what a normal map is doing as it calculates light and shadow in real time on an otherwise flat surface. We still need to maintain the silhouette of the model as best we can, meaning that the overall shape of the model will still look the same, even if the flat surface is highly detailed.

The good news is that using a normal map allows us to focus more polygons on the silhouette of the model. Currently, a normal map cannot change the silhouette of the model, but an even better type of mapping, called *parallax mapping,* can actually take into account the fact that items protruding from the surface of an object should occlude objects behind it.

## Vertex vs. Per-Pixel Lighting

The science of light is complex, to say the least. Due to the limitations of hardware, programmers have had to grossly oversimplify light calculations to calculate light in real time. They are just now able to program some decent lighting in games due to recent hardware advances. There are several ways in which lighting can be handled in games, but if it is calculated in real time it is probably either vertex lighting or per-pixel lighting. *Vertex lighting* (generally called *Gouraud shading*) uses a broad brush to determine the lighting of a surface, whereas per-pixel lighting uses a very fine brush to do so. Vertex lighting takes the brightness value of each vertex of a polygon and creates a gradient across the polygon face (Figure 10.1). This is not nearly as accurate a lighting model as *per-pixel lighting*, where the lighting is calculated for every pixel.

So what is a normal and how does it relate to the normal map? The normal is simply which way the face of a polygon is facing. Unlike

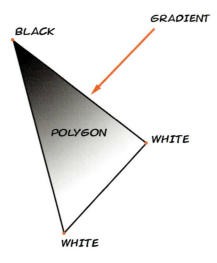

**Figure 10.1**
Vertex lighting.

the real world, in which a sheet of paper or the sides of a cardboard box have a back and a front (and, technically, sides) in a 3D world, a polygon is generally visible only when you are facing it. So, in a 3D world, if you get inside a cube, from the inside you will be able to see out of it because you are on the backside of all the polygons and the normals are all facing away from you. In some 3D games you can get your character in a position where you can see inside and through objects. In fact, in some games players can get themselves inside objects where they can see and shoot other players, but those players can't see them or shoot back. Most 3D modeling programs will show you an outline when you are behind a polygon to help you keep track of your objects or give you other tools to work in 3D, but games generally look at the normal "as is" unless specifically told not to.

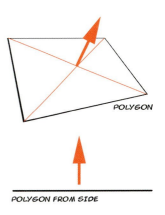

**Figure 10.2**
The normal map.

Normals are usually represented as an arrow pointing away from the visible face in a straight perpendicular line. This simple concept is important to understand, because the way a normal map functions is based on this bit of information (Figure 10.2).

In vertex lighting, for every normal on the mesh, the angle of the normal and the angle of the lights in the scene are calculated (often with their distances included as well) to determine the brightness of the vertex and the gradient between these points (Figure 10.3):

> Brightness = N (the normal) × L (the light vector, or the
> line from the light to the surface)

Now that you know what a normal is, the direction the polygon is facing, understanding what a normal map is will be easier. A normal map is an RGB texture that stores the normal information from a very high-resolution model in the various color channels of the texture (red, green, and blue representing the X, Y, and Z values of the normal vectors). This allows a single polygon to display the light and shadow information from a high-resolution model that has thousands

BRIGHTNESS = **N** (THE NORMAL) **DOT L** (THE LIGHT VECTOR)

**Figure 10.3**
The normal and the N × l calculation.

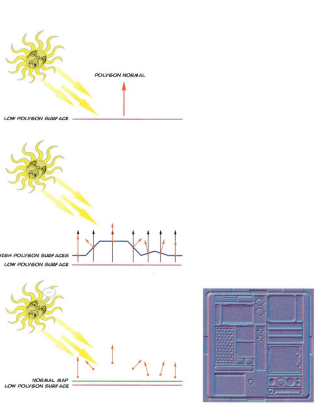

**Figure 10.4**
A normal map.

or even millions of polygons. Figure 10.4 shows what a normal map generally looks like.

## Creating Normal Maps in Photoshop

An easy way to create normal maps is to create a grayscale map in Photoshop and use the NVIDIA plug-in to convert it to a normal map. There are several techniques for building these maps: painting them, creating them from photos (source-based), and using parts of existing normal maps.

GRAYSCALE MAP          RESULTING NORMAL MAP

POLYGON                    NORMAL MAPPED POLYGON

**Figure 10.5**
Normal map creation using varying grayscale values and softer or harder edges.

## Painting Normal Maps

An easy way to create a normal map is to create grayscale height maps and use a filter (freely available from NVIDIA) to convert them into normal maps. In Figure 10.5, you can see the height map, the NVIDIA interface with 3D preview, and the resulting normal map. You can see that using various shades of gray and creating soft or hard edges, you can create almost any object you need in a normal map.

## Source-Based Normal Maps

A source-based normal map is one that is created from an image—usually a photo. Although this is not always desirable, you can get some good results from a photo. In most cases, when you're creating environments for a game, the textures that you will be creating won't all be for rounded, injection-molded plastic spaceship interiors. Most textures are for stones, concrete, tree bark, wood, and hard-edged objects—and a lot of other surfaces that are almost impossible to model and shoot normals for. You will often be in a situation where you have to use a photograph, or finished texture, to create a normal map. The steps to do this are as follows:

1. Start with a copy of your image and **desaturate** it. I often convert the image to **16** bit, since any banding in the image will show in the normal map. It will look like a topographical map (Figure 10.6).
2. Run the **Photocopy** filter. You will have to adjust the settings based on the source image, but the goal is to get the lower parts

**Figure 10.6**
Banding in the normal map.

**Figure 10.7**
Creating a normal map from a photo.

of the image to be black and the higher to be white, with little distortion. Figure 10.7 shows this and the following steps.

3. Darken the areas that are supposed to be deeper than the overall surface. In this example, I darkened the area where the bricks are exposed, since the plaster is on top of the layer of bricks and should be set back in relation to it.

4. I cleaned out a lot of the noise from the overall image, since normal maps are very sensitive and usually an excess of detail on a normal map translates into a noisy and/or puffy result.

5. I took a very small brush and darkened the major cracks in the wall and put a 2-pixel Gaussian Blur on the entire image. This entire process takes only a few minutes and adds a great sense of depth to the image.

6. You can build up more depth in your normal map by taking the normal map into Photoshop and creating a layer via copy and setting the Blending Mode to **Overlay**. This step alone will enhance the detail of the normal map.

7. If you blur this layer a few pixels, that adds more depth. You can repeat this process several times—duplicate the layer and blur it (making sure that the Blending Mode is still set on **Overlay**) and check the results every so often until you like what you see. This extra step is great for more organic textures because it builds depth in a way that makes the details more rounded. Hard details are still best painted in if you are working in Photoshop.

8. The last thing to do is to renormalize the map by running it through the NVIDIA filter and checking the **Normalize only** option. This step

**Figure 10.8**
Various strengths of the normal map created from the photo.

corrects any vector information encoded into the normal map that we might have corrupted during these steps (Figure 10.8).

### Use Parts of Existing Normal Maps

This method can be used in 2D as well as 3D. In 2D, you are simply cutting and pasting parts of existing normal maps and putting them together; in 3D, you are putting various parts or geometry together to create the normal map. The 2D parts can be moved about to be effective only as parts of a normal map, but the 3D parts can be moved, scaled, rotated, and reused in many more ways.

### Creating Normal Maps Using a 3D Program

The process for creating normal maps using a 3D application starts with the two models: a high-polygon model (the sky's the limit on detail) and a low-polygon model (needs to run in the game engine you are creating it for). It doesn't matter which one you create first, but there are some pros and cons to both approaches. After the two models are created, the process generally involves arranging the two models so that they are on top of each other and generate the normal map correctly. This step can be the most time-consuming and frustrating. When the application that generates the normal map is run, it is doing the following;

- Mapping an empty texture to the low-polygon model
- Calculating, for each pixel of the empty texture on the low-polygon model, the corresponding normal from the high-polygon model
- Recording that information in the texture map as an RGB value

**Figure 10.9**
Creating normal maps in a 3D application: the quick way.

This method is required for very highly detailed characters and some organic props, but the time and effort spent on this method for environmental art (walls, floors, control panels, and so on) is overkill—and often produces inferior results. If you can't achieve your result quickly in 2D and you have access to a 3D application, here is a method for the quick creation of normal maps in 3D: essentially, you model all your high-poly details as separate parts so that you can arrange them and shoot the normal map once (Figure 10.9). In fact, a simple prop with a few sides can more easily be modeled and normal maps shot by building all the separate faces of the model flat (similar to laying out UVs, only in 3D) and shooting the normal maps and assembling them in Photoshop. I have seen inordinate amounts of time (I am talking about days) go into normal map creation for things as simple as vents on a wall when it should have taken under an hour the first time and only moments in the future, since the asset can be reused.

## Assets for a Futuristic Interior

The assets for this futuristic interior mostly involve the creation of the textures for the shaders. The models themselves are purposely very simple for this exercise so that you can see clearly the power of the normal maps and other shaders when they're applied to even the simplest of geometry.

Texture list:

- Wall Panel
- Floor Panel

- Light/ceiling panel
- Column
- Door
- Monitor
- Pipes and hoses

## Wall Panels

Let's start with a wall panel. As we know, we are creating a shader that will involve multiple maps—diffuse (color), specularity, illumination, opacity, and a normal map—so we need to set the Photoshop file up so that each map corresponds exactly to each of the other maps. Say you are creating a light panel where the frame protrudes from the surface; the light panel is bright even in darkness, as though the light were on; the paint is scratched away, and the exposed metal shines brighter than the remaining paint around it. All the images created for use in the shaders that will produce all those visual effects need to line up exactly. If these images are not created in an organized fashion so that they line up perfectly, you will get many undesired effects that will shatter the illusion you are trying to create. Misaligned maps will create lit parts of a texture that should be dark, normal bumping where things should be flat (picture the image of a nail head in a wall and a few pixels over a bump that looks like a nail head). No map is immune! The specular map needs to line up perfectly with the materials in your texture. Scratches and chipped patches of exposed metal need to shine, and the shine needs to stop right where the exposed metal stops and the paint starts.
Of course, Photoshop layers make this easy. This approach also allows for the rapid iteration of changes in each of the maps. Setting the file up right will greatly speed up your work, since all the maps can be produced based on the first few layers you create. I usually start with a simple layout of the texture. For the wall panel, this is a black-and-white layout of the shapes of the panels and parts of the wall panel. You can see in Figure 10.10 the layers that compose the group for the shapes in the panel. From this I usually create the normal map right off, to see whether the concept can be achieved in 2D (Figure 10.11).

## Color

Start with the group that we just created for the layout of the panel and copy it. Name it **diffuse** or **color**. For the diffuse map, the stark black and white of the layout is all taken way down (use **Fill** and not Opacity to do this so that the layer styles are not affected). Having the shapes all on separate layers will make texture creation easier on each map, for various reasons. On the color map, you can use the various layers to apply subtle layer styles—a slight dark outer glow, for instance, to create the look of dirt in the cracks. You can use a color overlay to try out various colors quickly, and when you like what you have, you can sample the color to create a paint layer.

To create a great layer of peeling paint, use this common trick that will net you impressive results: create a new layer on the top of the

**Figure 10.10**
Black-and-white layout of the shapes of the panels.

**Figure 10.11**
Normal map to see whether the concept can be achieved.

stack and select the **paint bucket**. Check the **All layers** box, select a nice desaturated color, fill an area, and watch what happens. To get different results, try playing with the tolerance of the tool. You can also try masking off specific areas so that the paint only fills that area; this can be good for trim or panels. You can also use a pattern fill; that is how the caution stripes on the door were done in Figure 10.25.

**Figure 10.12**
Overlays for dirt and scratches and other elements such as stenciled writing or stickers. These overlays can be used on each texture you create, so all the surfaces of the space you are creating will have a consistency in the wear and tear and overall look.

Create the paint layer last and on top of the stack, but you need to move this layer under all the overlays for it to look right, with the weathering and stains on top of the paint. Try a one-pixel, very slight bevel on the paint to give it some perceived thickness. Use an equally subtle dark outer glow to help enhance this effect.

Having any parts that need illumination on their own dedicated layers makes it very easy to create the illumination map later on, too. This applies to all the maps—even the specular map is easier when you can quickly isolate a panel using Ctrl-click on a layer. By creating your overlays for dirt and scratches—and other elements of color, such as stenciled writing or stickers—on separate layers, you can use these layers as a basis for each new texture you create, so all the surfaces of the space you are creating will have a consistency in the wear and tear and overall look (Figure 10.12).

## Illumination

The illumination map is made by creating a new layer filled with black and Ctrl-clicking on the layers with the parts that will be illuminated—the color of the lights for this panel—and inverting the black to white on the new illumination layer (**Ctrl+I**). In this case, the only lights present are the two fluorescent-type tubes on the bottom of the panel. In Figure 10.13, you can see the difference between the texture with and without the illumination map present.

**Figure 10.13**
The texture with and without the illumination map present.

**Figure 10.14**
Rear: the diffuse texture with normal map applied. Middle: the specularity map by itself, and then all three applied to the mesh in the foreground (diffuse, specularity, and normal maps).

## *Specularity*

The specularity map is a copy of the entire texture that is darkened; because the various parts of the texture are on layers, we can Ctrl-click the layers to get precise control over the specularity of various elements of the surface, such as the paint. The paint is all chipped and peeling; by selecting this layer's transparency, we can take the brightness up or down to make the paint uniformly shiny or dull. We can also dodge in scratches and scrapes. Remember that the white will be shiny and the black dull, so the edges of panels and around handles will be scratched and shiny. You can also paint with a white brush on a separate layer if you want to have more control over the effect and the ability to redo and fix things more easily later. In Figure 10.14, you can see the texture with normal map, the specularity map, and then all three together in the foreground. Another thing to keep in mind is that deep cracks and spaces shouldn't have any specular reflection; this is one of the many reasons many normal maps often look like molded plastic.

**Figure 10.15**
Multiple layers of depth.

**Figure 10.16**
Grayscale value changes.

## Normal Map

The normal map starts out as a grayscale image. I do many iterations with the NVIDIA normal mapping filter in Photoshop several times until I get the desired result. There are a few things to keep in mind when you're creating normal maps in this fashion:

- Watch for banding in the normal map. If this is a problem, work at a higher resolution, take the image mode up to 16 bit, and make sure that the brush you are using is not only soft but that the "spacing" is set as low as possible under the brush tip shape of the Brushes palette.
- If you want to create multiple layers of depth, do this by working at multiple levels of grayscale. Two objects crossing each other will look as though they are on the same level and mashing together, rather than on separate levels, if they are using the same values. Make one darker so it seems further back. Figures 10.15 and 10.16 illustrate the effect of changing the grayscale values.

- Remember that normal maps are very sensitive to value changes. If you want to include dirt on your normal map, the difference in value for the surface it is sitting on should be very subtle. Brighten the surface slightly and the dirt will protrude; darken it and the dirt will look like pits and dents. You might want to consider adding dirt last, after you have tweaked the major height appearances of the normal map. If you need to increase the values of the overall normal map at any stage, that also means that the effect of the dirt protruding from the surface will increase and it will end up looking like huge lumps (Figure 10.17).

**Figure 10.17**
Dirt caution.

**Figure 10.18**
Wall panel variations.

- Save interesting objects that you build normal maps for and create a library of vents, panels, controls, and so on.

## Wall Panel Variations

By saving a copy of the file that you just created, you can make variations on the wall panel—without lights or half-sized or with different panel designs. By using the existing file, you can keep the texture visually consistent (Figure 10.18). In Figure 10.19, you can see more details for the open wall panel. This was constructed in the same manner as the other panels, only there is added detail—more panels and lights. Because there is so much detail in the normal map, I found that as I worked some parts looked good and others needed more work. I wanted to continue to make some parts more prominent, so I simply saved a copy of the normal map at that stage and kept working. Later I combined the versions of each normal map and kept the parts I liked best to create the final normal map. In this case, I wanted to make the panels more prominent, but that made the hose connectors too puffy, so I put the final normal map on top of the version with the good hose connectors and erased the connectors from the top layer. Remember to merge and renormalize. This is as complex as the geometry for the walls and floors gets at present (Figure 10.20).

**Figure 10.19**
Wall panel open.

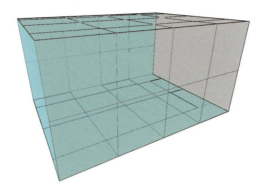

**Figure 10.20**
The geometry of the scene—
it's very simple.

**Figure 10.21**
Large floor panel.

## Floor Panels

Creation of the floor panels starts from the wall panels, but being on the floor, these textures can be more simple (Figure 10.21). They feature some diamond plate and caution stripes. I created a half-sized version with the caution stripe on it to be used around the edges of the hall (Figure 10.22).

## Columns

With the column, we introduce a slightly more complex mesh than the flat polygons of the floor and walls (Figure 10.23).

**Figure 10.22**
Half-sized floor panel.

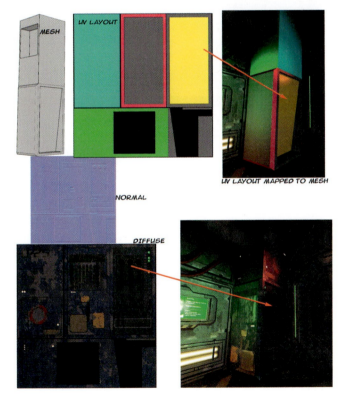

**Figure 10.23**
Column.

## Light/Ceiling Panels

The light panel (Figure 10.24) has only one unique texture for the grate. The others are wall panels and the lights themselves are from the wall panel with a light. There is also the introduction of the opacity map. Although the illumination map can be a little fuzzy

**Figure 10.24**
Light panel.

**Figure 10.25**
Door.

(so it appears that the area around the light is being lit), the opacity map needs to be precise if you want the grill to look clean. If it's fuzzy, there will be a fading of the texture.

### Doors

On the door texture, I included the frame parts as well (Figure 10.25). The surface behind the door is a wall, so I textured it accordingly.

### Monitors

The monitor (Figure 10.26) has a few overlays for the screen, and in addition to the illumination map, there is an actual light source in the scene that helps make it glow. The mesh is simply a line extruded, and the front face beveled.

### Pipes and Hoses

With the ability to add more polygons to our scenes, we are now able to include traditionally high-polygon (relatively speaking) objects such as hoses (Figure 10.27). Hoses are round and can be curvy—and round and curvy means polygon-intensive. Start with a horizontally tiling texture for a few hoses and a pipe or two. The fact that we can use a specular and normal map on the hoses allows us to create a really cool texture on the hoses (Figure 10.28). Figure 10.29 shows the final scene with and without the shaders in place.

**Figure 10.26**
Monitor.

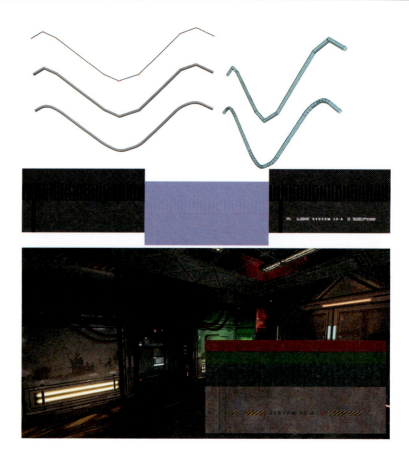

**Figure 10.27**
Pipes and hoses.

**Figure 10.28**
Hose detail.

**Figure 10.29**
Final scene.

**1.**

**2.**

**3.**

# Appendix A

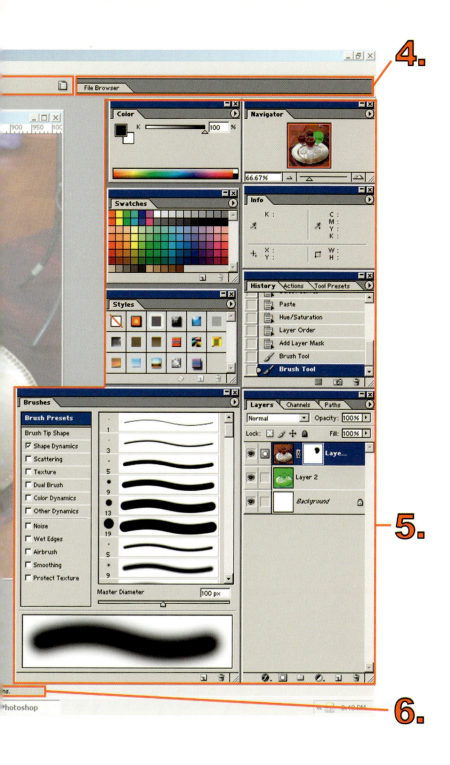

**4.**

File Browser

| Color | Navigator |

K      100   %

66.67%

| Swatches | Info |

K :      C :
          M :
          Y :
          K :

X :      W :
Y :      H :

| Styles | History | Actions | Tool Presets |

Paste

Hue/Saturation

Layer Order

Add Layer Mask

Brush Tool

**Brush Tool**

**Brushes** | **Layers** | Channels | Paths

| **Brush Presets** |   | Normal    Opacity: 100% |
| Brush Tip Shape | 1 | Lock:   Fill: 100% |
| ☑ Shape Dynamics | 3 |   |
| ☐ Scattering |   | Laye... |
| ☐ Texture | 5 |   |
| ☐ Dual Brush | 9 | Layer 2 |
| ☐ Color Dynamics |   |   |
| ☐ Other Dynamics | 13 | Background |
| ☐ Noise | 19 |   |
| ☐ Wet Edges |   |   |
| ☐ Airbrush | 5 |   |
| ☐ Smoothing | * |   |
| ☐ Protect Texture | 9 |   |

Master Diameter    100 px

**5.**

ns.

Photoshop

**6.**

# Photoshop Exercises

*One machine can do the work of fifty ordinary men. No machine can do the work of one extraordinary man.*

—Elbert Hubbard (U.S. author, 1856–1915)

## About Photoshop

Photoshop is the right hand of the game artist. Although there are many 3D applications, Photoshop pretty much stands alone as the 2D application of choice for game developers. The information pertaining to Photoshop in this book should apply to older versions of Photoshop, since I tried to stick to the basics—and those basics have been around for a while now.

I strongly encourage you to become familiar with every possible aspect of Photoshop. As you read this book, try the various tools that are mentioned. No amount of imagery can replace experimentation. See for yourself what the tools do; use them; master them. There are many books on Photoshop (thousands of them, I bet), ranging from simple overviews to exhaustive user manual regurgitations. There are topic-specific books that look at Photoshop's abilities from the angle of digital photography, Web site creation, scanning, text effects, and more. The Photoshop Help files are also a great way to learn about this powerful tool. These files are comprehensive and well written as well as presented in a traditional help file format that is easy to use. The help files allow you to view Photoshop tools and features in several ways: contents, site map, index, and search. I find the "Related Subtopics" listed at the end of most topics very useful when I am trying to chase down a specific bit of information pertaining to some aspect of Photoshop. Even if you simply skim over several topics and can't remember any specifics, if you are later faced with a problem pertaining to one of those topics, chances are that you will remember reading about it and will know right where to go to get the specific information you need to solve the problem.

So, where do you start with Photoshop? I strongly recommend that no matter where you start learning, you use the hotkeys and the right-click menus whenever possible. They are the most important things you can learn about Photoshop. Together these tools allow you to create great art much more quickly while being dangerously sedentary.

## The Photoshop Work Area

The *Photoshop Work Area* (Figure A.1) contains the following major elements:

- Menu bar
- Options bar
- Toolbar
- Palette well
- Palettes
- Status bar

**Figure A.1**
The main parts of the Photoshop Work Area are (1) the menu bar, (2) the options bar, (3) the toolbar, (4) the palette well, (5) palettes, and (6) the status bar.

## The Menu Bar

The *menu bar* contains standard menu items that you might recognize from other applications, such as File: Open, Save, New, and Export and Edit: Cut, Copy, and Paste, as well as other options that reflect the most common elements of Photoshop. The Layers menu contains commands for working with layers. The Image menu allows you to adjust, manipulate, and change the modes of an image. There are also menus for dealing with selections, filters, and the various view windows of Photoshop.

I will not list the menus in detail, because every feature contained in the menus is discussed in this chapter and the hotkey/right-click menu options are the way you should learn to work in Photoshop. Many people are taught the menus first, followed by the "faster way" to do things. I think this is the wrong approach. I guess the logic behind that approach is that you are learning a basis and adding to it, but you are not. What you *are* doing is learning a slow (and very different) way of doing something (clicking three or four times through a menu system) and afterward being presented with an entirely different way to do things. Being presented with a shortcut later on, after entrenching yourself in the menus, will feel like you are taking three steps back and slowing way down to speed up in the future. Most people will resist learning a new shortcut when it is that much of a speed bump. They will also fall back into the "menu habit" when they're focusing on their work. So do yourself a favor and learn the fastest way to do something first. The menus aren't going anywhere and will be just as slow when you do need to use them.

## The Options Bar

Almost all tools in Photoshop have several settings, or options; they are displayed in the tool's *options bar* instead of hidden in a menu. The options bar brings up information and options based on the tool that is selected. When using the Zoom tool, you will see options such as Resize to Fit, Fit on Screen, Zoom In and Out, and so on. If you are using the Paintbrush tool, for example, you will see options for Brush Size, Blending Mode, Opacity, and Flow. If you set up a tool and want to save the state of that tool (all its settings), you can save it in the tool *presets*. In Figure A.2, you can see the tool selected to the left and the various options available for that tool on the right; at the bottom is the menu of the options bar, where you can load, save, and reset tools.

### The Toolbar (Toolbox)

The *toolbox* holds all the tools that you will use for creating and manipulating your images. In a later section, "Toolbar Shortcuts," there is a more lengthy description of the toolbar.

### Palette Well

The *palette well* allows you to drag any palette in the work area into the palette well and dock it there. Palettes are hidden when they are in the palette well, but you will see a tab with the palette name on it. Clicking on the Palette tab will bring up the palette. The palette will be available until you click outside the palette.

### Palettes

*Palettes* are floating menus that contain information on layers, navigation, colors, styles, and text; almost any aspect of Photoshop can be displayed as a palette. Palettes can be resized, minimized, docked, and closed altogether. You can even use the Tab key to hide all active palettes and display them again as you had them arranged before you hid them. Here is every palette in Photoshop for your viewing pleasure (Figure A.3).

### The Status Bar

The status bar (Window>Status Bar) is located at the bottom of the window and displays the magnification of the image, the file size, and even instructions for using the currently selected tool.

## Hotkeys or Keyboard Shortcuts

Whatever you want to call them, whether *hotkeys* or *shortcuts*, pressing a key or key combination is much faster than clicking through numerous menus to get the tool you want. Many of us already know that Ctrl+c, V, or Z is a shortcut to cut, copy, or paste. Photoshop has lots of keyboard shortcuts, so don't feel intimidated. I try to learn new ones every so often to keep adding to my knowledge, and I still don't know most of them—there are a lot! You have the ability to create your own as well. Some of the basic ones I use most are:

F1: Help
F5: Brush style palette
F6: Color, Swatches, and Styles palette
F7: Layers, Channels, and Paths palette
F8: Navigator, Info palette

**Figure A.2**
The icon for the tool selected is to the left and the various options available for that tool on the right.

F9: Actions, History, Presets palette
Tab: Toggles off and on all the palettes on screen
Shift+Tab: Toggles palettes on screen, excluding the toolbar

The [and] keys make the brush size smaller or larger for the paintbrush, eraser, clone stamp, healing brush, dodge/burn/sponge, blur/sharpen/smudge, and other tools.

The numbers 1 through 0 on the keyboard will affect the opacity of the layer, from 0% to 100% in 10% increments.

## Toolbar Shortcuts

The toolbar (Figure A.4) has shortcuts, too. Using them allows you not only to work faster; they also will eventually help you eliminate the need to always have your toolbar open. As a result, you gain more screen real estate. This is true for the hotkeys for palettes and other windows, too. Even if you don't know all the hotkeys for a specific palette, just knowing what hotkey brings it up and takes it allows you to reclaim more of your workspace because you can quickly bring the palettes and tools you need up and down, rather than leave them all lying around your work area. You can also double-click the header bar on top of any window to minimize and maximize it.

Because you can select and hold down some of the tools in the toolbar to bring up other tools via the toolbar shortcuts, here is the complete list of keys for those tools:

A: Direct Select tool
B: Brush tool
C: Crop tool

**Figure A.3**
Here are all the palettes in Photoshop. Some I will talk about in depth; a few I just mention.

E: Eraser tool
G: Gradient Stamp tool
H: Hand tool
I: Measure tool
J: Healing Stamp tool
K: Slice Stamp tool
L: Polygonal Lasso tool
M: Rectangular Marquee tool
N: Notes tool

Adobe Online

Marquee Tool (M)        Move Tool (V)
Lasso Tool (L)          Magic Wand (W)
Crop (C)                Slice Tool (K)

Healing Brush (J)       Brush (B)
Clone Stamp (S)         History Brush (Y)
Eraser (E)              Gradient Tool (G)
Blur Tool (R)           Sponge Tool (O)

Selection (A)           Type Tool (T)
Pen (P)                 Rectangular Tool (U)

Notes (N)               Eyedropper (I)
Hand (H)                Zoom (Z)

Foreground Color        Switch colors (X)
Default Colors (D)      Background Color

Standard Mode (Q)       Quick Mask (Q)

Screen Modes (F)
Switch to ImageReady

**Figure A.4**
The Photoshop toolbar.

O: Sponge tool
P: Pen tool
R: Smudge tool
S: Clone Stamp tool
T: Horizontal Type tool
U: Line tool
V: Move tool
W: Magic Wand tool
Y: History Brush tool
Z: Zoom Stamp tool

## Ctrl Shortcuts

Holding down the Ctrl key and pressing another key will give you
even more options:

Ctrl+N: Opens New Document dialog box
Ctrl+A: Selects the entire area of the current layer
Ctrl+D: Deselects a selection
Ctrl+J: Duplicates the selected layer
Ctrl+K: Opens the Preferences dialog box
Ctrl+L: Opens the Levels dialog box
Ctrl+F4: Closes the current file
Ctrl+' (single quote key): Displays gridlines
Ctrl+; (semicolon): Sets toggle guides
Ctrl+R: Sets toggle rulers
Ctrl+U: Opens Hue/Saturation dialog box

Ctrl+O: Opens File dialog box
Ctrl+P: Opens Print dialog box
Ctrl+Z: Undoes last action
Ctrl+Tab: Jumps between open documents
Ctrl+c: Copies
Ctrl+X: Cuts
Ctrl+Alt+Shift+X: Opens Pattern Maker
Ctrl+V: Pastes
Ctrl+T: Sets Transform tool

Logically, adding more keys to the combination gives you even more options:

Ctrl+Shift+S: Opens Save As dialog box
Ctrl+Shift+F: Opens Fade dialog box
Ctrl+Shift+X: Sets Liquify Filter tool
Ctrl+Shift+N: Creates New Layer Preferences
Ctrl+Shift+I: Selects Invert
Ctrl+Shift+c: Copies all layers

Add even more keys to the equation:

Ctrl+Shift+Alt+N: Creates a new empty layer
Ctrl+Shift+Alt+S: Opens Save For the Web dialog box
Ctrl+Shift+Alt+X: Opens Pattern Maker dialog box

Finally we have navigation shortcuts. Holding down the Space bar will turn the cursor into the Hand tool and allow you to move around the image.

**Note:** Moving around the image is different from moving the image itself using the Arrow tool.

### Other Shortcuts

- Using the Page Up and Page Down keys when you're zoomed in will scroll the image one screen up or down.
- Holding the Ctrl key while using the Page Up and Page Down keys will scroll you from side to side.
- Holding the Shift key while using Page Up/Page Down scroll will move you in 10-pixel increments.
- Holding Shift while painting or erasing will make the line straight at 90- or 45-degree angles.

## The Bridge

The *bridge* (Figure A.5) allows you to view thumbnails of the images in a folder and drag them into Photoshop to open them. The fact is that no matter how descriptive your filenames, you still have to see an image before you can decide whether you want to use it or not. You can change the sizes of the thumbnail images from icon-sized to fairly large thumbnails. The navigation is easy, and the window is easily resized and moveable, making it even more useful. There is a

View window that allows for the viewing of file information, too. You can sort and manage files using the bridge. You can even process images: rename, move, and delete, and curious rotations are options. I find the Reveal Location in Explorer option useful. The Batch Rename feature is good, too—I do use that one.

## The History Palette

The *History palette* is like Undo on steroids (Figure A.6). You can use it to undo or redo multiple steps and even save a snapshot of the image. A snapshot is effectively a copy of the image you are working on. You can save the snapshot as a separate file. You can save multiple snapshots and save your work in steps. If you are working on a large and complex image, this capability can be very useful. Sometimes a Photoshop file can get so large that it starts to slow down your system. Say you are working on a complex wall image. Maybe you built up many layers to build the base wall and have many more layers on top of that. You can save a snapshot of the file (or use the Save As command, too) and flatten the layers that you consider final. This way the file is smaller, and if you need to go back and alter the wall layers you can drag them over to the newer file that you are working on and work on them again as layers.

One of the options that you will see associated with the History palette is Clear History. If Photoshop gives you a "low on memory" message, you can purge the history, which will free up some memory.

## Right-Click Menus

Initially, the easiest speed trick to learn is to use the right mouse button to bring up the context-sensitive menus associated with each tool in Photoshop. All you have to do is remember to use them! If you are working with a selection, the menu that pops up when the right

**Figure A.5**
The bridge allows you to view thumbnails of the images in a folder and drag them into Photoshop to open them.

**Figure A.6**
The History palette—Undo on steroids.

mouse button is clicked will pertain to selections; if you are working with the Zoom tool, the menu that pops up will contain the Zoom options. In fact, these little menus give you immediate access to options relevant to any active tool, palette, or selection you are using.

## Guides, Grids, Rulers, and the Snap

Guides, grids, and rulers are very important in game art. Snapping to the grid is a very helpful feature, even a necessity, so we will talk about that first.

### Snapping

Snapping allows you to place things exactly where you want them. When you drag an item within a certain distance of another item in Photoshop, you can have those two items snap to each other like magnets. This means that you will either be enough pixels away from something that you can see that it is not lined up right or the item will snap exactly to the item. This also means that you can't drag and place something only a few pixels away from something else, because snap will catch it and snap it to the item. You can turn snap off or use Nudge to position things, if you need to.

Things like selections, the crop tool, guidelines, painted lines, and images can be placed exactly where you want them using the *snap tool*. You can choose to turn snap off or choose what you snap to: guidelines, the grid, or the edge of the document. In Figure A.7, you can see the options of the snap tool. Precise placement can be very important in game creation. Not only high-end 3D game worlds but also user interfaces and menus require placement to the pixel. Mobile devices such as cell phones are just as precise and more limiting. The screens are very small, so every pixel counts and must be placed exactly in the right spot. If you open the options from the menu (lines, grid, and so on) and they are disabled, that is because the layer you want to snap on needs to be visible.

**Note:** Snapping guidelines to ruler units can be achieved by holding the Shift key when dragging a guideline.

## Rulers

*Rulers* run up the left side of the image window and across the top. You can turn them off and on with Ctrl+R (or View>Rulers).

You can set the ruler units to many different units of measure (right-click on the rulers), but in all likelihood you will be using pixels. Snapping to ruler units can be achieved by holding the Shift key while dragging out a guideline. Rulers will move and scale with your image, meaning that if you zoom into an image, you will see the ruler units adjust in size and position. In Figure A.8, you can see the rulers settings dialog box on the upper left; on the upper right is an image that is zoomed out. Notice that the image is still anchored at 0,0 and that the numbers on the rulers preceding 0,0 are negative numbers. The lower-left image is zoomed way in, so you can see that the ruler units have gotten larger to reflect the zoom. On the lower right, you can see that when the zoomed-in image is moved around, the rulers move with it.

## Guides and Grids

The guidelines and grid in Photoshop behave similarly, the difference being pretty evident (Figure A.9). A *guideline* is one line (you can drag out as many as you like), and the *grid* is a grid. You can change

**Figure A.7**
The options of the snap tool.

**Figure A.8**
The rulers settings dialog box is on the upper left; on the upper right is an image that is zoomed out. Notice that the image is still anchored at 0,0 and that the numbers on the rulers preceding 0,0 are negative numbers. The lower-left image is zoomed way in, so you can see that the ruler units have gotten larger to reflect the zoom. On the lower right you can see that when the zoomed-in image is moved around, the rulers move with it.

the color and style of a guideline and the color, style, distance, and number of grid lines.

Guidelines are lines that you can drag out over your image and are not actually part of the art. They won't print or be in the image when you export it to another format. You can move and delete these lines as well as lock them in place. The grid also does not print or appear in your exported files.

To see your grid, use the hotkeys listed in the previous section, or choose View>Show Grids. To see a guideline, you have to create one. Place your cursor on a vertical or horizontal ruler and click and hold the left mouse button and drag. The line will stay where you let go of the mouse button. To move a guide, hold your cursor over the line and press and hold the Ctrl key. When the cursor turns into a double-headed arrow, you can move the line. You can remove one guideline by dragging it outside the image window and into a ruler, and you can remove all of them by choosing View>Clear Guides. Remember that hiding and clearing are different. *Hiding* means that the guides can be unhidden, and *clearing* them removes them. You can use the History palette or the Undo feature to get them back in most cases.

**Figure A.9**
The guidelines and grid in Photoshop behave the same. A guideline is one line (you can drag out as many as you like), and the grid is a grid.

## Layers

The concept of *layers* was introduced in an earlier chapter. Here we will look at some of the specific features of Photoshop layers. Layers not only make life much easier for the texture artist, they are also critical to texture creation. Layers allow you to save your Photoshop file as many images on top of each other. You can control how each layer interacts with the one below it. In Figure A.10, you can see an illustration of the way layers work in Photoshop. Photoshop CS introduced the concept of *nested layers*, which allows you to create a collapsible grouping of layers that you can then place into other groups, thus creating subgroupings of layers. See Figure A.11.

### The Layers Palette

Using the *Layers palette*, you can create, delete, hide, copy, and move layers as well as apply many effects and styles to them. You can also combine layers, link them, and add layer masks and adjustment layers (we discuss them, too). You work with layers on the Layers palette. In Photoshop, there are several types of layers and several options associated with layers. Figure A.12 shows the parts of the Layers palette:

- Normal layer: This is a layer that is not modified or altered in any way.
- Layer effects: These are special effects you can apply to the layer. We look at these in depth in the next section.

**Figure A.10**
On the left side of this figure you can see three textures all created from one Photoshop file with various layers. To the right of the textures you can see the Layer palette for this file. Notice that this is the same file with different layers turned on and off. To the far right is an illustration of how the layers in Photoshop are stacked on top of each other and how the final result is seen in the Photoshop Image Window. This illustration reflects the actual layers used in the image to the left.

- Type layer: This is a layer that contains type, or text. Text can be edited.
- Background layer: The background is a bottom layer that is always locked and cannot be moved or have effects applied to it.
- Adjustment layer: An adjustment layer is a impermanent way to perform many adjustments to a layer that can be altered or discarded later, even after the file has been saved. We discuss these at length later in this appendix.
- Layer with Mask: The layer with a mask allows you to effectively erase parts of the layer by painting with black on the mask, but unlike erasing, with a layer and mask you have the ability to paint back parts of your layer using white. The original image remains unaltered. I almost never erase on a layer anymore but use a mask instead. It is not only undoable but easier to switch between black and white by pressing the X key. There is no need to use Undo or mess with the History palette when you can effectively erase and unerase your image.
- Thumbnail image: This is a small picture of the layer.
- Show/Hide icon: This icon indicates whether a layer is visible.
- Blending Modes: Blending Modes are discussed in detail a little later in this chapter.
- Layer Opacity: This adjusts how transparent a layer is; 0 is completely transparent and 100 is completely opaque.
- Layer Fill: Fill is similar to opacity, except that Layer Opacity affects everything in the layer and Layer Fill affects only the layer contents. Layer Effects remain 100% opaque.

**Figure A.11**
Photoshop CS introduced the concept of nested layers, which allows you to create a collapsible grouping of layers, which you can place into other groups, thus creating subgroupings of layers.

**Figure A.12**
The parts of the Layers palette.

## Layer Locks

- Lock Transparent Pixels: This allows you to paint on the layer but not on transparent pixels.
- Lock Pixels: You cannot paint on any part of the layer.
- Lock Position: You cannot move the layer, but you can make changes otherwise.
- Lock All: This completely locks the layer and allows no editing or changes at all.

## Layer Tools

- Layer Effects: These are special effects you can apply to the layer. We look at these in depth in the next section.
- Layer Mask: This allows you to create a mask. With a mask you can effectively erase parts of the layer, but unlike erasing you have the ability to paint back parts of your layer. The original image remains unaltered.
- New Layer Set: This allows you to create a new layer set, a folder in which you can store many layers. You can expand and collapse a layer set.
- New Adjustment Layer: This allows you to create an adjustment layer. We discuss these at length later in this chapter.
- New Layer: Click this to add a new layer. You can also drag a layer to this icon to duplicate it.
- Delete: This deletes the layer. You can click on this icon or drag the layer thumbnail to this icon.

### Using Layers and Layer Sets

The Layers palette lets you move and manipulate each layer or group of layers. To move layers, you simply drag them.

You can even drag layers into other Photoshop files. You can lock layers so that they can't accidentally be changed. One of the most powerful aspects of layers is the ability to name them, color-code them, and group them in sets. In some cases, one element of a texture may have several layers associated with it. Maybe you have many variations of an element in a texture, or maybe you built an element from many separate layers. Instead of scrolling through many layers in the Layers palette, you can group the layers and collapse them. In Figure A.13 is a texture with a layer set applied to it. In the Layers palette, on the upper right, you can see that there are many layers that scroll off the bottom of the Layers palette. Add to that Layer Effects (we discuss them next) and you get one long Layers palette. In the middle Layers palette, you can see that the vents and cracks have all been put into their own Layer sets. On the bottom Layers palette you can see that the cracks set has been opened and the other layer sets have been collapsed. You can see how much easier navigating a file like this can be using Layer sets.

In the coming sections, I will introduce you to layer effects and styles, layer blending modes, adjustment layers, and their options. These are some of the most powerful tools for texture creation.

### Layer Effects and Styles

Layer effects are powerful tools. I use layer effects a lot in the creation of textures because not only do they make your work very flexible, but if used correctly they can also make great-looking textures quickly and easily. Layer effects can be changed, copied, and turned on and off. This is a primary way that you can make a texture from a simple shape—remember our discussion in Chapter 1? By applying various effects such as drop shadows, inner and outer glows, bevels, overlays, gradients, strokes, and more, you can build up a texture.

**Note:** A *layer style* is a saved set of layer effects as well as a few other aspects of the layer, such as the opacity of the layer and the selected Blending Mode. If you find yourself repeatedly applying the same layer effects with the same settings, you can save a layer style and apply the effects in one click. You do this in the Layer Style window. Click New... to create the style based on the selected style, name it, and save it.

An important difference between layer effects and filters is that the filter permanently alters the pixels of the image and layer effects are in real time. If you put a drop shadow behind a square and then resize that square, the layer affects scale. A one-pixel stroke will always be exactly one pixel when you resize the object in the layer, whereas a one-pixel line that is part of the image will be subject to anti-aliasing and other resizing calculations and will get fuzzy, stretched, or disappear altogether. Figure A.14 illustrates this idea. Layer effects stay the same even if you resize your entire image. So, a one-pixel stroke that looks great on a 1024 × 1024 image will still

**Figure A.13**
A texture with a layer set applied to it. In the Layers palette on the upper right, you can see that there are many layers that scroll off the bottom of the Layers palette. In the middle palette, you can see that the vents and cracks have all been put into their own Layer sets. On the bottom palette, you can see that the cracks set has been opened and the other layer sets have been collapsed.

be one pixel if you resize that image down to 512 × 512 and could look wrong. You can scale layer effects up or down by a percentage to match the scaling of the image, but it would be nice if there were an option to scale effects automatically.

Complaints about the use of layer effects stem from a lack of patience in applying and experimenting with the effects. Photoshop gives you so many options and so much control that you can get any result you want. Why paint a drop shadow when you can pop one in and tweak it to look just right? If you need to alter the shadow or the element that it is under, you are not stuck having to repaint the shadow by hand. Figure A.15 shows a vent that has each of the layer effects applied in two ways.

There are several layer effects and an almost unlimited way to apply them, given the many options that each effect offers. Throughout the book we used layer effects and were more specific with their application. Most effects contain the same basic parameters that can be applied in various ways. Color, size, distance, blending mode, contour, and opacity are most of the common effects.

## Layer Blending Modes

*Blending Modes* are among the most useful tools in Photoshop for the texture artist. *Compositing* is the term for building textures using multiple layers, and Blending Modes are critical to this process. Adding cracks to a wall, stains to a floor, or making almost any

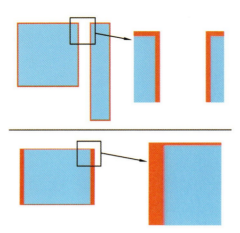

**Figure A.14**
A one-pixel stroke will always be exactly one pixel when you resize the object in the layer, whereas a one-pixel line that is part of the image will be subject to anti-aliasing and other resizing calculations and will get fuzzy, stretched, or disappear altogether.

element look like it is part of the texture and not just a separate image slapped on top is largely accomplished with layer Blending Modes. Although Blending Modes function the same every time you use them, they will create different effects based on the contents of the layer and the layers below it. Blending Modes are much simpler in their application than Layer Effects; you set the mode and adjust the opacity of the layer for the desired visual effect.

Blending Modes work by affecting the layer below the layer to which the mode is assigned. The layer underneath is called the *base* and the layer on top, the one with the mode applied, is called the *blend*. Blending Modes are grouped into six types:

- Normal and Dissolve
- Darken
- Lighten
- Contrast
- Invert/Compare
- HSL

**Note:** You can cycle through the modes without having to use the drop-down menu by pressing Shift+Alt and the + or – keys. You can also use the mouse wheel to scroll through the modes.

### Normal and Dissolve

There are six divisions of Blending Modes. The first set contains Normal and Dissolve. Normal is, well, normal; nothing is done to the layer. Dissolve will look like nothing is happening until you start to decrease the opacity of the layer. Then you will see random pixels disappear.

### The Darken Modes

The Darken modes are Darken, Multiply, Linear Burn, and Color Burn. With all the Darken modes, white disappears, and any pixel darker than white will darken the pixels in the base image. The various Darken modes darken the base image in different ways. Multiply looks at the pixels in the base and blend images and picks the darker

**Drop Shadow**

**Inner Shadow**

**Outer Glow**

**Inner Glow**

**Bevel and Emboss**

**Satin**

**Color Overlay**

**Gradient Overlay**

**Pattern Overlay**

**Stroke**

**Figure A.15**
This vent image has each of the layer effects applied in two ways. The vent image on the left has the layer effect applied with default settings. The image on the right has had the settings of the effects adjusted. The larger example image on the lower right shows the vent (top) with no effects and the vent (bottom) with a variety of effects applied and adjusted.

one. Linear Burn does the same thing, but it results in a darker image; blacks really come out. Color Burn darkens and increases the saturation of the colors in the base image.

### The Lighten Modes

The Lighten modes are Lighten, Screen, Color Dodge, and Linear Dodge. These modes knock out the darker pixels in the blend image; black is knocked out completely. The Lighten modes lighten the base image in different ways. Lighten compares pixels in the base and blend images and uses the lighter one. Screen is the opposite of Multiply. Color Dodge and Screen always result in a lighter image than the base. Color Dodge lightens the base image and adds saturation to the underlying colors. Linear Light has a similar but stronger effect that can result in more whites.

### The Contrast Modes

The contrast modes are Overlay, Soft Light, Hard Light, Vivid Light, Linear Light, and Pin Light. Contrast modes are kind of a blend of the Darken and Lighten modes. Grays disappear, and the lighter pixels brighten the image and the darker pixels tend to darken the image. Soft

Light makes the blend image act as though it were a soft light source. Hard Light looks at the brightness of the blend color and Screens lighter colors and Multiplies darker colors. Hard Light is meant to look like a spotlight using the blend as the light source cast on the base image.

### The Invert/Comparative Modes

Difference and Exclusion compare the blend layer to the base, and pixels that are identical become black. Difference looks at the two pixels and subtracts the darker pixel from the lighter. Blending with white inverts the color; blending with black makes no change. Exclusion creates an image lower in contrast than Difference.

### The HSL Modes

Hue, Saturation, Color, and Luminosity break up the color of the pixels in the blend layer and apply that information to the base. Hue applies the color of the blend without changing the Saturation or Brightness of the base, Saturation applies the amount of saturation of the Blend to the base, Color applies the color of the Blend to the Base, and Luminosity applies the brightness of the Blend to the Base.

### Hard Mix Mode CS

Hard Mix posterizes the layers below it based on the values of the layer that this mode is applied to. Pixels brighter than 50% gray will brighten the layer; darker pixels will darken the layer.

## Adjustment Layers

Adjustment and fill layers add a great deal of flexibility to texture creation. You can color, adjust tone, or fill a layer with color, patterns, or a gradient. You can use masks with adjustment layers. The adjustment layer I tend to use the most is Brightness/Contrast.

**Note:** Before creating an adjustment layer, make a selection and a mask will be created for the adjustment layer.

## Brushes

The *brush* is obviously an extremely important part of Photoshop. Brushes in Photoshop are very flexible and deep. The quick and simple use of a brush requires the selection of the *Brush tool* and a right-click to select a specific brush. Here you can also load other brushes and change the size and hardness/softness of the brush. You can also create your own brushes.

The *Brush palette* adds a deep level of control over your brush. You can specify the fade, randomness, spread, and other settings of your brush. You can even combine two brushes. As important as the brush is, I almost never use more than a standard hard/soft, large/small combination of the standard brush shapes, especially in the projects in this book.

### Cloning/Healing

These brushes are extremely useful to the texture artist. Quite simply, the *Clone tool* allows you to sample one part of an image and paint on another part of the image. The sample point moves as your brush does. If you are careful, you can be very accurate with the Clone tool and rebuild hard edges as well as remove defects from an image. The *Healing Brush* is similar to the Clone tool in its use, but it "corrects" the sample to match the area of the image. The Healing Brush matches the texture, lighting, and shading of the sampled pixels to the source pixels. See Figure A.16.

## Filters

Last but not least, we look at filters. Photoshop filters are typically discussed in the form of an example image with the effect of each filter shown on the sample image. Although that approach has its uses, I will not do it here, because not only has this been done a million times in other books and publications, but this approach doesn't really convey the power of using filters. A number of variables affect the result of using a filter(s): the image size, the foreground and background color, the settings of each filter, the combination of the filters you run, and of course the image you are running the filter(s) on. This section discusses the major filter groups and how they affect your image. You can also fade the effect of most filters, and I find this particularly useful. The Fade command allows you to change the opacity and blending mode of the filter as well as several of the other Photoshop tools.

### The Filter Gallery (CS)

New to Photoshop CS, the Filter Gallery allows you to see most of the filters as they are applied to the image. You can quickly click through the filters and see how they affect your image; see Figure A.17. You can also add another filter to a stack and move, hide, and delete them. This is incredibly powerful because you are no longer stuck running one filter at a time. Now you can go back and change the settings of an earlier filter and see the effects combined with the other filters in the stack.

**Note:** If you are working on a large image or on a slower computer, you can make a selection and run the filter on the smaller section much faster. After you run the filter on the selection, you can Undo the filter using Ctrl+Z and deselect the selection, then use Ctrl+F to run the filter on the entire image.

**Figure A.16**
The Clone tool and Healing Brush. The image on the left is the original, the middle image (1) the clone sample area, (2) the cloned area. Right, (3), is the Heal sample area, (4) the healed area.

**Figure A.17**
New to Photoshop CS, the
Filter Gallery allows you to
see most of the filters as they
are applied to the image.

## Artistic Filters

The first group of filters is the *artistic filters*, which can alter an image to make it look as though it has been painted by an artist in several styles.

## Blur Filters

The *blur filters* simply blur the image in various ways. You can use a blur to smooth an image you are overlaying, create a drippy stain, and so on.

## Brush Stroke Filters

The *brush filters* are similar to the artistic filters but focus on ink and brush effects rather than an artistic style.

## Distort Filters

*Distort filters* distort your image in various ways. You can make the image look like glass, or twirl and zigzag it. These filters are not fully represented in the Filter Gallery in Photoshop CS.

**Note:** You can use the Liquify tool for precise distortions of an image.

## Noise Filters

There are a few filters here that add or remove noise and artifacts from an image, but for texture creation Add Noise is the one you will use almost exclusively. Adding noise to a solid color gives the other filters something to work with. Running a filter on a solid color usually has little to no effect. Sometimes you even need to blur the noise a bit to get a better or different result.

## Pixelate Filters

These filters basically clump pixels together in various ways. I have not found the effect useful for texture creation.

## Render Filters

*Render filters* allow you to create 3D shapes, cloud patterns, and light effects, among others. For texture creation the clouds, Difference clouds, and Lighting Effects filters are very useful. In Photoshop CS, the Fibers filter was added. This filter creates a simple image of fibers that can be really useful for creating wood, bark, and other organic textures.

## Sharpen Filters

The *sharpen filters* basically increase the contrast of an image for the most part. I find that they create the conditions in an image that you are trying to avoid as a texture artist.

## Sketch Filters

*Sketch filters*, for the most part, use the foreground and background color as they process your image to make it look as if it were hand-drawn. These filters can be useful if you are creating a texture in which you want that effect. The Halftone Pattern creates a line effect across the image, which can be useful when creating computer monitors.

## Stylize Filters

*Stylize filters* displace pixels for various height effects, for the most part. These filters are also underrepresented in the Filter Gallery.

## Texture Filters

*Texture filters* can be useful to the texture artist, if used very sparingly. Actually, with the introduction of layer effects, I rarely use these filters. The Stained Glass filter can be useful, but not for stained glass, as you saw in Chapter 7.

## Other Filters

Under this last filter slot are the two filters most familiar to the texture artist: High Pass and the famous Offset filter. I also point you to a useful article on the High Pass filter. High Pass basically helps you remove hotspots. The Offset filter simply moves the image horizontally or vertically by an entered value. This filter is used a great deal to check for the seams in a texture. You can now use sliders instead of only numbers to move the image back and forth.

# Paths

Paths are wonderful and essential to the creation of lines that are not only organic and curvy but editable, too. This tool is useful not only for people who can't draw fancy lines, but can be useful for all, as it allows you to save, edit, and manipulate the paths in many ways.

Thus ends our quick look at the parts of Photoshop most useful to the texture artist. One of the best things that you can do to become a great texture artist is to master Photoshop. It may take a while, but it is well worth it.

# Index